SQL Server 7 Database Design

Thomas Moore

New Riders

201 West 103rd Street, Indianapolis, Indiana 46290

MCSE FAST TRACK: SQL SERVER 7 DATABASE DESIGN

Copyright © 1999 by New Riders Publishing

All rights reserved. No part of this book shall be reproduced, stored in a retrieval system, or transmitted by any means, electronic, mechanical, photocopying, recording, or otherwise, without written permission from the publisher. No patent liability is assumed with respect to the use of the information contained herein. Although every precaution has been taken in the preparation of this book, the publisher and author assume no responsibility for errors or omissions. Neither is any liability assumed for damages resulting from the use of the information contained herein.

International Standard Book Number: 0-7357-0040-0

Library of Congress Catalog Card Number: 99-62349

Printed in the United States of America

First Printing: June, 1999

03 02 01 00 99   7 6 5 4 3 2 1

Interpretation of the printing code: The rightmost double-digit number is the year of the book's printing; the rightmost single-digit number is the number of the book's printing. For example, the printing code 99-1 shows that the first printing of the book occurred in 1999.

TRADEMARKS

All terms mentioned in this book that are known to be trademarks or service marks have been appropriately capitalized. New Riders Publishing cannot attest to the accuracy of this information. Use of a term in this book should not be regarded as affecting the validity of any trademark or service mark.

SQL Server 7 is a registered trademark of Microsoft Corporation.

WARNING AND DISCLAIMER

Every effort has been made to make this book as complete and as accurate as possible, but no warranty or fitness is implied. The information provided is on an "as is" basis. The author and the publisher shall have neither liability nor responsibility to any person or entity with respect to any loss or damages arising from the information contained in this book.

Executive Editor
Mary Foote

Acquisitions Editors
Steve Weiss
Stacey Beheler

Development Editor
Christopher Morris

Managing Editor
Sarah Kearns

Project Editor
Brad Herriman

Copy Editor
Gayle Johnson

Indexer
Rebecca Hornyak

Technical Editors
William J. Anderson
James A. Cooper

Proofreader
Sheri Replin

Layout Technicians
Cheryl Lynch
Jeannette McKay

Contents at a Glance

INTRODUCTION

PART I WHAT'S IMPORTANT TO KNOW ABOUT EXAM 70-029

1. Developing a Logical Data Model   13
2. Deriving the Physical Design   29
3. Creating Data Services   43
4. Creating a Physical Database   151
5. Maintaining a Database   209
   Objective Review Notes   259

PART II INSIDE EXAM 70-029

6. Fast Facts Review   281
7. Insider's Spin on Exam 70-029   287
8. Hotlist of Exam-Critical Concepts   303
9. Sample Test Questions   331
10. Did You Know?   351

INDEX 353

TABLE OF CONTENTS

Part I What's Important to Know About Exam 70-029

1 Developing a Logical Data Model   13
Database Elements   14
Normalization Rules for Entity Definition   17
   First Normal Form   18
   Second Normal Form   18
   Third Normal Form   19
   Fourth and Fifth Normal Forms   19
Identification of Primary Keys   19
Foreign Key Selection and Referential Integrity   20
Business Rules and Data Integrity   22
Modeling Rules and Constraints   23
Denormalization   25
What Is Important to Know   27

2 Deriving the Physical Design   29
Performance   30
Maintainability   35
Extensibility   37
Scalability   38
Availability   39
Security   40
Physical Database Design   40
What Is Important to Know   42

3 Creating Data Services   43
The Syntax of Design   45
Dynamic SQL Model   45
Stored Procedures Model   46

Transact-SQL Cursors 47
  Cursor Types 47
Cursor Selection 49
  Resultset Size 49
  Data Volatility 50
  Cursor Features 51
  Performance 51
  Response 51
Sensitivity to Change 52
  Cursor Navigation 52
  Cursor Scope 53
Transaction Management 53
  Explicit Transactions 54
  Implicit Transactions 55
  Distributed Transactions 56
Data Consistency 57
  Atomicity 57
  Consistency 57
  Transaction Isolation 59
  Service Durability 59
Recoverability 59
  Automatic Database Recovery 60
  Backup/Restore 60
  Standby Servers 63
  Checkpointing 64
Isolation 64
  Share Locks 65
  Update and Exclusive Locks 65
  Intent Locks 66
  Schema Locks 66
  Implementing Locking 66
  Lock Manager 67
  Locking Configuration 68

Transaction Isolation 68
  Read Committed 69
  Read Uncommitted 69
  Repeatable Read 70
  Serializable 70
Using Isolation 70
Transaction Control 70
  Bound Connections 71
Deadlocks 72
  Avoiding Deadlocks 73
Locking 74
  Optimistic Locking 75
  Pessimistic Locking 75
@@trancount 76
SQL Standard Syntax 77
  INSERT 77
  DELETE 80
  UPDATE 82
  SELECT 85
  Joins and Subqueries 92
  Transact-SQL Scripts 100
  Views 121
  Stored Procedures 123
  Triggers 130
  Summarizing Data 133
  Session Level Configuration 139
  Accessing Data 143
CONTAINSTABLE 146
FREETEXTTABLE 147
Putting It All Together 147
  Example: Conditional Error Check 147
  Example: Referential Integrity 147
What Is Important to Know 148

4 Creating a Physical Database 151

Maintaining the Physical Implementation 152

File Management 152
- Creating Database Files 153
- Creating Filegroups 156
- Managing Database Files 157
- Managing Log Files 169

Maintaining Integrity 169
- Data and Referential Integrity 170
- Data Type Selection 170
- User-Defined Data Types 172
- NULL and NOT NULL 173
- Generated Values 173
- Constraint Implementation 179
- Index Maintenance 181
- Database Population 196
- Full-Text Implementation 203

What Is Important to Know 208

5 Maintaining a Database 209

Optimizing and Tuning SQL Server Implementations 210

Execution Plans 212
- Evaluation of Execution Plans 213
- Optimizing Performance 213

Query Execution Plans 224
- Evaluation of Query Plans 225
- Optimizing Performance 234

Locking Problems 240
- Locking Diagnosis 241
- Resolving Locking Problems 245

SQL Server Profiler 247
- Identifying Events Using Profiler 249

Putting It All Together 254

What Is Important to Know 258

Objective Review Notes 259

Part II Inside Exam 70-029

6 Fast Facts Review 281
What to Study 282
 Developing a Logical Data Model 282
 Deriving the Physical Design 283
 Creating Data Services 284
 Creating a Physical Database 285
 Maintaining a Database 286

7 Insider's Spin on Exam 70-029 287
Get into Microsoft's Mind-Set 290
Understand the Exam's Time Frame 291
Get Used to Answering Questions Quickly 293
Taking the Test 294
Where the Questions Come From 300
Different Flavors of Questions 301

8 Hotlist of Exam-Critical Concepts 303

9 Sample Test Questions 331
Questions 333
Answers and Explanations 347

10 Did You Know? 351

About the Author

Thomas Moore, MCSD, MCSE, MCT (certified in 1995), has been a computer programmer since 1981. Knowledgeable in many programming languages, including COBOL, Pascal, Visual Basic, C, Fortran, and RPG, Moore has development experience on many platforms, from PCs to supercomputers. He's been a database developer for ark, CICS, dBASE, and SQL Server, and has performed training for government agencies in Canada and the United States. He is also a LAN manager with seven years of experience. He also has 15 years of technical training experience with both private and public colleges and has done professional training (ATEC). In his trainer role, Moore has developed computer curricula, including exams, classroom materials, case studies, and other lessons.

About the Technical Reviewers

William J. Anderson wrote his first computer program in FORTRAN using keypunch cards in the '60s. He showed a real knack for the logic required to program, but his true love was golf. He was a member of the golf team at Michigan State University. Upon completing college, he became a professional golfer and earned a living giving lessons. In the late '70s, Anderson suffered a career-ending injury and was forced to find something other than golf at which to make a living. He rediscovered computers in the '80s. He was one of the first to install Novell networks in San Diego. He was also one of the first to provide the training that end users needed to operate their workstations on corporate networks. Anderson was a principal instructor for the San Diego branch of a national training company, earning Instructor of the Year honors from 1992 through 1995. He still teaches official curriculum as a Microsoft Certified Trainer and a Certified Novell Instructor. He is the president of his own consulting firm, specializing in Internet and WAN technologies. He hosts over 20 e-commerce Web sites on his servers. He also holds an MCSE, CNE, and MCP+Internet. Anderson can be contacted at bill@webshare.com.

James A. Cooper is an IT manager at a leading software company. He is an MCSE+Internet and MCT and has been working in the computer industry for over 10 years.

Dedication

To my darling wife, Joy Lambkin, who, through all my long hours of studying for exams, preparing course materials, writing books, and serving the needs of my contract clients, has always stuck by me and supported my efforts.

To my mother, Barbara Moore, who always believed in her son, regardless of the impossibility of the tangents chosen in life.

Acknowledgments

First and foremost, I must thank my mentor, Kenneth Rumble, who was instrumental in starting me on my way toward Microsoft certification. Ken's work ethic and study habits proved to be the guiding light in achieving success in this ever-changing environment. Without Ken, this book never could have happened. (Thanks for the San Jose lead, Ken.) Second, I would like to thank the entire project team at Macmillan Publishing, especially Chris Morris for his guidance in how to put together a book of this type. Finally, I would like to thank the students I have taught over the past 14 years or so, without whom I'm sure I could not have become the instructor I am. The many students (now friends) who still stay in touch have shown me that if you put your heart into it, you can really make a difference in other people's lives.

TELL US WHAT YOU THINK!

As the reader of this book, *you* are our most important critic and commentator. We value your opinion and want to know what we're doing right, what we could do better, what areas you'd like to see us publish in, and any other words of wisdom you're willing to pass our way.

As the Executive Editor of the Certification team at New Riders Publishing, I welcome your comments. You can fax, email, or write me directly to let me know what you did or didn't like about this book—as well as what we can do to make our books stronger.

Please note that I can't help you with technical problems related to this book, and that due to the high volume of mail I receive, I might not be able to reply to every message.

When you write, please be sure to include this book's title and author, as well as your name and phone or fax number. I will carefully review your comments and share them with the author and editors who worked on the book.

Fax: 317-581-4663

Email: certification@mcp.com

Mail: Mary Foote
Executive Editor
Certification
New Riders Publishing
201 West 103rd Street
Indianapolis, IN 46290 USA

Introduction

The *MCSE Fast Track* series is written as a study aid for people preparing for Microsoft Certification exams. The series is intended to help reinforce and clarify information you're already familiar with. This series is not intended to be a single source of student preparation. Instead, it's a review of information and a set of practice materials to help increase your likelihood of success when taking the exam.

WHY WE CREATED THIS BOOK: WORDS FROM THE AUTHOR AND PUBLISHER

Again, New Riders' *MCSE Fast Tracks* are *not* intended to be a single source of exam preparation. These books have been uniquely written and developed to work as supplements to your existing knowledge.

But exactly what makes them different?

- **Brevity.** Many other exam training materials seek Microsoft approval (you've probably seen the official Microsoft Approved Study Guide logo on other books, for example), meaning that they must include 50 percent tutorial material and cover every objective for every exam in exactly the same manner and to the same degree. *Fast Tracks* break that mold by focusing on what you really need to know to pass the exam.

- **Focus.** *Fast Tracks* are targeted primarily at those who know the technology but who don't yet have the certification. No superfluous information is included. *Fast Tracks* feature only what the more-experienced candidate needs to know to pass the exam. *Fast Tracks* are affordable study material for the experienced professional.

- **Concentrated value and learning power.** Frankly, we wouldn't be surprised if *Fast Tracks* prove to appeal to a wider audience than just advanced-level candidates. We've tried to pack as much distilled exam knowledge as possible into *Fast Tracks,* creating a digest of exam-critical information. No matter what level you're at, you may well see this digest on certification training as a logical starting point for exam study.

- **Classroom tested, instructor proven.** With tens of thousands of new certification candidates entering the training routine each year, trainers like Thomas Moore on the forefront of the certification education lines are finding themselves in front of classes comprised of increased numbers of candidates who have a measurable understanding of the technology and a desire for efficient, "just-the-facts" training.

Thomas Moore and New Riders Publishing pooled their thoughts and found that no books truly existed that provided an easy way to review the key elements of each certification technology without getting bogged down with elementary-level information and that presented the information from an insider's perspective.

Moore developed his instructional style and content to help this ever-increasing group of nonbeginners, and they, in turn, helped the author focus the material even more. The author then worked with New Riders to shape this classroom-tested material into a refined, efficient self-instruction tool. What you see in this book is the result of that interaction.

Think of *Fast Tracks* as the set of instructor's notes you always wished you could get your hands on. These notes only truly help you if you already know the material and are ready to take the exam. It's then that this book is designed to help you shine. Good luck and may your hard work pay off.

What This Book Covers

This book is specifically intended to help you prepare for Microsoft's Designing and Implementing Databases with Microsoft SQL Server 7.0 (70-029) exam—one of the electives available in the MCSE and MCSD programs.

PART I: WHAT THE SQL SERVER 7 DATABASE DESIGN EXAM (70-029) COVERS

The Designing and Implementing Databases with Microsoft SQL Server 7.0 certification exam measures your ability to design and implement a database solution by using Microsoft SQL Server version 7.0. The exam focuses on determining your skill in five major categories:

- Developing a logical data model
- Deriving the physical design
- Creating data services
- Creating a physical database
- Maintaining a database

The Designing and Implementing Databases with Microsoft SQL Server 7.0 certification exam uses these categories to measure your abilities. Before taking this exam, you should be proficient in the job skills discussed in the following sections.

Developing a Logical Data Model

Chapter 1, "Developing a Logical Data Model" has the following objectives:

Objectives for Developing a Logical Data Model

- Group data into entities by applying normalization rules.
- Identify primary keys.
- Choose the foreign key that will enforce a relationship between entities and that will ensure referential integrity.
- Identify the business rules that relate to data integrity.
- Incorporate business rules and constraints into the data model.
- In a given situation, decide whether denormalization is appropriate.

Deriving the Physical Design

Chapter 2, "Deriving the Physical Design" has the following objectives:

Objective for Deriving the Physical Design

- Assess the potential impact of the logical design on performance, maintainability, extensibility, scalability, availability, and security.

Creating Data Services

Chapter 3, "Creating Data Services" has the following objectives:

Objectives for Creating Data Services

- Access data by using the dynamic SQL model.
- Access data by using the stored procedures model.
- Manipulate data by using Transact-SQL cursors.
    - Choose the appropriate type of cursor.
    - Define the appropriate level of sensitivity to change.
    - Choose the appropriate navigation.
    - Choose the scope of the cursor—specifically, global or local.
- Create and manage explicit, implicit, and distributed transactions to ensure data consistency and recoverability.
    - Define the transaction isolation level.
    - Design transactions of appropriate length.
    - Avoid or handle deadlocks.
    - Use optimistic locking appropriately.
    - Implement error handling by using `@@trancount`.
- Write INSERT, DELETE, UPDATE, and SELECT statements that retrieve and modify data.

- Write Transact-SQL statements that use joins or subqueries to combine data from multiple tables.

- Create scripts using Transact-SQL. Programming elements include control-of-flow methods, local and global variables, functions, and error-handling methods.

- Design, create, use, and alter views.
  - Modify data through a view.
  - Query data through a view.

- Create and execute stored procedures to enforce business rules, to modify data in multiple tables, to perform calculations, and to use input and output parameters.
  - Implement error handling by using return codes and the RAISERROR statement.
  - Choose appropriate recompile options.

- Create triggers that implement rules, enforce data integrity, and perform cascading updates and deletes.
  - Implement transactional error handling.

- Create result sets that provide summary data. Query types include TOP n PERCENT and GROUP BY—specifically, HAVING, CUBE, and ROLLUP.

- Configure session-level options.

- Access data from static or dynamic sources by using remote stored procedures, linked servers, and openrowset.
  - Evaluate where processing occurs when using OPENQUERY.

Creating a Physical Database

Chapter 4, "Creating a Physical Database" has the following objectives:

Objectives for Creating a Physical Database

- Create and manage files, file groups, and transaction logs that define a database.

- Create tables that enforce data integrity and referential integrity.
    - Choose the appropriate data types.
    - Create user-defined data types.
    - Define columns as NULL or NOT NULL.
    - Define columns to generate values by using the IDENTITY property, the uniqueidentifier data type, and the NEWID function.
    - Implement constraints.
- Create and maintain indexes.
    - Choose an indexing strategy that will optimize performance.
    - Given a situation, choose the appropriate type of index to create.
    - Choose the column(s) to index.
    - Choose the appropriate index characteristics—specifically, FILL-FACTOR, DROP_EXISTING, and PAD INDEX.
- Populate the database with data from an external data source. Methods include bulk copy program and Data Transformation Services (DTS).
- Implement full-text search.

Maintaining a Database

Chapter 5, "Maintaining a Database" has the following objectives:

Objectives for Maintaining a Database

- Evaluate and optimize the performance of an execution plan by using DBCC SHOW CONTIG, SHOWPLAN_text, SHOWPLAN_ALL, and UPDATE STATISTICS.
- Evaluate and optimize the performance of query execution plans.
- Diagnose and resolve locking problems.
- Identify SQL Server events and performance problems by using SQL Server Profiler.

Hardware and Software Recommended for Preparation

The *Fast Track* series is meant to help you review concepts with which you already have training and hands-on experience. To make the most of the review, you need to have as much background and experience as possible. The best way to do this is to combine studying with working on real networks using the products on which you will be tested. This section describes the minimum computer requirements you will need in order to build a solid practice environment.

Computers

The minimum computer requirements to ensure that you can study on everything you'll be tested on are one or more workstations running Windows 95 or Windows NT Workstation, and two or more servers running Windows NT Server, all connected by a network.

Workstations: Windows 95 and Windows NT

- Computer on the Microsoft Hardware Compatibility list
- 486DX 66MHz (or better)
- 16MB of RAM (minimum)
- 340MB hard disk (or larger)
- $3^1/_2$-inch 1.44MB floppy drive
- VGA (or Super VGA) video adapter
- VGA (or Super VGA) monitor
- Mouse or equivalent pointing device
- Two-speed CD-ROM drive (optional)
- Network interface card (NIC)
- Presence on an existing network or use of a two-port (or more) mini-port hub to create a test network

- MS-DOS 5.0 or 6.x and Microsoft Windows for Workgroups 3.x preinstalled
- Microsoft Windows 95 (or 98)
- Microsoft Windows NT Server

OBJECTIVE REVIEW NOTES

The Objective Review Notes feature of the *Fast Track* series lists each subobjective covered in the book. Each subobjective is listed under the main exam objective category—just where you'd expect to find it. I strongly suggest that you review each subobjective, make note of your knowledge level, and then return to the Objective Review Notes chapter repeatedly and document your progress. Your ultimate goal should be to review this section by itself and know if you are ready for the exam.

Here is how I suggest you use the Objective Review Notes:

1. Read the objective. Refer to the part of the book where it's covered.

2. If you already know this material, check "Got it" and make a note of the date.

3. If you need to brush up on the objective area, check "Review it" and make a note of the date. While you're at it, write down the page numbers you checked, since you'll need to return to that section soon enough.

4. If this material is something you're largely unfamiliar with, check the "Help!" box and write down the date. Now you can get to work.

5. You get the idea. Keep working through the material in this book and in any other study materials you have. The more you understand the material, the quicker you can update and upgrade each Objective Review Notes section from "Help!" to "Review it" to "Got it."

6. Cross-reference using all your exam preparation materials. Most people who take certification exams use more than one resource. Write down where this material is covered in other books, software programs, and videotapes you're using.

Think of this as your personal study diary—your documentation of how you'll pass this exam.

PART II: ROUNDING OUT YOUR EXAM PREPARATION

Part II of this book is designed to round out your exam preparation by providing you with the following chapters:

- "Fast Facts Review" is a digest of all the "What Is Important to Know" sections from all Part I chapters. Read this chapter right before you take the exam: It's all here in an easy-to-review format.

- "Insider's Spin on Exam 70-029" grounds you in the particulars of preparing mentally for this exam and for Microsoft testing in general.

- "Hotlist of Exam-Critical Concepts" is your resource for cross-checking technical terms. Although you're probably up to speed on most of this material already, double-check yourself anytime you run across an item you're not 100 percent certain about; it could make a difference at exam time.

- "Sample Test Questions" provides a full-length practice exam that tests you on the material covered in Part I. If you mastered the material there, you should be able to pass with flying colors here.

- "Did You Know?" is the last-day-of-class bonus chapter. It briefly touches on peripheral information. It's designed to be helpful and of interest to anyone using this technology to the point that they want to be certified in its mastery.

PART I

WHAT IS IMPORTANT TO KNOW ABOUT EXAM 70-029

MCSE Fast Track: SQL Server 7 Database Design is written as a study aid for people preparing for Microsoft Certification Exam 70-029. The book is intended to help reinforce and clarify information with which the student is already familiar. This series is not intended to be a single source for exam preparation, but rather a review of information and set of practice tests to help increase the likelihood of success when taking the actual exam.

Part I is designed to help you make the most of your study time by presenting concise summaries of information that you need to understand in order to succeed on the exam. Each chapter covers a specific exam objective area that is outlined by Microsoft:

1 **Developing the Logical Data Model**

2 **Deriving the Physical Design**

3 **Creating Data Services**

4 **Creating a Physical Database**

5 **Maintaining a Database**

About the Exam

Exam Number	70-029
Minutes	90*
Questions	51*
Passing Score	705*
Single Answer Questions	Yes
Multiple Answer with Correct Number Given	Yes
Multiple Answer Without Correct Number Given	No
Ranking Order	No
Choices of A–D	Yes
Choices of A–E	No
Objective Categories	7

Note: These exam criteria will no longer apply when this exam goes to an adaptive format.

Objectives

- Group data into entities by applying normalization rules.
- Identify primary keys.
- Choose the foreign key that will enforce a relationship between entities and ensure referential integrity.
- Identify the business rules that relate to data integrity.
- Incorporate business rules and constraints into the data model.
- In a given situation, decide whether denormalization is appropriate.

CHAPTER 1

Developing a Logical Data Model

DATABASE ELEMENTS

This chapter looks at the fundamental structure of a database to derive a logical model.

A *database* is a single organizational structure that stores large amounts of information in a manner that facilitates the quick retrieval of meaningful information. The content of a database includes far more than just data divided into tables. When you're preparing to design a database, you must thoroughly understand the interrelationship of a database's elements.

Entity structuring accommodates the initial stages of database design. When you're designing an appropriate logical model, the data must be organized into separate elements called *entities* that will later make up the physical tables within a database. Entities can be categorized as kernel, associative, or characteristic. An entity is characterized by its attributes. Attributes are used to define the data elements of an entity. The key attribute is referred to as an entity's *identifier,* much as a person's name identifies that person as being an individual, different from all others. Entities are usually interdependent: Each holds information that relates to other entities. These relationships can be defined by their correlated dependencies. The development of the actual physical tables will undergo various changes from the point a rough plan is put on paper. Often, at the outset of the design phase, the entity structure is represented by rough drawings that organize the data elements (fields and columns). Once a database developer has all the data elements, the division of elements into a logical entity structure can begin. Entities, attributes, identifiers, and dependencies are characterized as follows:

- **Entity.** An *entity* is the basic division of a database. In the logical design, entities will be representative of the tables that will be present when the database development process moves into the physical design phase. Entities can be divided into three basic types: kernel, associative, and characteristic. Each of these types represents a reason why the entity exists as a separate individual, unique from all the others.

    - **Kernel entity.** A *kernel entity* exists on its own; it doesn't define or provide descriptive information for other entities. An example of a kernel entity would be a product listing in an inventory model. The information contained in each kernel entity of a table represents the heart of the database model.

- **Associative entity.** An *associative entity* is needed to allow multiple kernel entities to be tied together. In the inventory system, a sales entity would be needed to tie a customer kernel entity to the products he has purchased. This same sales entity could be tied to another kernel entity, such as salespeople.

- **Characteristic entity.** A *characteristic entity* provides additional information for a respective kernel or associative entity. Information contained in characteristic entities can be updated independently of the related entity. A product entity could have a characteristic parts entity. A given product could be made up of a number of parts. A part that becomes unavailable could affect the product's availability. Changes over time to parts information could be made more easily if a parts entity existed, instead of your having to make changes against the product's kernel.

- **Attribute.** An *attribute* is a descriptive element or property of an entity. It is represented by fields when the logical design progresses to the physical design stage. A product would have a description entity and entities relating its color, size, and so on.

- **Identifier.** An *identifier* is a special kind of attribute. The identifier is usually a single attribute that defines one unique element of an entity. The use of identifiers allows for the individual selection of records from an entity. As the design progresses to the physical stage, identifiers will become the primary and foreign keys within tables, allowing tables to be tied together through association or relationships. A product's identifying attribute is usually a unique product ID.

- **Dependency.** A *dependency* is a circumstance where one entity either can't exist or has little meaning without at least one other entity in the database. When a dependency exists, it becomes a table relationship in the physical database design. There are three basic types of entity dependencies and they are illustrated in the following figures. These illustrations were drawn using SQL Server 7's diagram tool and the Pubs database that is provided as a sample SQL Server database.

- **One-to-one dependency.** A *one-to-one dependency* is the rarest form of relationship, since each record in one entity correlates to exactly one record in the other. In a one-to-one relationship, the entities can often be combined into a single entity. We will discuss this further under the topics of normalization and denormalization.

- **One-to-many dependency.** A *one-to-many dependency* is the most common form of relationship. One record in a primary entity has ties to many records in a secondary entity. One salesman has many sales, or one product has many parts, or, as shown in Figure 1.1, one title has many sales.

- **Many-to-many dependency.** A *many-to-many dependency* exists when many records in one entity can relate to many records in another entity. One product can be stored in a number of warehouses and a single warehouse can have many products. In this situation, the dependency will be facilitated through the use of three entities: a product entity, a warehouse entity, and a product/warehouse entity that allows the other two to be connected. A many-to-many relationship is physically designed as two one-to-many relationships (see Figure 1.2).

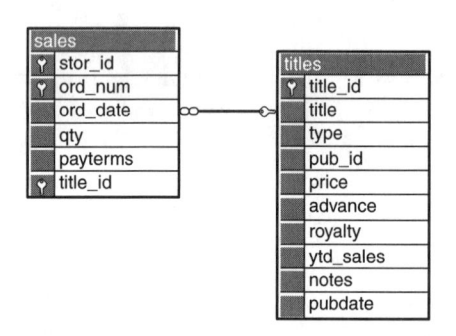

FIGURE 1.1
A one-to-many dependency (one title has many sales).

- **View.** A *view* represents a subset of table(s) attributes that can be designed to facilitate a particular special circumstance. You might not want all fields and/or records of a database to be visible. A view can provide this functionality. The management of permissions and other administrative tasks is far easier to implement than if this had to be done on the entire content of a table.

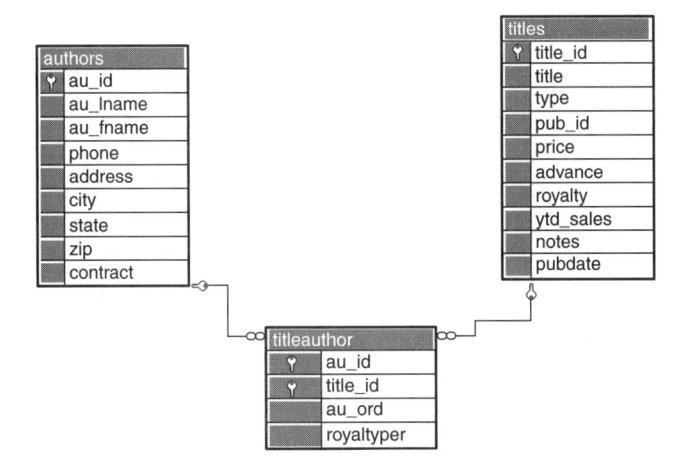

Normalization Rules for Entity Definition 17

authors
- au_id
- au_lname
- au_fname
- phone
- address
- city
- state
- zip
- contract

titles
- title_id
- title
- type
- pub_id
- price
- advance
- royalty
- ytd_sales
- notes
- pubdate

titleauthor
- au_id
- title_id
- au_ord
- royaltyper

FIGURE 1.2
A many-to-many dependency (one author writes many titles; one title can have many authors).

- **Index.** An *index* is used to quickly retrieve information from a database. If a search of a database must be performed on an element other than the primary key, an alternative index will drastically improve the performance of this search. Suppose a customer's information must be found. If the customer number isn't known, but another element, such as the name or phone number, is, this element can be used against an alternative index to find the desired information.

Other database elements include *rules*, *check*s, *stored procedures*, *triggers*, and *constraints*. These elements are all interrelated and let you maintain data integrity and provide additional functionality to the database. Each of these elements is discussed in more detail in later chapters.

NORMALIZATION RULES FOR ENTITY DEFINITION

The process of *normalization* is the division of entities within a table in an attempt to provide the most efficient use of storage. At times, *denormalization* is subsequently performed to improve response time and use of resources. The process of designing the logical structure of a database is an attempt to provide a degree of normalization combined with aspects of denormalization to produce optimum storage efficiency while still providing acceptable levels of performance and resource utilization. Denormalization will be discussed later in this chapter.

> **NOTE** You might get questions on the exam which pertain to applying the theory of Normalization. You must know when it is necessary to denormalize. You must also recognize what rules are broken when looking at samples of data.

There are three basic rules to normalizing a database structure. These three rules are known as "normal forms" of database design. Using normal forms provides these basic advantages:

- No-data redundancy contributing to data integrity
- Index columns for faster sorting and searching
- Smaller entities that reduce table locking and data contention
- Query optimization

The three rules are discussed in the following sections.

First Normal Form

An attribute of an entity shouldn't have more than one definable piece of data or repeating groups. A full name should never be used. For example, a field called customer name could be divided into first name and last name and would, therefore, break the first normal form rule. The first name is a piece of data that is independent from the last name and therefore should be a separate attribute.

Second Normal Form

A non-key attribute of an entity must depend on the entire primary key, not just a portion of the key. For example, if the primary key of an orders entity contained two fields, customer ID and product ID, the attribute field product description wouldn't belong because it has no connection to the customer ID, only the product ID. This would break the second normal form rule.

Third Normal Form

A non-key field must not depend on another non-key field. The most obvious example of this rule is in the case of address information. The zip code is dependent on the address area; the city is dependent on the address itself. A large corporation or government agency may choose to have zip code information stored in a separate table and not within the base data to a perfect normalized form. Although in most table designs this situation is denormalized, in a pure normal form, a separate entity would be used to provide additional address information, such as city and zip code, based on the address.

Fourth and Fifth Normal Forms

Two other normal forms do exist but aren't commonly implemented. It's entirely possible that by adhering to a third normal form, you may actually accomplish the fourth and fifth forms. Fourth normal form dictates that a third normal form have no multivalued dependencies. In other words, every value of an attribute must appear in at least one row with every other value of the other attribute. Fifth normal form is intended to eliminate joint dependency constraints. This is a theoretical consideration that is thought to have no practical value. If you disregard these forms, the design of the database might be less than perfect, but it should have no loss of functionality.

IDENTIFICATION OF PRIMARY KEYS

A primary key is not necessarily required for all tables in a database. However, the provision of a primary key does allow for a considerable number of benefits and should be considered for every table. When defining a primary key, you should keep a number of factors in mind. The primary key normally defines uniqueness in a table in that every record of a table has its own unique primary key. Also, when defined, a primary key should not be permitted to not have any content. If a primary key is empty or null, you have a situation where data integrity is difficult (if not impossible) to maintain.

A primary key should be defined as a single attribute that doesn't allow duplicates or NULL content. The primary key should be as small as possible. It's possible to create a compound primary key that uses multiple attributes or a key that contains a large number of bytes, but in the physical design this will increase the overhead and response time associated with data retrieval.

Under SQL 7, the primary key constraint is used to identify the primary key. SQL 7 mandates that primary keys be unique, one per table, and non-NULL in content. SQL 7 will also create a unique index for the specified column(s).

FOREIGN KEY SELECTION AND REFERENTIAL INTEGRITY

A foreign key is used to tie one entity to the primary key of another for the purpose of creating a dependency. An attribute or combination of attributes can act as a foreign key. A foreign key doesn't have to be unique. In fact, foreign keys are often in a many-to-one relationship with a primary key in another entity. Foreign key values should be copies of the primary key values. No value in the foreign key except NULL should ever exist unless the same value exists in the primary key. In SQL 7, a foreign key may be NULL. If any part of a composite foreign key is NULL, the entire foreign key must be NULL.

A foreign key constraint works in conjunction with primary or unique constraints to enforce referential integrity among specified tables. In a database diagram, a foreign key constraint is automatically placed on specified attributes when you create a dependency relationship to a table from another table to which a primary key or unique constraint is attached. A relationship is created to enforce referential integrity between these two related entities.

You can use the database diagram feature to create a relationship between tables in SQL 7. You can use drag-and-drop functionality to relate a field or column of one table to another by dragging to the title bar. This will create a relationship with the primary key. You can use the Create Relationship dialog box, shown in Figure 1.3, to specify any additional information about the relationship. To access the database diagram feature to create a relationship, do the following:

1. Start the Enterprise Manager and open the object collections by clicking the + to expand the drop-down list for the database holding the related tables.

2. Select the Database Diagrams folder. You will see all existing diagrams in the right panel.

3. Double-click an existing diagram or right-click the folder and select New Database Diagram to access the diagram editor.

4. Tables can be added from the list of available tables for a new diagram. Once a diagram exists, you can right-click anywhere in the diagram and select New Table to add additional tables.

5. To open the Create Relationship dialog box, drag the related key from one table to the primary key of the table it is to be related to.

6. Select the desired options from the check boxes shown:

    - Check existing data on creation: Enforces the constraint on existing data.

    - Enable relationship for INSERT and UPDATE: Causes the relationship to be enforced on any Insert and Update procedure.

    - Enable relationship for replication: Enforces the relationship during the replication process.

These options are further defined when constraints and referential integrity are discussed later in this book.

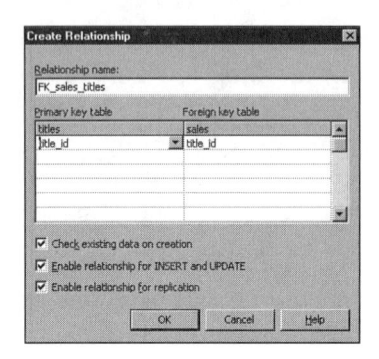

FIGURE 1.3
The Create Relationship dialog box.

BUSINESS RULES AND DATA INTEGRITY

A *business rule* is the implementation of a portion of company policies and procedures that helps enforce the integrity or correctness of data. A business rule will be defined in the logical design as a limitation placed on the data. The database server can enforce an attribute that cannot exceed an upper limit or one that must have a value from a selection of choices. Also, data type requirements can be more strictly enforced to provide additional control over attributes that contain alphanumeric information but require a specific format or picture.

When you implement business rules, you can immediately take action to correct the data before it is permanently saved to the database. A company can have a guideline that customers not be allowed to owe more than $1,000, or it can limit the free delivery of a product to one of three states. Using Check constraints with SQL Server easily enforces these types of situations.

These types of constraints can be placed at the entity or attribute level. From the Tables tab of the Properties dialog box, you can implement a SQL expression (as shown in the following example) to define the constraint. To access the Properties dialog box, shown in Figure 1.4, right-click any table within a database diagram and select Properties.

```
State = 'TX' or State = 'NM'
ZipCode LIKE '[0-9][0-9][0-9][0-9][0-9]'
Balance < 1000
```

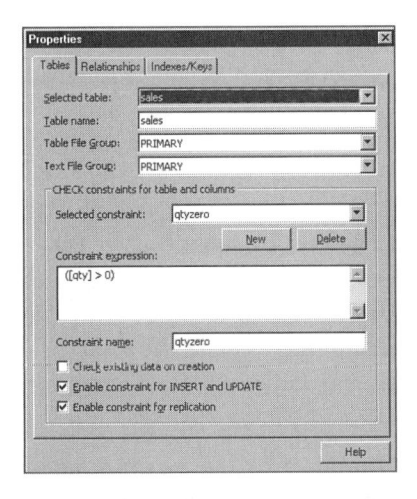

FIGURE 1.4
The Tables tab of the Properties dialog box.

By defining business rules that apply to your database during the logical design phase of development, you allow for a smoother implementation. Also, as the logical design becomes further defined, other rules that were missed in the initial process will be easier to spot.

MODELING RULES AND CONSTRAINTS

SQL 7 provides an extensive modeling tool, the Database Diagram (also called the Database Designer). This tool provides many functions, including the following:

- You can enact changes directly to the contents of each table in a database diagram using this tool.
- You can create a number of special-purpose diagrams combining as many of the tables from the database as you want.
- You can view a table in any of five different views to help manage the size and layout of your diagram.
- You can create the table and define its columns in your database diagram.
- You can alter the table's appearance in your diagram so that the information you need is visible when you need it.

When you save your table or the diagram, the table is created in your database. Any edits or adjustments can be performed from the database diagram, including the addition of rules and constraints to be enacted at the table or column level.

Two modes of operation exist for the designer:

- **You may view and edit individual tables by selecting a table, right-clicking, and choosing a design table.** It's recommended that you create a table in stages. Even though you might know the desired content of a table, you should initially create the table base and save it to the database before you define rules, constraints, keys, and so on.

- **You may view and edit a group of related tables by creating or selecting a previously created database diagram.** When you change a table's design in a database diagram, any data that is stored in the table is preserved to the extent possible. When you're satisfied with your basic design, you can add constraints, indexes, and any additional columns you require.

A table can appear only once in a given diagram. However, you can create a table that has a structure similar to an existing table. By duplicating the existing table within a diagram, you can easily create a new table with some of the same column names. You can then delete unwanted columns, add new columns, and assign a new table name to the newly created table.

It is possible to delete tables from your diagram without affecting the database. If you want to, you can delete a table from the diagram, all existing diagrams, and the database itself. Note that the actual deletion doesn't occur until you save your diagram.

The tool provides much documentation functionality. Once a diagram has been completed, you can adjust several aspects of the view, add text annotations, and print a hard copy.

> **NOTE** It is important to become comfortable with viewing models using this feature. You will see numerous exhibits on the exam which utilize database diagrams created using this modelling tool. Pay particular attention to relationships including one-to-many, many-to-many, one-to-one and also those which connect a FK to a PK within the same table.

Denormalization

Once you have a logical design completely normalized, rarely will you keep it in that state as you proceed to the physical design of the actual database. Although normalization gives you a great deal of storage efficiency and might result in increased performance in some situations, there are a number of drawbacks to a completely normalized database. You should consider the tradeoffs between storage efficiency, performance, and maintainability in your final design.

If you go too far with the normalization process, you might actually reverse the effect you're trying to achieve. Although normalization will reduce data redundancy, result in smaller tables with fewer rows, and provide a logical and consistent form, it will also require joins for the implementation and will not allow for summary, duplicate, or other data that a user might expect to find in a single table. Normalizing a database design too far can decrease performance and make it difficult to alter the underlying table structure and might make it harder to work with the data.

Denormalization may occur at any number of levels. At the absolute extreme, a database schema under SQL 7 can be completely duplicated to a number of servers across the network by implementing SQL replication. This could be warranted if you need to distribute the access to the data across slow network links or to multiple remote locations. Many advantages are gained through database replication, because the data is more easily available at the locations where it will be used. The drawback of this is increased maintenance of a number of servers. Also, if database replication isn't configured properly, it could monopolize a WAN. In addition, if there are network problems or a poor setup, the data might not be synchronized to a level that keeps it up-to-date. Data can be maintained as an exact duplication against a number of servers, but this would require a high-speed network and the configuration of a two-phase commit.

Other, simpler examples of planned denormalization would be to maintain complete address information for customers, suppliers, employees, and so on in the tables with the rest of their general information. This is what most users expect, and it is difficult to maintain a separate address table. There are no defined rules for denormalization, but some definite guidelines will help you understand what level might be appropriate in a given situation.

Data warehousing schemas often use a denormalized approach referred to as a star or snowflake schema. This schema structure takes advantage of typical decision support queries by using one central "fact" table for the subject area and many dimension tables containing denormalized descriptions of the facts.

There are also several other situations to consider. If a join requires the implementation of more than three tables, denormalization should be considered. In some situations where the number of columns in a table can grow very large, a denormalized structure would split the table into more easily handled portions and use a one-to-one relationship to connect the information.

The completed structure will have to be modified over time as the live use of the database warrants. Never consider a database design to be perfect or complete. It often takes a number of years of actual use to determine the best levels of normalization and denormalization to use.

What Is Important to Know

The following list summarizes the chapter and accentuates the key concepts to memorize for the exam:

- Normalization rules govern the efficient design of a database to minimize data redundancy.
- Denormalization is the process of purposefully adding redundancy to improve system performance and reduce associated overhead.
- Primary keys are defined to provide a unique mechanism for referring to each row in a table, thus giving you quick access to desired records.
- Foreign keys are used within a table as a pointing mechanism to the primary key of another table for the purpose of establishing relationships between tables.
- Business rules coincide with the company's business goals. When you implement a database design, business rules and constraints help you maintain data integrity and focus the system design to meet business goals.
- In the implementation of any database model, a balance between normalization and denormalization is required.

OBJECTIVE

- Assess the potential impact of the logical design on performance, maintainability, extensibility, scalability, availability, and security.

CHAPTER 2

Deriving the Physical Design

This chapter looks at many of the considerations you must take into account when implementing SQL Server. Six factors will be addressed: performance, maintainability, extensibility, scalability, availability, and security. Each of these factors can affect the overall system.

A perfect design, were it to exist, would outperform user expectations. A server and its objects would never require maintenance. No additions would ever be needed to keep a system up-to-date. Thousands of users could access a single server at the same time with no loss of performance. All data, and information obtained from it, would be exactly what was required to solve all business problems and would be available exactly when needed to address any situation. No possible breaches in security could ever occur, and technology would remain stagnant without ever evolving.

Since this is the real world, where technology changes almost daily, and business requirements for any implementation constantly need updating, a developer must take measures to ensure that a system meets optimum levels (as close to perfection as possible).

The six factors are discussed in detail in the following sections. It is important to note that most of these factors are covered in other areas of this book. They are discussed here as introductory topics in the overall implementation of a system.

Performance

Many aspects of the design affect the database's performance. Wise decisions must be made early in the logical design to ensure that the database's performance will be at optimum levels. Even so, once the physical structure has been determined and placed into active service, some fine-tuning will be required in order to get the best performance.

SQL 7 provides a number of tools to help you optimize the performance of the database and the SQL Server engine itself. One proven tool for measuring performance is NT's own Performance Monitor. As with previous versions of SQL Server, several counters are provided. SQL integrates these counters into the Performance Monitor environment. SQL Performance Monitor uses NT authentication to perform its activities. An NT account must be granted permission to connect to SQL Server and must be a member of the SQL Server public role.

When trying to measure performance using Performance Monitor, you must remember that there will be some overhead directly related to Performance Monitor itself because each counter consumes some RAM and processor time while executing tasks. Carefully consider the number of counters utilized within Performance Monitor at any one time.

You can monitor performance from a remote workstation. SQL Server Performance Monitor attempts to connect to SQL Server using the default named pipe *Server_name*\pipe\sql\query. If SQL Server is not configured to listen on named pipes, SQL Server Performance Monitor won't be able to connect. It's important to note, then, that when using Performance Monitor, you can't connect to a server running on Microsoft Windows 95 or 98 because SQL Server can't listen on named pipes when running on Windows 95 or 98. An alternative named pipe can be configured and set up if you want to allow an application to connect under a name other than that provided for by the default. A DB-Library alias must be added from that computer name to the separate local pipe name. You can do this using the SQL Server Client Configuration utility, shown in Figure 2.1.

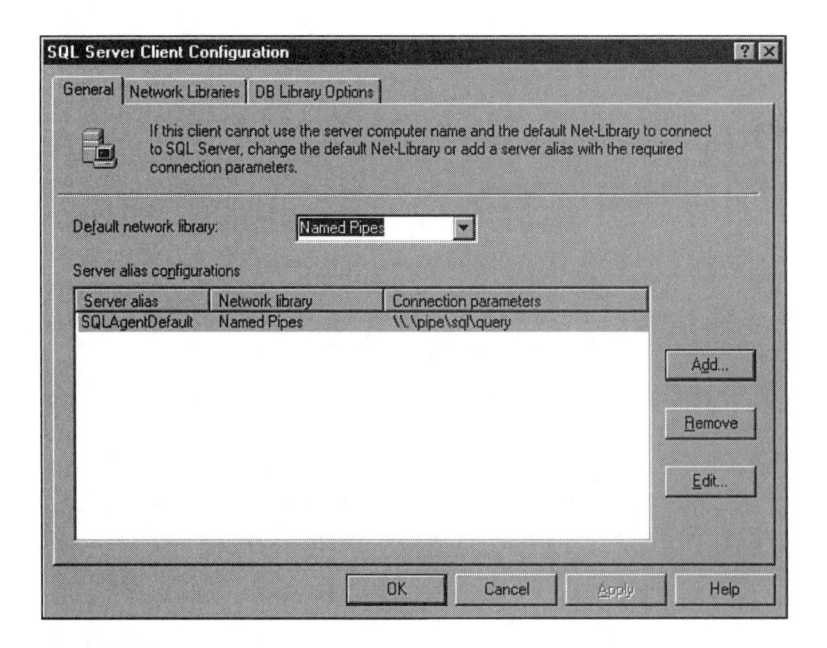

FIGURE 2.1
The SQL Server Client Configuration utility.

SQL Server also provides the Profiler to monitor events pertaining to the engine. Monitoring engine events with SQL Server Profiler allows you to use a graphical tool to monitor server activity. With the Profiler, you can monitor much engine activity, including the following:

- Login connections, failures, and disconnections
- Transact-SQL SELECT, INSERT, UPDATE, and DELETE statements
- Batch activity and status
- Stored procedure activity
- Errors written to the SQL Server error log
- Locks acquired or released on a database object
- Cursors that are opened

Event data can be captured and saved to a file or table for later analysis. We will revisit the monitoring tools later when we discuss database maintenance.

As always, the use of stored procedures can greatly improve performance. SQL Server optimizes and compiles a stored procedure when it is executed. It will then maintain this information in memory for as long as possible, dramatically reducing the overhead of subsequent calls to the same stored procedure.

Driver performance data can also be profiled. Using the ODBC utility in the Control Panel, you can configure the DSN log file to supply a location to store information obtained through the use of a data connection. You can also control this functionality programmatically. This topic is fully covered in the SQL Server Books Online.

Several details affect SQL Server's performance, from software to hardware to network considerations and more. In the logical design of a database, a number of important criteria affect performance. When you design and implement a database, you should identify the large tables in the database and the more complex processes the database will perform. Additionally, you must consider the effect on performance of increasing numbers of users accessing the database. Denormalization strategies can help you improve performance. The addition of a column or columns to an entity that contains preaggregated data can improve the efficiency with which reporting is performed. Also keep in mind that if a database has a number of small tables, a considerable amount of work is required to combine the related data. Extra processing can reduce the database's performance.

The correct use of indexes, RAID, and file groups is important for achieving optimum performance. Limit indexes to a single column and field and keep them as small as possible. Implement hardware or software RAID using top-of-the-line disk controllers and hard drives. Use file groups to simplify tasks performed by the database engine. Each of these aspects will be dealt with in full later.

Another important aspect to be aware of is the selection of appropriate hardware. In most companies, the database server is one of the most active computers in the environment. Therefore, it's important to provide the highest hardware levels possible to this server. Consider the fact that, in an NT environment, the servers do a great deal of the processing. It is less important to have powerful desktop machines, and it's extremely important that the servers—especially the database servers—are high-quality.

Hardware selection is a corporate-wide investment. Upgrades can be costly, but it's easy to justify the cost of hardware improvements when you consider the benefits. If your network is using 16-bit network cards, considerable work must be performed by the network infrastructure for the communication of data over the wire. Using 32-bit cards in most cases can almost double performance.

Is your company still working on a coaxial 10Base2 network? The maximum speed of this type of cabling is 10MBps. A changeover to twisted-pair cabling can be costly, but let's look at these costs a little more closely. Most network cards, especially those that support Plug and Play, can use either cable type without computer configuration changes. Performance can be improved to 100MBps with appropriate cable grade and strong supporting equipment. Cable problems and other network failures affect only a single computer or set of computers on a distributed hub, not the entire network.

Disk controllers come in a variety of levels, costs, and supported features. By selecting a high-end controller with its own dedicated processor, you take the work of disk reads and writes away from the main CPU and give its processors more time to perform other operating system tasks.

Implementing multiple controllers and multiple hard drives gives you many added benefits. First, you have the benefit of hardware redundancy and fault tolerance, providing for safeguards and less down time upon failures. Second, if you implement disk striping (with or without parity), you can gain substantial performance improvements in the area of disk accesses.

If sufficient budgetary funds are available, use a multiprocessor server with as much RAM as you can cram in. NT is a symmetric multiprocessing operating system that fully benefits from hardware with multiple processors. Careful consideration must be taken, though: This hardware can be very expensive. Unlike Windows 95 and 98, NT loves RAM to an endless degree. Windows 95 and 98 can use only 64MB of RAM; any more is disregarded by the operating system. NT will use all available RAM. NT's file caching algorithm will attempt to predict the files needed and have them waiting in RAM when reads are requested. Reading from RAM is much faster than reading from disk, so more RAM can make a huge difference in responses to user queries.

SQL Server allows you to preallocate RAM and use it for its tasks. When configured, NT will dedicate this block of RAM to SQL Server. Like NT, SQL Server loves RAM and can cache more data and prepared procedures if large amounts of RAM are available. A big bonus here is that RAM is cheap. For a very small investment, you can dramatically improve any NT computer.

So, how much does this upgrading really cost? In a worst-case scenario (replacing network cards and cabling, reorganizing the network), you're probably looking at about $300 per workstation with a time investment of two to three weeks, depending on network size. This cost can be as low as $100 per workstation if network cards are sufficient and cable distances to the hubs are short.

You can pay in excess of $20,000 for a good server with multiple processors and a full RAID implementation. To warrant this expense, you would make this investment only in high-volume servers performing mission-critical tasks where optimum performance can mean the success or failure of an implementation and of the company itself. A server sufficient for most installations can be obtained for around $10,000.

My suggestion, based on many years of dealing with management and cost-justifying hardware, software, and user training, is to select a server with the highest level of processor(s) possible that fits into your budget. Implement a SCSI or a similar brand of controller that supports 10 or more drives and has a dedicated processor. Fill up all available RAM slots with the highest available chip size that fits into your budget. Use 32-bit Plug and Play network cards and throw the old 10Base2 and 16-bit cards away—as far away as possible so that they are never accidentally used.

Consider the design of fact tables as a method to improve query performance in a large data warehouse schema. As you design a fact table, remove any columns that are not required for the analysis of business operations. If the data doesn't represent a business transaction, or if the data can be obtained using aggregate functions or an aggregate column, the data can probably be removed from the fact table.

Using triggers is a good way to obtain functionality without undue overhead. The time involved in running a trigger is spent mostly in referencing other tables, which can be either in memory or on the database device. The deleted and inserted tables are always in memory. The location of other tables referenced by the trigger determines how long the operation takes.

> **NOTE** These ideas represent only some of the performance capabilities provided in SQL 7. We will revisit performance issues in every chapter of this book. Keep in mind that a high-performance database is an important aspect of database development and should, therefore, be a major consideration as you prepare for the exam.

Maintainability

Each of the SQL Server objects created in the design will require some degree of maintenance. These interrelated components each require special consideration criteria if a data structure is to be productive over time. Improvements in SQL 7 reduce some of the administrative chores associated with previous versions. However, it's important to remember that, like all other IT systems, databases have a definable life cycle and undergo constant modifications. Making the correct decisions during the logical design can make these maintenance tasks much easier to perform.

You should include a method of implementing backups, including a practiced disaster recovery plan, as part of a regular maintenance routine. The archiving of historical data should also be considered during the design. Periodic archive procedures will keep space available for the database. Occasionally running the SQL Server Profiler will help you detect data usage and aid in the further design of indexes not included in the original plan.

A database design is easiest to maintain when the structure and interrelationships between tables is kept simple. When you ensure a first normal form in a database, each data element is separate from all others; thus, changes to data are easier to implement. Avoid creating too many small tables with complex relationships. In doing so, you make the task of maintenance very involved and complex. Again, a balance between normalization and denormalization will provide the best results.

A powerful feature of SQL 7 is its ability to implement full-text queries. By entering a simple English phrase, the user can produce desired output. This feature, although desirable for someone who is unfamiliar with SQL syntax, doesn't occur automatically. Synonyms must be developed and maintained to permit this feature to work. Consider the following example. A table has columns for Customer Name and Balance. A user could enter an English query similar to this:

```
Give me all clients who owe money for more than 30 days
```

To allow for this type of query, you would need to develop and configure these synonyms:

```
Client = Customer Name
```

and

```
Money = Balance
```

Because it's difficult to predict all the English words that a person might choose to describe individual data items, the proper configuration of English text queries can be a difficult task. The development and implementation of these queries is discussed in full in Chapter 4, "Creating a Physical Database."

Full-text support for SQL Server data involves the ability to issue queries against data stored in character columns, but this requires administration to create and maintain the underlying indexes that facilitate these queries. Full-text indexes are stored in the file system but are administered through the database. There is only one full-text index per table. One or more full-text indexes within the same database are gathered into a full-text catalog.

Full-text indexes are created, managed, and dropped using stored procedures. This complete process is discussed in Chapter 4.

Full-text administration is carried out at several different levels. At the server level, properties are set to facilitate the options of full-text queries. These properties will affect operation on a server-wide basis. At the database level, metadata (data that reflects information about the database and its objects) for one or more full-text catalogs can be created and dropped in an enabled database. At the catalog level, administrative facilities must be used to populate a full-text catalog. At the table level, a table must be registered as supporting full-text queries. Then metadata is created for that table's full-text index. A registered table must be activated before it can participate in the next full-text catalog population. At the column level, columns that support full-text queries can be added to or dropped from an inactive registered table. At all levels, there are facilities to retrieve metadata and status information.

The administration utilities available in SQL Server include the Full-Text Indexing wizard, SQL Server context menus for tables, and the Full-Text Catalog object in the Enterprise Manager. Administration can also be performed through a set of stored procedures and scalar functions.

Other maintenance procedures will be discussed later in this book. Maintaining databases requires ongoing proactive actions to be performed under SQL Server. As a preparation for taking the exam, you should examine the internal utilities and practice using the related Transact-SQL commands and stored procedures.

EXTENSIBILITY

SQL 7 provides much extensibility through new features, programmable objects, and the restructuring of the data storage architecture. There has always been some degree to which objects could expand within the system, but these new changes provide levels of expansion that couldn't be achieved previously.

> **NOTE:** Throughout the history of Microsoft certification, exam content has always focused on new features and changes to the environment. This is true of just about every exam in every certification. Considering the number of changes and their drastic effect on the environment, you should spend a great deal of time in your exam preparation looking at what's new in SQL 7.

Extensibility refers to adding features to a design after it has been implemented. Producing a database schema that is fully extensible requires a little forethought and planning for the usage of the database in the future.

To provide extensibility in moving from a logical to a physical data model, it is to your advantage to implement the design of systems around a three-tier model, separating user, business, and data services into separate elements. Not only does this provide for extensibility, but it also leverages SQL as a back-end database server and improves maintainability. As you design a structure, try to isolate all operations, keeping unrelated items as separate elements and keeping interrelated objects and processes together. This applies not only to a system's data elements but also to business rules and user interface considerations.

Physical data modeling involves the careful layout and definition of tables, columns, and relationships. Using the Database Diagram tool you can see illustrations of the physical design and enact relationships through drag and drop procedures.

SCALABILITY

How many users can a given system support? As the number of users grows, will the current design need modifications to provide for the growing numbers? SQL 7 provides numerous features that support scalability:

- The same server across Windows 95 and Windows NT platforms
- Dynamic row-level locking

- Very large database (VLDB) improvements
- Improved query optimizer
- Intraquery parallelism
- VLM support
- Replication improvements
- Distributed queries
- Parallel backup and restore
- Full integrity protection
- Distributed transactions

To provide for scalability in a database model, all of the following offer advantages and produce a more scalable design:

- Planned redundancy/replication
- Normalization/denormalization
- A three-tier development
- Implementation of transactions
- The separation of error checking across tiers

Availability

Has the data been made available in a timely fashion to people who need that information for business decisions? Is there a reasonable level of response time when system traffic is heaviest? These questions represent the ultimate goal in the finished product. Selecting a distribution model will help you make the appropriate data available. Also, the initial setup of the hardware and implementation of domain planning can ensure that information is truly available to all that need it. Replication involves the copying of complete tables and/or table subsets in the form of articles to another server. In replication, redundant data is maintained to place the data closer to the users who will need it or to allow for load balancing in case one server has too many users to handle all access to the contained data. We will discuss replication later in this book.

Security

Providing the facilities of a system while still maintaining security can be somewhat of a challenge—a challenge that should be kept in mind through all stages of design. Designing and implementing the security model for SQL 7 produces truly integrated capabilities, whereas previous models provided only pseudo-integration between NT and SQL Server. By utilizing this flexible model, you can easily meet security requirements while still providing access to data resources.

When implementing users and their permissions, try to keep the number of people who can actually create objects to a minimum. If too many people have creation privileges, SQL Server spends a great deal of time checking object permissions. When a user creates an object, the user becomes the owner of that object. If that object is used to create other objects, as in the case of a table being used to create a view or a view being used to create another view, SQL Server must check permissions for each object in the chain that has a new owner.

Even if only two people are creating objects, a complex ownership chain can exist from object to object. Often, two developers share each other's tools. For example, one developer could create a view from another developer's table, and that view could be used for a second view created by the table's developer. This would cause two ownership breaks.

You can have many ownership breaks requiring permissions to be checked, even though they may have already been checked a few steps earlier. In the previous example, if other objects were created, permissions would have to be checked many more times, even though there are only two owners.

Physical Database Design

A thorough overview of some of the physical database models will serve you well on the exam. Use the sample databases and create some of your own and ensure that you are comfortable with the looks of these designs through the various SQL Server tools.

Using a three-tier object model is an important mechanism in today's technologically advanced operations. You can easily have a worldwide

Physical Database Design 41

distribution center that uses geographically dispersed SQL Servers and Microsoft Transaction Servers to form a complex network of data that is efficient and that responds quickly to queries of enterprise users.

An MTS server will isolate the transactions occurring from multiple users and perform interactions with SQL Server in a comfortable manner. Using a three-tier architecture in this manner lets a larger number of users make requests more frequently. If accuracy and consistency of the environment are desired, distributed transactions can be used that let multiple servers take part in a transaction yet maintain the consistency in operations. In a three-tier model, the MTS server helps take some of the workload from the server to allow it to function more efficiently and concentrate solely on data manipulation functions.

In simpler models, a two-tier environment can be beneficial. If a heavy load is not expected by a large number of concurrent users, the simple interaction of a client application against SQL Server can handle most business operations. With new security mechanisms in SQL Server 7, it is possible to assign permissions to an application where it is not desired to give users these same permissions.

> **NOTE** Permissions are not considered a topic for the exam. However, if you are preparing for the Administration exam, you should spend a great deal of time looking into the new SQL Server 7 security implementations.

When preparing for the Implementation exam, consider the elements of the physical design in complete sections. Try to separate a particular portion of an application and look at all components related to that particular procedure. It will help if you scope out a procedure using a database diagram, table structure, or constraint definition and follow through to the coding, or paying particular attention to the scope of the procedure.

What Is Important to Know

The following list summarizes the chapter and accentuates the key concepts to memorize for the exam:

- The fine-tuning of a database implementation is never completed. Adjustments (tweaking) should be made regularly. Monitor performance during live use after implementation.
- Provide for the optimum hardware levels that can be cost-justified and fit into the budget.
- Simplify the database structure and avoid over-normalization. Select performance or storage efficiency for best results.
- Use a three-tier model to allow for the highest degree of extensibility, scalability, and maintainability.
- Use replication and redundancy to allow for most availability.
- Keep ownership of database objects to as few people as possible.

OBJECTIVES

- Access data by using the dynamic SQL model.
- Access data by using the Stored Procedure model.
- Manipulate data by using Transact-SQL cursors.
  - Choose the appropriate type of cursor.
  - Define the appropriate level of sensitivity to change.
  - Choose the appropriate navigation.
  - Choose the scope of the cursor, global or local.
- Create and manage explicit, implicit, and distributed transactions to ensure data consistency and recoverability.
  - Define the transaction isolation level.
  - Design transactions of appropriate length.
  - Avoid or handle deadlocks.
  - Use optimistic locking appropriately.
  - Implement error handling by using `@@trancount`.
- Write INSERT, DELETE, UPDATE, and SELECT statements that retrieve and modify data.
- Write Transact-SQL statements that use joins or subqueries to combine data from multiple tables.
- continues...

CHAPTER 3

Creating Data Services

OBJECTIVES continued

- Create scripts by using Transact-SQL. Programming elements include control-of-flow methods, local and global variables, functions, and error-handling methods.

- Design, create, use, and alter views.
  - Modify data through a view.
  - Query data through a view.

- Create and execute stored procedures to enforce business rules, modify data in multiple tables, perform calculations, and use input and output parameters.
  - Implement error handling by using return codes and the RAISERROR statement.
  - Choose appropriate recompile options.

- Create triggers that implement rules, enforce data integrity, and perform cascading updates and deletes.
  - Implement transactional error handling.

- Create result sets that provide summary data. Query types include TOP *n* PERCENT and GROUP BY (specifically, HAVING, CUBE, and ROLLUP).

- Configure session-level options.

- Access data from static or dynamic sources by using remote stored procedures, linked servers, and openrowset.
  - Evaluate where processing occurs when using OPENQUERY.

The Syntax of Design

This chapter focuses on the physical design of a database and its related applications. We look at the command structures used in the database design and the design of SQL Server objects that relate to the daily tasks of a developer. This chapter is the first of two that represent the heart of the material on the certification exam. In the previous two chapters, the concentration centered on development of the logical model; in this chapter, we look closely at the physical model, actual SQL Server objects, and the commands used.

There are two mechanisms that execute any given SQL statement. An SQL statement can be "static," thus representing the same syntax to be applied against data. The second mechanism, "dynamic," is built on-the-fly by using a combination of string expressions and variables. In SQL Server 7, each method can be optimized by the engine; in previous versions, only static SQL maintained in stored procedures could be fully optimized. The optimization of SQL statements now occurs in a more versatile fashion, which allows for the optimization of any form of SQL statement. Thus, performance is improved over multiple operations of both static and dynamic SQL (whether it is used in stored procedures or through a direct data query execution). The following sections compare and contrast static and dynamic SQL.

Dynamic SQL Model

Unlike static SQL statements, which are hard-coded in the program, dynamic SQL statements can be built at runtime and placed in a string variable. Dynamic SQL is generally slower than static SQL. When a program containing dynamic SQL statements is compiled, the dynamic SQL statements are not stripped from the program, as in static SQL. Instead, they are replaced by a function call that passes the statement. To gain some of the processing speed of static SQL, you can have a dynamic SQL statement utilize prepared execution. For a statement that executes once, there is really no advantage in performing a prepared execution. For repeatedly accessed statements, however, the overhead for preparation occurs only once, and future instances of the execution will occur much more quickly. The alternative is to set the SQL statement to execute immediately, which provides less flexibility.

SQL statements, whether prepared or not, can contain replaceable parameters, as shown in the following example of the DELETE operation:

```
DELETE CUSTOMERS WHERE FIRSTNAME = ? AND LASTNAME = ?
```

A prepared and executed statement can contain parameters, whereas an execute immediate statement must conform to Transact-SQL syntax. Parameter statements utilize a question mark placeholder for information that will be supplied at runtime, as shown in the previous example. Using dynamic SQL statements, you can write an application that prompts a user for information (such as database object names) that is unavailable at compile-time. In the following SQL syntax examples, the options for a prepared execution and an immediate execution are illustrated. Note the extra step of preparation prior to the execution:

```
PREPARE statement name [INTO :sql data structure] FROM :string
 variable

EXECUTE prepared statement name [USING DESCRIPTOR :sql data
 structure |
USING :string variable [,...]]


EXECUTE IMMEDIATE :statement string variable
```

STORED PROCEDURES MODEL

Stored procedures supply a facility for storage and optimization of processes that are frequently executed against a database and its objects. Stored procedures can be permanently stored as a database object, or they can be temporary and exist only for the duration of a given process. You can utilize parameters within stored procedures to further provide diversity to any implementation.

The optimization of a stored procedure happens automatically the first time that a procedure runs after SQL Server restarts. It also happens if an underlying table used by the procedure changes. If a new index is added that the procedure might benefit from, however, optimization does not automatically happen (until, for example, the next time SQL Server restarts and the procedure runs). The sp_recompile system procedure forces a recompile of a procedure the next time it runs. The following example marks every stored procedure and trigger that accesses the MyTable table, so that they are recompiled the next time they execute:

```
sp_recompile MyTable
```

The optimization, preparation, and execution processes used by SQL Server involve a five-step operation. The first four of these steps prepare the code to execute, and the final step is the actual execution. The four processes used in preparation are used to parse the statements, optimize for the underlying table, and compile the result. Any parameters that are needed are then received and the statement executes. In the case of prepared execution, the overhead is accommodated once, and future executions use the compiled version. You should not use prepared execution if a procedure is used only once during an SQL Server session.

TRANSACT-SQL CURSORS

A *cursor* is a tracking point through a resultset and is the basis for the creation of a resultset. As a database designer/implementor, you need to fully understand the features that are provided by the different types of cursors, and the resulting impact on performance of the application and the database engine.

Cursor Types

There are essentially four separate cursor types available in SQL Server, each providing different characteristics for the control of data, manipulation of data, resources utilized, and recognition of data changes. You use the Transact-SQL statement, DECLARE CURSOR, to select from one of these four available cursors. SQL Server allows for the use of both ANSI SQL 92 syntax structures and Transact-SQL.

The following is the syntax for SQL-92:

```
DECLARE cursor name [INSENSITIVE] [SCROLL] CURSOR
FOR select statement
[FOR {READ ONLY | UPDATE [OF column list]}]
```

And here is the syntax for Transact-SQL Extended:

```
DECLARE cursor name CURSOR
[LOCAL | GLOBAL]
[FORWARD_ONLY | SCROLL]
[STATIC | KEYSET | DYNAMIC]
[READ_ONLY | SCROLL_LOCKS | OPTIMISTIC]
FOR select statement
[FOR UPDATE [OF column list]]
```

The four cursor types that SQL Server supports are listed as follows:

- **Static.** Static cursor types consume few resources and remain constant, not reflecting the changes made to the data once the cursor is initiated. Although Static cursors can be most efficient for small data sets, they can utilize a very large amount of resources in larger data sets because they store the entire content into tempdb. Many developers may recognize a static cursor as a "Snapshot" or "Insensitive" cursor because it bases its data on a specific point in time, and does not reflect external changes without having the cursor closed and reopened.

- **Dynamic.** Dynamic cursor types consume extremely small amounts of resources. A Dynamic cursor detects changes made to the encompassed data and also recognizes additional records and the deletion of existing records after cursor initiation. The Dynamic cursor type can be closely compared to a Keyset cursor—it provides for more liveliness as records are added and deleted from the dataset from external sources.

- **Forward-only.** The Forward-only cursor is traditionally considered to be a cursor type for front-end applications written in other languages. A Forward-only cursor is actually an option that SQL Server provides for the limitation of scrollability within the data provided for in Static, Dynamic, or Keyset cursors—not a cursor itself. A Forward-only option does not permit reverse scrolling. When used, the cursor must progress through the data set in order, from the beginning to the end. Data is not actually retrieved from the database until it is fetched. Once data is fetched, any updates made by other users are not realized. If a cursor is opened and data is not yet fetched, however, another user can enact changes to the data. These changes are reflected back to the implementation when it is actually fetched. If a change is made to data that would affect the position of the data in a resultset created by using ORDER BY, the new position could alter the Forward-only cursor and cause data to be fetched a second time. When a database API cursor attribute or property is set to forward-only, SQL Server implements it as a Forward-only dynamic cursor.

- **Keyset-driven.** This model consumes very few resources (fewer than a Dynamic cursor), while allowing for the detection of changes. Although the Keyset cursor recognizes changes to existing data, it does not recognize additional records accessed after cursor initialization, and maintains the key values of records deleted by external sources. The number of records maintained in memory at any one time is dependent upon the size of the fetch buffer, which defaults to 10 records. Using the SET FETCH_BUFFER statement can make modifications to the size of the fetch buffer. Unlike a Static cursor, values that change between fetches do not cause records to move around if the changes affect the ORDER BY clause. Records are not removed from the Keyset if changes are made that disqualify a record from matching the condition of the WHERE clause.

Cursor Selection

To choose the appropriate cursor for any given application, you must first consider several factors within the implementation. The scope of these considerations include the following:

- The amount of data in the resultset
- The need for implementation of data changes
- The features required of the cursor
- The visibility of external data changes
- The speed in feeding results to a client
- The effect on application and engine performance

Resultset Size

The amount of data in the resulting set is one of the main factors in the selection of a cursor. The size of the recordset directly affects the performance of the implementation and presents a couple of options for cursor selection. In general, if a recordset will be extremely large, you should stay away from any of the cursor models that store the entire data of the set into memory. In an application model, this means using a client-side cursor; for a server-side application, use Keyset or Dynamic cursors. When using a Static cursor, the size of the rows in the result set cannot exceed the maximum row size for an SQL Server table. In these situations, you should select one of the key-based cursor types that fetch data for local storage only when the data will be viewed or prepared for viewing/editing. If a resultset is relatively small, then the default cursor settings are probably sufficient. Keep in mind, however, that these settings do not provide for updates.

> **NOTE:** The default cursor settings are Forward-only, Read-only, one row at a time, and entire result set. Default result sets must be used for any Transact-SQL statement or batch of Transact-SQL statements that generate multiple result sets.

Data Volatility

The volatility, or changeability, of the data being used presents several different options for performing updates with various cursor types. Not all cursors allow for updates to be made to the resultset, and those that do handle these changes in different ways. It is important, therefore, to consider how each of the cursors handles the implementation of changes. Remembering that the defaults do not allow for data changes, you must select a cursor model that does allow for alterations. Both Keyset and Dynamic cursors allow you to change the data within the resultset. The number of records within a resultset does not change in a Keyset model, but it can increase or decrease in a Dynamic model.

Problems can be presented in changes to records within the recordset if those records are available to other users. Another user can delete a record that matches an existing key. If a change is made to a record in a Keyset cursor for a record that is deleted by another user, it causes an exception in the system. Such exceptions can be handled, but they are less likely to occur in a Dynamic cursor. @@FETCH_STATUS returns information that can detect a record that cannot be fetched because of such a deletion (see Table 3.1 for the return values of @@FETCH_STATUS).

TABLE 3.1

RETURN VALUES FROM @@FETCH_STATUS

Value	Result
0	FETCH statement was successful.
-1	FETCH statement failed or the row was beyond the result set.
-2	Row fetched is missing.

Cursor Features

Keyset-driven or Static cursors must be used if you want to do absolute fetches. To fetch a row from a specific row within the cursor, you utilize the FETCH ABSOLUTE statement; you can fetch rows from an absolute position from the beginning or end of a resultset. If a positive integer is used as an argument, then the position is determined from the beginning of the resultset. If it is negative, the row before the end of the cursor is fetched. If it is zero, no rows are fetched.

Static and Keyset-driven cursors increase the usage of tempdb. Static server cursors build the entire cursor in tempdb; Keyset-driven cursors build the keyset in tempdb.

Performance

By using a Dynamic cursor, you can achieve the results of allowing for updates while also recognizing deletions and additions made by operations that are external to the cursor. So, you might ask, why not use a Dynamic cursor in all situations? The solution is simple when you determine the total functionality of the implementation and look at performance and response time as additional cursor-selection criteria. As previously observed, the resultset features of Dynamic cursors do not allow for all implementations. There are also performance ramifications to consider with a Dynamic cursor. Dynamic cursors open very quickly and have very little overhead because they do not have usage involved with interaction against tempdb in the creation of temporary tables. Overall, a Dynamic cursor is a good cursor selection when working with large resultsets that are not hampered by the feature limitations. After Dynamic cursors are opened, however, they can perform more slowly than other models and should not be used in operations that leave the resultset opened for prolonged periods of time. In these instances, consider using a Keyset or Static cursor. Also worthy of note is that an Inner join can outperform a Dynamic model in resultsets that involve multiple tables.

Response

The fastest way to transmit data to a client is to use the default recordset cursor type. This being an extremely limited model selection criteria where other features are needed require particular scrutiny. When an implementation needs to perform a positioned update or utilizes multiple active statements, default result sets cannot be used. Although a Static cursor provides superior performance and response in a small resultset, response and performance improvements in larger sets should utilize other cursor types.

> **NOTE** When selecting a cursor, functionality is usually chosen over response and performance. After all, what good is a fast-moving implementation if it doesn't perform the required tasks?

SENSITIVITY TO CHANGE

An Insensitive cursor is a read-only cursor that does not reflect modifications to data from any sources external to the cursor. A Read-Only cursor presents changes made by other users but does not allow for changes to the internal data. In SQL-92 syntax, the Insensitive option is used to set the cursor criteria. When using a cursor declared using the Insensitive option, a copy of the data is temporarily made and stored into tempdb. The cursor then makes use of this data and answers all requests.

It is worth noting that you cannot mix the options of the two different forms of cursor declaration. Any use of the options of the SQL-92 syntax prevents the use of any of the options in the Transact-SQL form.

Cursor Navigation

Once a scrollable cursor is opened, you can maneuver through the data by performing a "fetch". If the options you set permit it, scrolling can be performed in either direction. A fetch can be performed in an absolute manner, as defined earlier, or relative to the current position. The fetch command has several different options that provide for full resultset navigation:

- **FETCH FIRST.** Fetches the first row in the resultset.
- **FETCH NEXT.** Fetches the next row after the current row fetched.

- **FETCH PRIOR.** Fetches the previous row before the current row fetched.
- **FETCH LAST.** Fetches the last row in the resultset.
- **FETCH RELATIVE #.** Fetches the row defined by the integer relative to the current position.
- **FETCH ABSOLUTE #.** Fetches the row that corresponds to the row number in the resultset.

Cursor Scope

If you declare the scope of the cursor to be local, then that cursor is restricted to the batch, stored procedure, or trigger in which the cursor was created. The name that you supply for the cursor can be used only during that process. If you need to reference a local cursor after a process ends, then you can use an output parameter within a called stored procedure that declares the local cursor. The called process declares the cursor and uses the parameter to pass the cursor back to a calling process that can assign it to a cursor variable. The calling process can use a cursor variable to keep the cursor open after a process finishes. In this case, the cursor is not closed until all variables that hold a reference to the cursor finish or go out of scope. If no output parameter is used, then the cursor terminates after the end of the process in which it was declared.

If you declare a cursor as global, then the cursor name can be used in any process that is executed by a connection, without needing to pass a reference to the cursor back and forth between processes. The cursor use terminates only after the connection disconnects.

TRANSACTION MANAGEMENT

Normally, SQL Server automatically commits transactions. You do not have to specify or control any of the operations if this "AutoCommit" behavior is desired. In many instances, more control is desired in the implementation of transactions. In such instances, you can develop logic that allows for the committing or rolling back of transactions, based on certain conditions being met.

Explicit Transactions

The use of transactions as a whole allow for changes to be made to a cached copy of the resultset with no changes made to the actual data until explicitly committed. A database implementation can use this feature to allow a long series of changes to be entered, and then give the choice for committing the entire set of changes or rolling back the changes as if none of them were ever performed. When a beginning point and ending point is defined for a transaction, you explicitly control the transaction-handling mechanisms within SQL Server. As a database implementor, you code scripts by using the BEGIN TRANSACTION, COMMIT TRANSACTION, COMMIT WORK, ROLLBACK TRANSACTION, or ROLLBACK WORK statements to define explicit transactions.

The BEGIN TRANSACTION statement defines an explicit starting point for transactions. There are two ending points to a basic transaction. COMMIT TRANSACTION forces the changes onto the actual data. ROLLBACK TRANSACTION places the data back to its original state (before the transaction began or the last savepoint). The short form "TRAN" can be used instead of the complete word "TRANSACTION" for all statements that include the term. The SQL syntax for the use of a transactional operation is as follows:

```
BEGIN TRANSACTION [transaction name | @transaction name variable]

ROLLBACK [TRANSACTION] [transaction name |
@transaction name variable |
savepoint name |
@savepoint variable]

COMMIT [ TRANSACTION [transaction name | @transaction name variable]
]
```

Although the ROLLBACK (or ROLLBACK WORK) statement provides the same functionality as ROLLBACK TRANSACTION, it provides less flexibility in the defined syntax. The COMMIT WORK statement is similar. You may choose to use these statements to simplify the syntax of a simple procedure when specific names and/or variables are not needed. The WORK options can be provided, however, as indicated in the SQL syntax description that follows (there are no further options to these statements):

```
ROLLBACK [WORK]

COMMIT [WORK]
```

Implicit Transactions

The SET IMPLICIT_TRANSACTIONS ON statement places SQL Server into implicit transaction mode. Using this method, transactions need only to be committed or rolled back; in essence, everything becomes a transaction. With each transaction completion, SQL Server automatically starts a new transaction. When a connection is operating in implicit transaction mode, you don't have to do anything to indicate the start of a transaction. This process causes a continuous series of transactions to be implemented.

Transactions are automatically implemented for the following set of database interaction statements utilized within Transact-SQL:

- ALTER TABLE
- FETCH
- REVOKE
- CREATE
- GRANT
- SELECT
- TRUNCATE TABLE
- DROP
- OPEN
- UPDATE
- DELETE
- INSERT

Transactions remain in effect until you issue a COMMIT or ROLLBACK statement. New transactions are started, and this process continues until the mode is turned off by using SET IMPLICIT_TRANSACTIONS OFF. Implicit transaction mode is set by either using the Transact-SQL SET statement or through database API functions and methods.

Distributed Transactions

In more advanced implementations, you may want to execute a transaction that spans more than one server; that is, it updates information in databases stored on separate machines. In fact, SQL Server treats any transaction that spans more than one database as a distributed transaction, even if the databases both reside on the same machine. To perform this type of procedure, it is necessary to envelop the process and only commit the entire transaction after all portions of the transaction can complete. This is known as a *two-phase commit*, and it guarantees the greatest control over data validity and consistency. SQL Server's transaction manager handles this type of implementation. The two-phase operation involves a preparation phase, in which all servers isolate the necessary data and prepare for the transaction; and a second phase, in which the transaction is actually committed. All distributed transactions operate as a local transaction.

Preparation Phase

When SQL Server receives a commit request for a distributed transaction, it sends a prepare command to all resource managers involved in the transaction. Each resource manager then does everything required to make the transaction durable, and all buffers holding log images for the transaction are flushed to disk. Upon completion of this phase, each resource manager reports back the manager where the transaction was initiated. Each manager indicates whether the preparatory measures were successful or whether they failed.

Committal Phase

Upon successful completion of the preparatory phase by all managers, commit commands are sent to each resource manager involved in the process. The resource managers can then complete the committal of the transaction. If all the resource managers report a successful committal, the transaction manager then sends a success notification to the application. Any transaction that fails within the preparation phase causes a rollback command to be sent to each resource manager, and indicates that a failure is sent to the application.

> **NOTE:** For a more complete look at the distributed transaction coordinator within SQL Server and the handling of its implementation, check SQL Server Books Online, *"About Guide to Microsoft Distributed Transaction Coordinator."*

DATA CONSISTENCY

When referring to database consistency, keep in mind that consistency is only one element that presents issues to a database implementation. Use the acronym ACID to remember appropriate implementation standards. ACID refers to atomicity, consistency, isolation, and durability (discussed in the following sections).

Atomicity

Transactions should be implemented as an all-or-nothing state. It is difficult to locate the position where a transaction fails if portions of a transaction are committed while other parts fail. Atomicity guarantees that either the whole transaction is committed or the entire transaction is rolled back. This becomes particularly important if transactions also incur the possibility of network or other communication-oriented failures.

Consistency

Data should always be consistent over multiple sources, as within the replication of databases or a portion thereof to multiple servers. Each server should reflect the same data. SQL Server replication supplies a loose level of consistency, whereas distributed transactions using a two-phase commit provide for a tighter consistency level. Consistency levels can be further defined and implementation can be provided for different levels of consistency, as required. When using distributed applications, it is generally considered a database standard to break consistency definitions into these three different levels:

- Immediate guaranteed consistency
- Latent guaranteed consistency
- Convergence

In transactions, consistency is maintained by guaranteeing that any data added or modifications made to the database complies to the rules set up for the data. All internal data structures, such as b-tree indexes or doubly linked lists, must be correct at the end of the transaction.

A database implementor is responsible for starting and ending transactions at points that enforce the logical consistency of the data. The developer must define the sequence of modifications and leave the data in a consistent state, relative to the organization's business rules. SQL Server provides several mechanisms to help ensure the physical integrity of each transaction: data locking, transaction logging, and transaction committal and rollback statements.

Immediate Consistency

Using two-phase commit operations in a distributed transaction environment, SQL Server can provide for tight consistency in databases. To implement this in a network environment, it is necessary to have a high-speed connection between the data sources. Without this high-speed connection, data may become unavailable for a prolonged period of time and produce undesirable locking situations.

Latent Consistency

In general, absolute consistency is not always needed. Because of the additional hardware and infrastructure requirements needed to implement immediate consistency, often a compromise is made that allows the data to be out-of-date for a short period of time. Even at this level, however, it is important that a guarantee be made that the data is accurate after the entire process is complete. Latent consistency is a common replication implementation that sends transactions that update data to be executed on a server that holds a copy of the data. The data at the two sources will not match for the period of time it takes to send and execute the transactions.

Convergence

This scenario puts priority on the exactness of the data in multiple locations without regard to its correctness. Similar to the process used in Microsoft Access, synchronization changes are merged from multiple sources. If data cannot be duplicated from one dataset to another, transactions may be discarded. This causes other problems, such as a series of transactions that depend on each other's completion to be implemented.

By allowing changes at only one location and implementing other consistency technologies, these problems can be avoided. For this reason, convergence is often discarded as a method of maintaining consistency.

Transaction Isolation

Transactions must be isolated from each other so that each transaction is a complete unit of work, unrelated to other transactions being implemented by other system users. Two transactions enacting against the same data should not be allowed to interfere with each other. For example, in a banking scenario, if a user attempts to transfer money from one account to another, the increase can be made to an account temporarily providing a higher balance. When the money is drawn from the other account, it can be locked for whatever reason, possibly a hold on the account. When the transaction is backed off, the temporary increase in the first account is rolled back. A second transaction cannot be permitted to draw on the increased balance until after the first transaction has committed to the transfer.

Service Durability

A system must be able to provide for transaction services, even in the event of a hardware failure or some other unforeseen problem. Durability provides for the recording of transactions for future updating to the actual data when the service comes back online.

RECOVERABILITY

To provide a full database service, the environment must be able to fully recover in a minimum amount of time so that day-to-day operations can continue. SQL Server provides for data recovery at several different levels:

- Automatic Recovery
- Backup/Restore
- Standby Server
- Checkpoint

Automatic Database Recovery

Each time SQL Server starts, it recovers every database, rolling forward any transactions that have committed and rolling back transactions that haven't. This process can not be disabled because it provides for data consistency and guarantees system-wide atomicity. In the event of a server failure, the process of automatic recovery resets the environment the next time the server starts and the SQL Server engine proceeds through its startup process.

SQL Server also provides for the implementation of automatic checkpointing, which is discussed in more detail in the checkpoint section later in this chapter. You can use the sp_configure stored procedure to set the recovery interval option to set the maximum number of minutes for database recovery. This option determines how often SQL Server saves committed transactions.

Backup/Restore

The Backup and Restore statements will replace the Dump and Load statements in future versions of SQL Server. For the time being, you should consider the Backup and Dump statements to be identical with the Restore and Load statements in all handling. Microsoft recommends, therefore, that Backup and Restore be used for all related operations.

Backup and Restore is a necessary tool, regardless of any safety or other precautions that were taken against the loss of data. There are many historical examples of companies and individuals who disregarded backup procedures and paid dearly, as well as many instances of properly implemented backups saving the day. Backups are called upon in the event of media failures, unrecoverable user errors, or the permanent loss of a server. Backups can also be used as a mechanism for moving or copying data from one place to another. The SQL backup procedure provides for many options, as defined in the following syntax examples.

Backing up a database:

```
BACKUP DATABASE {database name ¦ @database name variable}
TO <backup device> [, ...n]
[WITH
[BLOCKSIZE = {blocksize ¦ @blocksize variable}]
[[,] DESCRIPTION = {text ¦ @text variable}]
[[,] DIFFERENTIAL]
```

```
[[,] EXPIREDATE = {date ¦ @date variable}
¦ RETAINDAYS = {days ¦ @days variable}]
[[,] FORMAT ¦ NOFORMAT]
[[,] {INIT ¦ NOINIT}]
[[,] MEDIADESCRIPTION = {text ¦ @text variable}]
[[,] MEDIANAME = {media name ¦ @media name variable}]
[[,] [NAME = {backup set name ¦ @backup set name variable}]
[[,] {NOSKIP ¦ SKIP}]
[[,] {NOUNLOAD ¦ UNLOAD}]
[[,] [RESTART]
[[,] STATS [= percentage]]
]
```

Backing up a transaction log:

```
BACKUP LOG {database name ¦ @database name variable}
{
[WITH
{ NO_LOG ¦ TRUNCATE_ONLY }]
}
¦
{
TO <backup device> [, …n]
[WITH
[BLOCKSIZE = {blocksize ¦ @blocksize variable}]
[[,] DESCRIPTION = {text ¦ @text variable}]
[[,] EXPIREDATE = {date ¦ @date variable}
¦ RETAINDAYS = {days ¦ @days variable}]
[[,] FORMAT ¦ NOFORMAT]
[[,] {INIT ¦ NOINIT}]
[[,] MEDIADESCRIPTION = {text ¦ @text variable}]
[[,] MEDIANAME = {media name ¦ @media name variable}]
[[,] [NAME = {backup set name ¦ @backup set name variable}]
[[,] NO_TRUNCATE]
[[,] {NOSKIP ¦ SKIP}]
[[,] {NOUNLOAD ¦ UNLOAD}]
[[,] [RESTART]
[[,] STATS [= percentage]]
]
}
<backup device> :: =
{
{backup device name ¦ @backup device name variable}
¦
{DISK ¦ TAPE ¦ PIPE} =
{'temp backup device' ¦ @temp backup device variable}
}
<file or filegroup> :: =
{
FILE = {logical file name ¦ @logical file name variable}
¦
FILEGROUP = {logical filegroup name ¦ @logical filegroup name
➥variable}
}
```

When using the backup procedure, there are three different standards for performing database backups (as discussed in the following sections):

- Full Database Backup
- Transaction Log Backup
- Differential Backup

Full Backup

Full backups need to be performed on a regular basis. A full backup stores the entire contents of a database on to the selected media. It is a standard practice to keep a rotational set of backups and store at least one copy of the backup off-site (where it cannot be damaged by predictable or natural disasters). This is particularly important when the database contains mission-critical information. Full backups should be combined with regular transaction backups to optimize the time it takes to recover data in the event of a problem. The frequency of backups depends on the importance of the data, the minimum level of acceptable downtime, and the possibility of incurring problems.

Full backups are usually scheduled or manually performed during levels of low database usage. Although SQL Server performs backups in a dynamic fashion, allowing the data to remain live during the backup, a response-time degradation occurs while the backup is in progress. Along with the backup of user databases, system bases and file backups should also be a regular part of this regime. Only full database backups of the Master database can be created.

Log Backup

A log backup writes the transaction log contents to the media. This backup process is used in conjunction with a full or differential database backup, and is implemented to allow for faster recovery of data and point-in-time restoring of data. To allow for a point-in-time recovery, you must use log backups. To restore to a specific point-in-time, you restore the last full backup prior to the time and then restore all or part of any log backups to the desired time.

Differential Backup

A differential backup is an option of a full backup that only saves data that has changed from the point of the previous full backup. You can use differential backups to reduce the amount of time it takes to perform a backup. Unlike transaction log backups, differential backups do not allow you to restore the data to a specific point-in-time; it only allows for the restore to the point-in-time that coincides with the time of the actual backup.

Standby Servers

A standby server, also referred to as a warm backup, is a technique that is used to bring the level of downtime caused by any unforeseen problems to a minimum. The idea is that any operation performed on one server is duplicated over to the second. If something happens to the first server, the second can quickly be placed into operation and take over as the primary server.

The backup process can be used to create this server by restoring the desired databases onto the secondary or backup/standby. At periodic intervals, the transaction logs from the primary server are applied on the secondary server, keeping the two servers identical by using the latent consistency process referred to previously in this chapter.

If a problem does arise that requires the standby server to be needed, it is a simple operation to enable the server to take over activities. The implementation of this type of environment can be made to be "automatic fail-over." Either Microsoft Cluster Server is used, or the fail-over can be implemented manually without using this secondary product. The manual changeover is not a difficult one to implement. The problem is that users' computers have internal pointers to the primary server by name, and the secondary server according to network rules will have a different name. To activate the second server, you need only rename the server with the same name used on the primary machine, implement a couple of configuration changes, and reboot.

When the standby server is required to perform as the production server because of failure, use the RECOVERY clause and apply the final transaction log backup from the primary server, if access to the database on the primary server is still possible. If not, the server may be slightly out of date and need some minor data upgrading to achieve a "current status." Regardless, you will lose any uncommitted transactions from the point prior to the failure.

A standby server starts with its databases set to a read-only mode between log restores. To bring a standby server completely online after the final transaction log is applied, a final restore statement is required. The final restore statement recovers the database without creating an undo file, making the database available for users to modify, and the databases are set to a nonread-only state.

Checkpointing

Checkpointing is the process in which committed transactions that still reside in memory are written to the database. There are two forms of checkpointing: automatic and manual. SQL Server automatically checkpoints a database periodically. The frequency of this automatic checkpoint is based on the time needed to recover the database and the "recovery interval" of the configuration option.

The database owner using the CHECKPOINT statement can execute a manual checkpoint at any time. You may want to perform a manual checkpoint prior to a backup or any time you want to guarantee that committed transactions are applied to the database. Checkpointing minimizes the amount of time needed to recover a database by recognizing a point in which all transactions have been applied.

Isolation

In a scenario where data can be changed by a number of users or applications, some control must be taken to guarantee that one user's changes do not adversely affect the others. Several situations arise in the daily interactions against a database that permits multiple users to gain access to and change data. While a user is interacting with a table to enact alterations, control over the activities permitted against the data protects the validity of the data, while allowing the freedom to view records in a table that is not being changed. Also, while waiting for transactions to complete, it is possible for a process to perform other operations. SQL Server 7 institutes several levels of locking that protect the data, and there are a number of configurable isolation elements that can optimize process execution and improve upon this situation. Optimistic and pessimistic locking, as well as the different object-level locks, will be discussed later in this chapter.

There are a variety of locks used in SQL Server. In general, the server controls the locking behavior as it is needed. You can supply locking hints to change the default behavior that SQL Server does normally use, but it is usually best to let the server control the locking. (Locking hints are discussed later.) The lock groups that SQL Server uses include the following:

- **Share Locks.** Created by non-update operations.
- **Update Locks.** Placed on resources that can be updated to prevent deadlocking.
- **Exclusive Locks.** Prevents any other transaction from acquiring a lock applied during an update operation.
- **Intent Locks.** Indicates that the server desires a lock.
- **Schema Locks.** Placed to prevent access during schema alterations.

Share Locks

The default handling of isolation is to lock a page of data that houses the record being changed by a process. Although row-level locking is possible, it is more expensive because a number of locks might have to be set within a single page of data. Data cannot be changed on the entire page of data, as long as the cursor is located on a given row. The locking mechanism used by SQL Server is referred to as a "share lock." A share lock allows multiple processes to read and hold share locks on a resource. No other process can update the data while a share lock is in place. SQL Server, depending on the functionality needed, automatically adjusts locking. Locking can also be changed through configuration mechanisms or the declaration of a cursor with a higher degree of locking.

Update and Exclusive Locks

Performing an update to a row of data requires a shared lock to be converted to an exclusive lock. An exclusive lock prevents any transaction from updating or reading the data contained within the lock. The actual lock can be at a row or page level. If it is at a page level, this lock can encompass a number of records. At times, update locks are used to prevent deadlock situations. Similar in features to an exclusive lock, an update lock can be set only once by a single process, preventing access to the data contained within the lock for the duration of the lock. If a transaction modifies data, the update lock is converted to an exclusive lock. If no changes are required to be made, the update lock changes to a shared lock.

Intent Locks

Intent locks can be used to improve performance. Applied at the table level, an intent lock prevents other processes from obtaining an exclusive lock. Because an intent lock is applied at the table level, performance is improved by not requiring the engine to examine every page and/or row to determine whether any locks are applied. Intent locks come in three common locking forms: shared, exclusive, and shared/exclusive. A shared intent lock indicates the intention of the process to read data. An exclusive intent lock indicates the proposal to change some of the underlying table objects. A shared/exclusive intent lock allows concurrent reads to objects within the table that will not change, while protecting the table objects that will be altered. There can be only one shared/exclusive intent lock placed on a table.

Schema Locks

The final style of locks used by SQL Server is a schema lock. A shared schema lock (or *Sch-S* lock) allows other processes to perform transactions, including those that alter the data to be performed on a table while a query is being compiled. While a Sch-S lock is in place, another process can obtain an exclusive lock to alter data in the underlying table. A Sch-M, or modify schema lock, is required to perform a data definition language operation to a schema, such as adding an additional column to a table definition. A DDL operation cannot be performed while another process holds an exclusive lock on a table.

Implementing Locking

Locking can be implemented at several levels of granularity within SQL Server. RID (Row identifier) locking is used to individually lock a single row within a table. Key-level locking is a row lock within an index that protects key ranges in serializable transactions. Page-level locking is based on an 8K data page or an index page. An extent lock locks a contiguous group of eight data or index pages. A table-level lock locks an entire table, including all data and indexes. A DB (database) lock locks the entire database. The granularity of locking does not affect the types of locks being implemented. SQL Server automatically locks resources at a level that is appropriate for the task.

Lock Manager

The Lock Manager object in SQL Server provides a series of counters that allow monitoring of overall server lock activity. This helps gauge user activity and resource usage, and identify performance bottlenecks.

Table 3.2 shows the available lock manager counters:

TABLE 3.2

AVAILABLE LOCK MANAGER COUNTERS

Counter	Function
Lock Blocks	The current number of lock blocks that are in use. A lock block represents an individual locked resource, such as a table, page, or row.
Lock Blocks Allocated	The current number of allocated lock blocks. At server startup, the number of allocated lock blocks, plus the number of allocated lock owner blocks, depends on the SQL Server Locks configuration option. If more lock blocks are needed, the value increases.
Lock Owner Blocks	The number of lock owner blocks. A lock owner block represents the ownership of a lock on an object by an individual thread.
Lock Owner Blocks Allocated	The current number of allocated lock owner blocks. At server startup, the number of allocated lock owner blocks, plus the number of allocated lock blocks, depends on the SQL Server Locks configuration option. If more lock owner blocks are needed, the value dynamically increases.
Table Lock Escalations	The number of times that locks on a table were escalated (fine-grained locks, like row locks, are converted into coarser grain locks, like page locks).

Locking Configuration

Using an advanced option of sp_configure, you can alter the locks option to set the maximum number of available locks. In doing so, you limit the amount of memory used by SQL Server for locking. The default is 0, which enables SQL Server to dynamically allocate and deallocate locks, based on system requirements.

Locking configuration can further be controlled by using deadlock priority or setting the lock timeout duration as previously described. You may also wish to set transaction isolation levels, use locking hints on SQL statements, and/or configure locking granularity for an index.

TRANSACTION ISOLATION

The isolation level required by an application determines the locking behavior that SQL Server uses. Although locking can solve concurrency control problems, you can further maintain correctness of data by using appropriate isolation levels. A low isolation level can increase concurrency, but the data may lose accuracy. On the other hand, if a high isolation level is utilized, the data may be correct, but the capability of processes to perform tasks against the data at the same time can be negatively affected.

Transaction isolation levels available in SQL Server determine the degree to which the data is protected against interference from other processes. Use HOLDLOCK when you require a degree of locking that is higher than that of the default handling by SQL Server. Normally, SQL Server frees a locked resource, once it is no longer needed. By holding the lock, the data is secure for the entire duration of the cursor.

A hold lock sets the isolation level of SQL Server to repeatable read. This is an extremely secure technique, but it should be used sparingly and with caution because it prolongs the time a lock is in place, preventing other processes from updating data.

Alternatively, you can open a cursor by using the FOR BROWSE option, which supplies you with a snapshot of the data. You will be unable to detect changes made by other user. Because a snapshot is used for manipulations, no lock is placed on the original data. FOR BROWSE is a requirement if you are performing an "Update Where Current Of" or

"Delete Where Current Of" operation. You can combine the two capabilities (allow repeated reading, updating data in a browsing mode) by setting HOLDLOCK first and then opening the cursor FOR BROWSE.

SQL-92 defines four levels of isolation:

- Read committed
- Read uncommitted
- Repeatable read
- Serializable

Read uncommitted provides the lowest level of isolation, whereas serializable provides for the highest degree of isolation. SQL Server uses read committed as the default if no other setting is defined. Process must utilize repeatable read or a higher isolation level if data update losses are to be prevented. If a process uses serializable, any overlapping processes are guaranteed to be serializable. That is, they are fully isolated from one another and are essentially handled as if they were to occur in sequence, one after another. Use SET TRANSACTION ISOLATION LEVEL statement to implement the desired isolation level for your implementation.

Read Committed

Shared locks are held while the data is being read and the data can be changed before the end of the transaction, resulting in *non-repeatable reads* or *phantom data*. Phantom data is data that was not originally in the resultset but was added by another process after the cursor was opened. This option is the SQL Server default.

Read Uncommitted

Implements dirty read locking, which means that no shared locks can be obtained and no exclusive locks are honored. When this option is set, it is possible to read dirty, uncommitted data; values in the data can be changed and rows can appear or disappear in the data set before the end of the transaction. This option has the same effect as setting NOLOCK on all tables in all SELECT statements.

Repeatable Read

Locks are placed on all data that is used in a query, preventing other users from updating the data, but new phantom rows can be inserted into the data set by another process and will be included in later reads. Concurrency in this setting is lower than the default isolation level and should be utilized only when necessary.

Serializable

A range lock is placed on the data set, preventing other users from updating or inserting rows into the data set until the process is complete. Concurrency with this setting is much lower and should only be used when necessary. This option has the same effect as setting HOLDLOCK on all tables in all SELECT statements.

USING ISOLATION

To set any of the possible levels of transaction isolation, you can provide an environment setting, as shown in the syntax example that follows. It is also possible to request specific levels of isolation on a statement-by-statement basis. (Statement options will be explored in further syntax examples later in this chapter.)

```
SET TRANSACTION ISOLATION LEVEL
{READ COMMITTED |
READ UNCOMMITTED |
REPEATABLE READ |
SERIALIZABLE}
```

TRANSACTION CONTROL

The durability of data can be controlled through transactions. After a transaction is complete and is committed, it is important that its effects become permanent in the system. This cannot always be guaranteed in today's read ahead, dirty write technology. Although SQL Server takes strides to accomplish this through automatic checkpointing, there are a few considerations, configuration options, and statements that optimize this process. SQL Server's automatic recovery options are set to fast recovery by default, which means that the default value of the database recovery interval is set to zero.

Controlling transactions can mean the implementation of savepoints within a transaction, controlling the flow of committal and rollback through developed logic, monitoring for errors in procedure execution, and configuring transaction handling to allow for implicit transactions. Committal, Rollback, and Implicit transactions were discussed earlier in this chapter; and we will fully address error handling in a later topic. Using savepoints enables the partial rollback of information within a transaction. It is important to note that transaction savepoints should be implemented only at a point that does not interfere with the integrity of the transaction and the database as a whole. Consider the use of a transaction committal unless the situation warrants the use of a savepoint.

Savepoints are useful in situations in which errors can occur. If an infrequent error requires the coding of an inspection process, then a savepoint can provide a higher degree of efficiency. Savepoints, committal, and rollbacks are expensive, however. Use the SAVE TRANSACTION command with a savepoint name or a variable containing the savepoint name, as indicated by the following SQL syntax:

```
SAVE TRANSACTION {savepoint name ¦ @savepoint variable}
```

Bound Connections

A *bound connection* is a tie between processes, which allows two or more connections to share the same transaction space if used locally. Bound connections also share locks. A bound connection can allow work to be performed on the same data without having any lock conflicts. A bound connection can be created from connections in the same application, from multiple applications having separate connections, or from multiple applications that are located on separate servers.

To implement bound connections, an established connection has to obtain a bind token. It does this by using the stored procedure sp_getbindtoken. This token is a character string that uniquely identifies each bound process. The bind token has to be sent by using some communications technique to the other connections that will participate. The other connections need to bind to the first connection. Binding to an established connection must be performed by using the initially created token. Because there is no mechanism to query for a token, the initial process has to use a global variable, SQL Server table, or interprocess communication technique to get the unique token string to the secondary process. Once the token string is known, the secondary process must bind to the first. The secondary process that performs this binding uses the stored procedure sp_bindsession.

Bound connections can be used locally on a single server or across servers that utilize the distributed transaction coordinator. A distributed bound connection requires a bit of additional handling because it is not identified by a character string bind token. A distributed bound connection uses a distributed transaction identification number that is used by sp_bindsession. An additional advantage of using bound connections is that it allows for the implementation of a three-tier architecture. A three-tier architecture improves the flexibility of a system and makes it easier to implement changes in the future. For example, an application that inserts a sales record into a table and then creates a process to authorize the sale with the credit card company can use bound processes to allow the authorization process to access the sales record without a lock \conflict.

DEADLOCKS

A *deadlock* is a condition that can occur when two or more resources are locked by two separate processes. If each process requires the resource that the other needs, you have a deadlock. The deadlock occurs because each process waits for the other to release its lock on the resource before continuing with the remainder of its operation. Normally, SQL Server solves the deadlock by selecting a deadlock victim. You can configure a preferred victim by using the SET DEADLOCK_PRIORITY statement. The setting can be LOW if the current process is to be the chosen victim, or it can be NORMAL if SQL Server is to use the standard technique for resolving a deadlock.

The normal resolution technique used by SQL Server to resolve a deadlock is to select the "least-expensive" process as a victim. Whichever of the processes is determined to be the easiest to undo is chosen as the victim and its activities are rolled back to allow the other process to resume. The victim application is notified by the return of an error code (1205).

Avoiding Deadlocks

Minimizing the number of deadlocks that can occur requires a complete design strategy. There are several things that can accommodate the reduction of deadlocks because they are usually caused by a poorly developed application. Deadlocks cannot be completely avoided, but minimizing their occurrence is simply a matter of careful design. Within applications that access the same set of resources, make sure that you access these resources in the same order every time. If possible, avoid interactions within transactions that may slow the completion of a transaction. Keep transactions as short as possible and maintain processing to a single batch. Use as low an isolation level as possible within transactions. Use bound connections to control data element access. These strategies are discussed in the next few sections.

Access Objects in the Same Order

If all transactions access objects in the same order when running, deadlocks are less likely to happen. Fewer deadlocks occur because the locking of resources occurs in the same order. Any resources to be locked prevent second transactions from starting their processes until the first transaction completes, commits, and frees its lock. To make it easier to maintain the same order of resource access, use stored procedures for data modifications.

Avoid User Interaction

Batches execute much more quickly without user interaction. Locks are in effect for shorter periods of time and the whole system benefits, not only from fewer deadlocks, but also from faster processing overall. A transaction that waits for user interaction can hold up the entire system for prolonged periods of time. Distractions of the user for a variety of reasons can hold up transaction completion for extended periods. By default, SQL Server does not implement a timeout for transactions that execute for prolonged periods. Even if a deadlock situation does not arise, other transactions that access the same resources are blocked, waiting for the transaction to complete.

A timeout value does not exist for the execution of transactions, nor is there a method for obtaining lock information without attempting to actually perform a lock on a resource. A SET LOCK_TIMEOUT statement is available if you want to get feedback on a prolonged lock and thus cancel the transaction that attempts to lock a resource. If implemented, you have to retry the transaction at a later time and it may not be desirable for all implementations, especially for those whose lock timing is unpredictable. Resource Timeout can also be set by using `sp_configure` with advanced options, but it isn't desirable because of its global implications. The default value for resource timeout is 10 seconds.

Minimize Transactions Size

A deadlock often occurs when multiple transactions execute at the same time against the same database. If the transactions are lengthy, then resources are locked for longer periods of time, increasing the chance of a deadlock. By keeping transactions in a single batch, you minimize network roundtrips, reducing possible delays in completion of transactions and releasing locks.

Use Low Isolation Levels

Determine the lowest isolation level that a transaction can reasonably be set at without needlessly affecting the accuracy of the data (for example, read committed rather than serializable). Implementing read committed allows a transaction to read data previously read (not modified) by another transaction, without waiting for the first transaction to complete. Using a lower isolation level, such as read committed, holds shared locks for a shorter duration than a higher isolation level, such as serializable.

Use Bound Connections

When you use bound connections, two or more connections that are opened by the same application can cooperate. Any locks that are acquired by either of the connections do not interfere with each other.

LOCKING

Essentially, there are two ways that a developer looks at locking for the implementation of any shared data application: optimistic or pessimistic. As the terms indicate, *optimistic* locking sets up locking for the shortest period of time because it is expected that the data will never be updated by more than one process at a time. *Pessimistic* locking takes the reverse viewpoint and is utilized when changes to data are frequently made by a number of different processes, and when the possibility of simultaneous access increases. SQL Server defaults to pessimistic locking, but because this locking strategy increases the duration of locks, it is worth looking at the locking strategy that an application really requires. If a change is made to an optimistic strategy, gains can be made in improved performance and less overhead. If you do make this change, however, you increase the need for error handling in an application, and you must control what happens in the event of multiple accesses of the same data.

Optimistic Locking

Optimistic concurrency is based on the assumption that multiple processes are unlikely to access the same data at the same time. An optimistic strategy places locks on the data only for the amount of time that the data actually is being modified at its source (committed). If a problem occurs, such as the attempt to change data that has been changed by another process at some point between the initial fetch of the data and the attempt to commit, then a transaction is forced to start over.

Pessimistic Locking

In pessimistic locking, resources are locked for the entire duration required by the process. Once data has been fetched, locks are immediately implemented. In this respect, errors are less likely to occur when a committal of changes is executed. A process that uses a pessimistic locking strategy is all but guaranteed successful completion. The only element that might come in to play to stop the process is a deadlock or communications failure.

The desired locking strategy or concurrency is chosen by using the SET CONCURRENCY statement, which affects all subsequent uses of the OPEN statement. The statement and options that can be used are defined here:

SET CONCURRENCY {LOCKCC ¦ OPTCC ¦ OPTCCVAL ¦ READONLY}

- **LOCKCC.** The default setting when SET ANSI_DEFAULTS is on. This setting specifies an intent to update locking. If a FETCH statement is issued, an exclusive lock is placed on the data before it is fetched. This setting is identical to a cursor declaration with the use of FOR UPDATE/ FOR BROWSE. If a cursor is declared in this manner, the SET statement is ignored. This setting provides for a pessimistic locking strategy.

- **OPTCC.** The default setting if SET ANSI_DEFAULTS is not on. This setting specifies an optimistic strategy with control based on a row-versioning indicator (usually a timestamp column, if available) or all non-text, non-image columns.

- **OPTCCVAL.** This setting specifies an optimistic strategy with control based on all non-text, non-image columns.

- **READONLY.** This setting specifies read-only cursors. Any data that is retrieved by a FETCH statement cannot be modified.

If you choose to use the OPTCC or OPTCCVAL setting, an UPDATE WHERE CURRENT OF statement can fail if the row changed since the last FETCH statement. The application has to be designed to handle this situation.

@@TRANCOUNT

This object returns an integer value that indicates the number of active transactions for the current user. It can be used as a form of error handling to test for open transactions that might need to be committed. Each time the BEGIN TRANSACTION statement is executes, @@trancount is increased by one. Thus, if one or more transactions is still open, the value returned is greater than zero. The object is usually utilized in conjunction with conditional statements and test conditions applicable to the application.

In the following example, an attempt is made to remove a single customer that has a negative balance. If more than one customer is found with this situation, the transaction will not execute and is rolled back. @@trancount checks to see whether the transaction was committed; if not, it is rolled back.

The following example is provided for illustration purposes (other implementations that perform the same tasks may actually be preferred):

```
BEGIN TRANSACTION
UPDATE Customers SET Balance = 0
WHERE Balance < 0
IF @@ROWCOUNT = 1
COMMIT TRAN
IF @@TRANCOUNT > 0
```

```
BEGIN
   PRINT 'Transaction effects more than one user'
   ROLLBACK TRAN
END
```

SQL Standard Syntax

The primary focus of database implementation is that of correctly applying SQL syntax within an application, in a static or dynamic fashion. SQL Server supports two forms of SQL syntax: ANSI SQL 92 and its own proprietary Transact-SQL. There are some significant differences between these two versions, as was discussed previously. Basic SQL knowledge and implementation can easily be applied to either syntax. The concentration in preparation for the exam should be on Transact-SQL, paying particular attention to changes within SQL Server 7 and its implementation of SQL.

INSERT

The INSERT statement adds a row or rows to a table or view. The SQL syntax for the INSERT statement and its usable options are defined as follows:

```
INSERT [INTO] {<table sources>}
{
   {[(column list)] VALUES ({DEFAULT ¦ constant expression}[,...n]) ¦
➥select statement ¦ execute statement}
   ¦DEFAULT VALUES}
<table sources> :: =
{<table or view> ¦ (select statement) [AS] table alias [(column
➥alias [,...m])]
   ¦ <table or view> CROSS JOIN <table or view>
  { {INNER ¦
      {FULL ¦ LEFT ¦ RIGHT}[OUTER] [<join hints>] JOIN}
      <table or view> ON <join condition> }
      ¦ <rowset function>}
[, ...n]
<table or view>::=
{ table name [ [AS] table alias ] [ WITH (<table hints> [ ...m]) ] ¦
➥view name [ [AS] table alias ] }
<table hints> ::=
{ INDEX(index name ¦ index id) ¦ HOLDLOCK ¦ PAGLOCK ¦ READCOMMITTED
¦ REPEATABLEREAD
   ¦ ROWLOCK ¦ SERIALIZABLE ¦ TABLOCK ¦ TABLOCKX }
<join hints> ::=
{HASH ¦ LOOP ¦ MERGE}
<rowset function> :: =
{ OPENQUERY (linked server, 'query') ¦ OPENROWSET ( 'provider name',
 ➥  {'datasource'; 'user id'; 'password' ¦ 'provider string'},
   {[catalog.][schema.]object name ¦ 'query'}) }
```

Important issues with regard to the appropriate use of the INSERT statement are as follows:

- DEFAULT is not valid for an identity column.
- If a constant expression is used, it cannot contain a SELECT or EXECUTE statement.
- Any valid SELECT statement that returns rows of data to be loaded into the table can be used to obtain the values for the insert.
- If the EXECUTE option is used with INSERT, each result set returned must be compatible with the columns in the table or in the *column list*.
- If the EXECUTE option returns data with the READTEXT statement, each individual READTEXT statement can return a maximum of one megabyte (1,024K) of data.
- The EXECUTE option can also be used with extended procedures and it inserts the data returned by the main thread of the extended procedure. Output from threads other than the main thread is not inserted.
- INSERT cannot be used with multitable views, views containing aggregates (AVG, COUNT, MIN, MAX, SUM), or expressions in the view's column definition.
- Only one index per table can be specified.
- Any index specified for a view is ignored, and SQL Server returns an error message.
- SQL Server does not allow more than one table hint from each of the following groups:
  - Granularity hints: PAGLOCK, NOLOCK, ROWLOCK, TABLOCK, or TABLOCKX
  - Isolation hints: HOLDLOCK, NOLOCK, READCOMMITTED, REPEATABLEREAD, SERIALIZABLE
  - NOLOCK and READPAST are only allowed in SELECT statements; and not in DELETE, INSERT, or UPDATE statements
- SQL Server must be able to provide a value based on the definition of the column; otherwise, the row cannot be loaded. SQL Server automatically provides a value for the column if:
  - It has an IDENTITY property. The next incremental identity value is used.

- It has a default. The default value for the column is used.
- It has a timestamp data type. The current timestamp value is used.
- It can contain null values.

♦ *Column list* and *values list* must be used when inserting explicit values into an IDENTITY column, and the IDENTITY_INSERT setting must be true for the table.

♦ Columns created with the unique identifier data type store specially formatted 16-byte binary values. No automatic value is generated. The NEWID() function should be used to provide a globally unique identifier (GUID).

SQL Server applies a number of rules whenever rows are being inserted. These rules are necessary to maintain the validity and correct format of the data during insert operations (particularly when using character data types and working with default inserts).

When loading a value into columns that have a character data type, the padding or truncation of trailing blanks is performed if ANSI padding is off. Variable-length character columns have trailing blanks removed, leaving at least one character in the resulting string. Variable-length binary columns are stripped of any trailing zeroes. Using SET ANSI_PADDING ON can reverse this feature. For more information, see SET ANSI_PADDING. An empty string, not a null, is loaded into a column with a varchar or text data type (the default operation is to load a zero-length string). If the compatibility level for the database is less than 70, the value is converted to a single space. If you insert a null value into a text or image column, a valid text pointer is not created and 8K-text page is not allocated.

You cannot perform an INSERT or DELETE operation that violates a constraint or rule. You also may not insert a value that is incompatible with the data type of the column. Both of these situations return an error that results in complete statement termination. If an arithmetic error (overflow, divide by zero, or a domain error) occurs during an expression evaluation in an INSERT, UPDATE, or DELETE operation, SQL Server handles it as an error and aborts the remainder of the batch.

If no join type is specified in an INSERT, UPDATE, or DELETE statement, SQL Server defaults to an INNER join—returning all matching pairs of rows and discarding unmatched rows from both tables.

You must have insert permission for the table you are inserting into. These permissions default to members of the sysadmin fixed database role, database owner, and table owner. These members can transfer this permission to other users.

The following examples illustrate the use of the INSERT statement with a variety of options. An INSERT operation can be used in a number of useful procedures. For further examples of its use, see the syntax guide for the INSERT statement in SQL Server Books Online. Further information on related commands (such as joins) are found later in this book.

- A simple insert (values must match column order):
    ```
    INSERT MyTable VALUES (1, 'Test String')
    ```
- An insert of data using column names (the order is unimportant if names are used):
    ```
    INSERT MyTable (MyColumn2, MyColumn1) VALUES ('Test String', 1)
    ```
- Load data using DEFAULT VALUES (assuming that all columns can initiate without explicit values):
    ```
    INSERT INTO MyTable DEFAULT VALUES
    ```
- Insert data using the TOP clause in a SELECT statement:
    ```
    INSERT INTO MyTopTenTable SELECT TOP 10 * FROM MyTable
    ```
- Load data using EXECUTE:
    ```
    INSERT MyTable EXECUTE add_new_data
    ```

DELETE

The DELETE statement removes row from a table. As indicated by the following SQL syntax, the DELETE operation has a lot of flexibility. Note the use of locking strategies (table hints) as an alternative to environment locking through the use of SET CONCURRENCY (discussed previously).

```
DELETE [ FROM {table name ¦ view name}]
{FROM <table sources>}
[ WHERE
{ <search conditions> ¦ {[ CURRENT OF{{[ GLOBAL ] cursor name } ¦
↪cursor variable name }]}}
    [OPTION (<query hints> [, ...n])]
    <table sources> :: =
    { <table or view>¦ (select statement) [AS] table alias [ (column
↪alias [,..m]) ]
        ¦<table or view> CROSS JOIN <table or view>¦ <table or view>
```

```
    {{ INNER ¦ { FULL ¦ LEFT¦ RIGHT} [ OUTER ] [ <join hints> ] [
➥JOIN ]}
        <table or view> ON join condition>}
        ¦ <rowset function>}
    [, ...n]
    <table or view> :: =
    { table name [ [AS] table alias ] [ WITH (<table hints> [...n]) ]¦
➥view name [ [AS] table alias ]}
    <table hints> ::=
    {INDEX(index name ¦ index id) ¦ HOLDLOCK¦ PAGLOCK¦ READCOMMITTED¦
➥REPEATABLEREAD
            ¦ ROWLOCK¦ SERIALIZABLE¦ TABLOCK ¦ TABLOCKX}
    <join hints> ::=
    { HASH ¦ LOOP ¦ MERGE }
    <query hints> :: =
    { { HASH ¦ ORDER } GROUP ¦ { CONCAT ¦ HASH ¦ MERGE }
        UNION¦ FAST number rows ¦ FORCE ORDER¦ ROBUST PLAN}
    <join condition> :: =
    {table name ¦ table alias ¦ view name}. column name <logical
➥operator>
    {table name ¦ table alias ¦ view name}. column name <logical
➥operator>:: ={ = ¦ > ¦ < ¦ >= ¦ <= ¦ <> ¦ != ¦ !< ¦ !> }
    <rowset function> :: =
    {OPENQUERY (linked server, 'query')
        ¦ OPENROWSET( 'provider name', {'datasource'; 'user id';
➥'password' ¦ 'provider string'},
    {[catalog.][schema.]object name ¦ 'query'}
}
```

Important issues regarding the appropriate use of the DELETE statement are as follows:

- If a join hint is also specified for any particular pair of joined tables in the FROM clause, it takes precedence over any join hint specified in the OPTION clause.

- If a WHERE clause is not supplied, DELETE removes all the rows from the table. To delete all the rows in a table, use TRUNCATE TABLE. The operation is performed much more quickly because each deleted record does not need to be logged in the transaction log.

- If a WHERE CURRENT OF clause is supplied, the row from the table that corresponds to the current row in the cursor is deleted.

- DELETE cannot remove data from tables on the nullable side of an outer join.

You must have DELETE permissions on the table you are deleting from. These permissions default to the table owner. The table owner can transfer these permissions to other users. SELECT permissions are also required if the statement contains a WHERE clause.

If two cursors exist with the same name—one local and one global—the GLOBAL keyword indicates that the global cursor should be used. If GLOBAL is not specified, the local cursor is used. This is also true in an UPDATE operation.

The following examples illustrate the use of the DELETE statement with a variety of options. A delete operation can be used in a number of useful procedures. For further examples of its use, see the syntax guide for the DELETE statement in SQL Server Books Online. Further information on related commands (such as joins) are found later in this book.

- A simple delete with no parameters (all rows will be deleted):
  ```
  DELETE MyTable
  ```
- To delete a set of rows:
  ```
  DELETE FROM MyTable WHERE Balance < 0
  ```
- To delete the current row of a cursor:
  ```
  DELETE FROM MyTable WHERE CURRENT OF MyCursor
  ```
- Deletion based on a subquery:
  ```
  DELETE FROM MyTable WHERE Customer_ID IN
  ( SELECT Customer_ID FROM Customers WHERE TypeCode = 'CHQ' )
  ```
- Deletion using SELECT with the TOP clause:
  ```
  DELETE MyTable FROM (SELECT TOP 10 * FROM MyTable) AS mtt
  WHERE MyTable.Customer_ID = mtt.Customer_ID
  ```

UPDATE

The UPDATE statement makes changes to existing data in a table. When updating records in an existing table, it is important to consider isolation and locking strategies (see the sections in this chapter on isolation and locking for further information). The SQL syntax for the update operation is as follows. Note that it is possible to indicate isolation levels and locking strategies, both termed as table hints, for singular statement operations. This is an alternative to SET ISOLATION and SET CONCURRENCY.

```
UPDATE {<table or view>} SET
{ column name = {expression ¦ DEFAULT}¦ @variable = expression}
➥[,...n] [FROM
{<table or view> ¦ (select statement) [AS] table alias [ (column
➥alias [,...m]) ]
   ¦ <table or view> CROSS JOIN <table or view> ¦ INNER [<join
➥hints>] JOIN
```

SQL Standard Syntax

```
    <table or view> ON <join condition> ¦ <rowset function> }[, ...n]]
    [WHERE <search conditions> ¦ CURRENT OF
    { { [GLOBAL] cursor name } ¦ cursor variable name} }]
    [OPTION (<query hints>, [,...n] )]
    <table or view> :: =
    { table name [ [AS] table alias ] [ WITH (<table hints> [...m]) ] ¦
➥view name [ [AS] table alias ] }
    <table hints> ::=
    { INDEX(index name ¦ index id) ¦ FASTFIRSTROW ¦ HOLDLOCK ¦ PAGLOCK
➥¦ READCOMMITTED
            ¦ REPEATABLEREAD ¦ ROWLOCK ¦ SERIALIZABLE ¦ TABLOCK ¦ TABLOCKX
➥}
    <join hints> ::=
    { HASH ¦ LOOP ¦ MERGE }
    <query hints> :: =
    { { HASH ¦ ORDER } GROUP ¦ { CONCAT ¦ HASH ¦ MERGE } UNION ¦ FAST
    √number rows
        ¦ FORCE ORDER ¦ ROBUST PLAN }
    <join condition> :: =
    { table name ¦ table alias ¦ view name }. column name <logical
➥operator>
    { table name ¦ table alias ¦ view name }. column name <logical
➥operator>:: = {= ¦ > ¦ < ¦ >= ¦ <= ¦ <> ¦ != ¦ !< ¦ !>}
    <rowset function> :: =
    { OPENQUERY (linked server, 'query')
            ¦ OPENROWSET ( 'provider name', {'datasource'; 'user id';
➥'password' ¦ 'provider string'},
        {[catalog.][schema.]object name ¦ 'query'})}
    <search conditions> ::=
    { [ NOT ] <predicate> [ { AND ¦ OR } [ NOT ] <predicate> ] } [,
➥...n]
    <predicate> ::=
    { expression { = ¦ <> ¦ != ¦ > ¦ >= ¦ !> ¦ < ¦ <= ¦ !< } expression
➥¦ string expression [NOT] LIKE string expression
        [ESCAPE 'escape character'] ¦ expression [NOT] BETWEEN
➥expression AND expression
            ¦ expression IS [NOT] NULL ¦ expression [NOT] IN (subquery ¦
➥expression [,...n])
            ¦ expression { = ¦ <> ¦ != ¦ > ¦ >= ¦ !> ¦ < ¦ <= ¦ !< }
    {ALL ¦ SOME ¦ ANY} (subquery) ¦ EXISTS (subquery)
    }
```

Important issues regarding the appropriate use of the DELETE statement are as follows:

- Any column prefix specified in the SET clause must match the table or view name specified after the UPDATE keyword.

- UPDATE can be used to change existing rows in one or more tables.

- Modifying a text, ntext, or image column with UPDATE initializes it, assigns a valid text pointer to it, and allocates at least one data page (unless updating the column with NULL).

- If an update query may alter more than one row while updating both the clustering key and one or more text, image, or Unicode columns; the update operation fails and SQL Server returns an error message.

- If an update to a column or columns participating in a clustered index causes the size of the clustered index and the row to exceed 8,092 bytes, the update fails and an error message is returned.

- The UPDATE statement is a logged operation; if you are replace or modify large blocks of text, *n*text, or image data, use the WRITETEXT or UPDATETEXT statement instead of the UPDATE statement. The WRITETEXT and UPDATETEXT statements (by default) are not logged.

- Variable names can be used in UPDATE statements to show the old and new values affected. This should only be used when the UPDATE statement affects a single record; if the UPDATE statement affects multiple records, the variables will contain the values for only one of the updated rows.

You must have update permissions for the table that contains the data you are changing. These permissions default to the table owner; the table owner can transfer these permissions to other users. SELECT permissions are also required for the table being updated if the UPDATE statement contains a WHERE clause, or if *expression* in the SET clause uses a column in the table.

The following examples illustrate the use of the UPDATE statement with a variety of options. An update operation can be used in a number of useful procedures. For further examples of its use, see the syntax guide for the UPDATE statement in SQL Server Books Online. Further information on related commands (such as joins) is found later in this book.

- A simple update (all rows will be altered):

    ```
    UPDATE MyTable SET TypeCode = 'CHQ', Balance = Balance * 1.09,
    Description = NULL
    ```

- To update a group of rows with a WHERE clause:

    ```
    UPDATE MyTable SET Balance = Balance * 1.09 WHERE TypeCode = 'CHQ'
    ```

- To update data by using information from another table:

    ```
    UPDATE MyTable SET TInterest = Check.Interest + Saving.Interest
    FROM Check, Saving
    WHERE Check.Customer_ID = Saving.Customer_ID AND Customer_ID =
    Check.Customer_ID
    ```

- To update data by using the TOP clause in a SELECT statement:

```
UPDATE MyTable SET TInterest = 0 FROM
  (SELECT TOP 10 * FROM MyTable ORDER BY LastName) AS mtt
  WHERE MyTable.Customer_ID = mtt.Customer_ID
```

SELECT

SELECT retrieves rows from the database. It enables the selection of one or many rows or columns from one or many tables by using several optional clauses, including GROUP BY, FROM, and WHERE. The SELECT statement is the heart of SQL and can be used as a portion of many other statements, as illustrated in the UPDATE, DELETE, and INSERT statements. The SELECT statement is an extremely powerful statement, as shown by the variety of implementations using the following SQL syntax. SELECT can create result-sets that represent a singular table, and combine multiple tables and/or produce joined tables that have particular special features (examined separately, later in the chapter).

> **NOTE** You can expect a variety of SELECT statements on the exam. Because it is such an important aspect of working in SQL, it is strongly recommended that you try as many of the options as possible (specifically, but not limited to, those that relate to unions and joins).

```
SELECT [ ALL ¦ DISTINCT ] [ TOP n [PERCENT] [ WITH TIES] ] <select
➥list> [ INTO new table ]
   [ FROM <table sources> ] [ WHERE <search conditions> ] [ [ GROUP
➥BY [ALL] group by expression [,…n]]
   [HAVING <search conditions> ] [ WITH { CUBE ¦ ROLLUP } ] ]
   ➥   [ ORDER BY { column name [ ASC ¦ DESC ] } [,…n] ][ COMPUTE { {
AVG ¦ COUNT ¦ MAX ¦ MIN ¦ SUM }
   ➥   (expression) } [,…n] [ BY expression [,…n] ][ FOR BROWSE ][
OPTION (<query hints>) ]
   <select list> :: =
   { [ { <table or view> ¦ table alias }.]* ¦ { column name ¦
➥expression ¦ IDENTITYCOL ¦ ROWGUIDCOL }
       [ [AS] column alias ] ¦ new column name = IDENTITY(data type,
➥seed, increment)
       ¦ GROUPING (column name) ¦ { table name ¦ table alias}. RANK ¦
➥column alias = expression
       ¦ expression column name } [,…n]
   <table sources> :: =
```

```
   { <table or view> ¦ (select statement) [AS] table alias [ (column
➥alias [,…m]) ] ¦ <table or view>
      CROSS JOIN <table or view> ¦ <table or view>
      { { INNER ¦ { FULL ¦ LEFT ¦ RIGHT } [ OUTER ] [ <join hints> ]
➥[ JOIN ] } <table or view> ON
          <join condition> }
          ¦ <rowset function> } [,…n]
   <table or view> :: =
   { table name [ [AS] table alias ] [ WITH (<table hints> […n]) ] ¦
➥view name [ [AS] table alias ] }
   <table hints> ::=
   { INDEX(index name ¦ index id [,…n]) ¦ FASTFIRSTROW ¦ HOLDLOCK ¦
➥NOLOCK ¦ PAGLOCK
          ¦ READCOMMITTED ¦ READPAST ¦ READUNCOMMITTED ¦ REPEATABLEREAD
➥¦ ROWLOCK
          ¦ SERIALIZABLE ¦ TABLOCK ¦ TABLOCKX ¦ UPDLOCK }
   <join hints> ::=
   { HASH ¦ LOOP ¦ MERGE }
   <query hints> :: =
   { { HASH ¦ ORDER } GROUP ¦ { CONCAT ¦ HASH ¦ MERGE } UNION ¦ FAST
➥number rows
          ¦ FORCE ORDER ¦ MAXDOP number ¦ ROBUST PLAN }
   <join condition> :: =
   { table name ¦ table alias ¦ view name }. column name <logical
➥operator>
   { table name ¦ table alias ¦ view name }. column name <logical
➥operator>:: = {= ¦ > ¦ < ¦ >= ¦ <= ¦ <> ¦ != ¦ !< ¦ !>}
   <rowset function> :: =
   { CONTAINSTABLE [ [ AS] table alias] ( table, { column ¦ *},
➥'<contains search condition>' )
          ¦ FREETEXTTABLE [ [ AS] table alias] ( table, {column ¦ * },
➥'freetext string' )
          ¦ OPENQUERY (linked server, 'query') ¦ OPENROWSET ( 'provider
➥name',
       { 'datasource'; 'user id'; 'password' ¦ 'provider string' },
➥{[catalog.][schema.]object name ¦ 'query' })
   <search conditions> ::=
   { [ NOT ] <predicate> [ { AND ¦ OR } [ NOT ] <predicate> ] ¦
➥CONTAINS ( {column ¦ * },
          <contains search condition>' ) ¦ FREETEXT ( {column ¦ * },
➥'freetext string' )
          ¦ fulltext table. fulltext key column = fulltext table.[KEY] }
➥[ ,…n]
   <predicate> ::=
   { expression { = ¦ <> ¦ != ¦ > ¦ >= ¦ !> ¦ < ¦ <= ¦ !< }
➥expression ¦ string expression [NOT] LIKE string expression
      [ESCAPE 'escape character'] ¦ expression [NOT] BETWEEN
➥expression AND expression
          ¦ expression IS [NOT] NULL ¦ expression [NOT] IN (subquery ¦
➥expression [,...n])
          ¦ expression { = ¦ <> ¦ != ¦ > ¦ >= ¦ !> ¦ < ¦ <= ¦ !< }{ALL ¦
➥SOME ¦ ANY} (subquery) ¦ EXISTS (subquery)
   }
```

Important issues regarding the appropriate use of the SELECT statement are as follows:

- The FROM clause is almost always present because it is required, except when the SELECT list contains no column names.

- Duplicate rows appear in the result set only if the ALL keyword is specified immediately following the SELECT keyword. Use DISTINCT to show only unique rows in the result set. Null values are considered equal for the purposes of the DISTINCT keyword.

- When creating a derived table, the SELECT statement does not support the use of the INTO, ORDER BY, COMPUTE, or COMPUTE BY clauses. A derived table is a SELECT statement in the FROM clause, referred to by an *alias* or a user-specified name.

- When selecting an existing identity column into a new table, the new column inherits the IDENTITY property, unless one of the following conditions is true:

  - The SELECT statement contains a join, GROUP BY clause, or aggregate function.
  - Multiple SELECT statements are joined with UNION.
  - The identity column is listed more than once in the select list.
  - The identity column is part of an expression.

- If any of these conditions is true, the column is created NOT NULL instead of inheriting the IDENTITY property. All rules and restrictions for the identity columns apply to the new table.

- Earlier versions of SQL Server joins (using the *= and =* syntax in the WHERE clause) cannot be used within the same statement as SQL-92-style joins.

- The FOR BROWSE option specifies that updates be allowed while viewing data in client applications using DB-Library. To permit browsing, the table must include a time-stamped column, and a unique index.

- It is not possible to use HOLDLOCK in a SELECT statement that includes the FOR BROWSE option.

- The order of the clauses in the SELECT statement is significant. Although any of the optional clauses can be omitted, they must appear in the appropriate order when used.

- SQL Server raises exception 511 and rolls back the current executing statement if either the SELECT statement produces a result row; an intermediate work table row exceeds 8,060 bytes; or the DELETE, INSERT, or UPDATE statement attempts action on a row exceeding 8,060 bytes.

- In SQL Server, an error occurs if no column name is given to a column created by a SELECT INTO or CREATE VIEW statement. For more information, see the discussion of trace flag 246 in Trace Flags.

SELECT INTO

SELECT INTO creates a temporary or permanent table. A temporary table can be used to temporarily store information for reporting purposes, and so on. The advantage of using the INTO format is to free up the source table while future procedures can be enacted on the newly created table.

Important issues regarding the appropriate use of the SELECT statement with the INTO option are as follows:

- When used in a SELECT statement, IDENTITY must be used with an INTO clause.

- If you wish to select into a permanent table, execute sp_dboption and turn on the SELECT INTO/BULKCOPY option. If SELECT INTO/BULKCOPY is on in the database where the table is to be created, a permanent table is created. If SELECT INTO/BULKCOPY is not on in the database where the table is to be created, permanent tables cannot be created by using SELECT INTO; only local or global temporary tables can be created. To create a temporary table, the table name must begin with a number sign.

- SELECT INTO is a two-step operation. The first step creates the table. The user executing the statement must have CREATE TABLE permission in the destination database. The second step inserts the specified rows into the new table.

- SELECT INTO is done with minimal logging, so it tends to be faster when copying large amounts of data. The SELECT INTO/BULK COPY option invalidates all subsequent log backups, and a FULL or DIFFERENTIAL backup must be performed before any backups of the transaction logs can be taken.

Embedded SELECT INTO

SELECT [select list] INTO {:host variable [,...]} select options

The SELECT INTO statement retrieves one row of results and assigns the values of the items in the SELECT list to host variables. It is important that you set the data type and length of the host variables so that they are compatible with the values assigned to them. The syntax follows:

```
EXEC SQL SELECT LastName INTO :name FROM MyTable WHERE Customer_ID =
➥:id
```

GROUP BY and HAVING

The GROUP BY clause produces individual groupings and the HAVING clause can further define the rows to be included (see the example that follows). Additional columns can be used in an aggregate function (such as sum or average). The GROUP BY clause is an excellent technique for producing summary listings. The following example shows the appropriate syntax to list any advances over $25,000 for those with a year-to-date sales value:

```
SELECT pub_id AS ID,
  SUM(advance) AS "Total Advance" ,
  AVG(price) AS "Average Price"
FROM titles
WHERE ytd_sales > 0
GROUP BY pub_id
HAVING SUM(advance) > $25000
ORDER BY pub_id
```

Important issues regarding the appropriate use of the SELECT statement using the GROUP BY and HAVING clauses are as follows:

- The HAVING clause excludes rows that do not meet its conditions. Typically, the HAVING and GROUP BY clauses are used together. It is possible to specify the HAVING clause without the use of a GROUP BY clause, in which case the HAVING clause behaves the same as a WHERE clause.

- Columns in the SELECT list must also be in the GROUP BY clause or be parameters of aggregate functions.

- Columns in a HAVING clause must have only one value per group.

- A query with a HAVING clause should have a GROUP BY clause. If it does not, all the rows not excluded by the WHERE clause are considered to be a single group.

ORDER BY

The ORDER BY clause specifies the order of the results from the SELECT. In the following example, the output is listed in Type sequence.

```
SELECT title_id as Title, pub_id AS Publisher, Type
FROM titles
WHERE ytd_sales > 0
ORDER BY Type
```

Important issues regarding the appropriate use of the SELECT statement using the ORDER BY clause are as follows:

- Use a column name or an expression in the ORDER BY clause; specifying a column heading cannot perform sorting.

- If the ORDER BY clause is not specified, groups returned with the GROUP BY clause are not in any particular order. It is recommended that you always use the ORDER BY clause to specify a particular ordering of the data.

COMPUTE BY

A COMPUTE BY clause allows you to see both detail and summary rows. You can calculate summary values for subgroups and/or the entire result set. If the BY option is not specified, only final summary values are shown—not those for subgroups. The following example lists the year-to-date total sales and prints the report by type, giving totals for each type.

```
SELECT Type, Ytd_sales
FROM Titles
ORDER BY Type, Ytd_sales
COMPUTE SUM(Ytd_sales) BY Type
```

Important issues regarding the appropriate use of the SELECT statement with the COMPUTE clause are as follows:

- The DISTINCT keyword is not allowed with row aggregate functions.

- The columns in a COMPUTE clause must appear in the statement's SELECT list.

- SELECT INTO cannot be used in the same statement as a COMPUTE clause because statements that include COMPUTE do not generate normal rows.

- If you use COMPUTE BY, an ORDER BY clause must also be specified. The columns listed after COMPUTE BY must be identical to or a subset of those listed after ORDER BY. They must be in the same left-to-right order, start with the same expression, and not skip any expressions.

- When using an expression with a COMPUTE clause, remember that when used as a row aggregate function, an expression is usually the name of a column, and one COMPUTE clause can apply the same function to several columns or several functions to one column.
- You cannot use SELECT INTO with the COMPUTE clause or inside a user-defined transaction.
- In a SELECT statement with a COMPUTE clause, the order of columns in the SELECT list overrides the order of the aggregate functions in the COMPUTE clause. ODBC and DB-Library programmers must be aware of this order requirement to put the aggregate function results in the correct place.
- *n*text, text, or image data types cannot be specified in a COMPUTE or COMPUTE BY clause.

You must have select permission on the tables being used. These permissions default to the owner of the table or view. The table or view owner can grant these permissions to other users by using the GRANT statement. If the INTO clause is used to create a permanent table, the user must have create table permission in the destination database.

The following examples illustrate the use of the SELECT statement with a variety of options. A select operation is one of the most frequently used processes in a number of useful procedures. For further examples of its use, see the examples section for the SELECT statement in SQL Server Books Online. Further information on related commands (such as joins) is found later in this book.

- A simple select choosing all columns:
    ```
    SELECT * FROM MyTable
    ```
- In order:
    ```
    SELECT * FROM MyTable ORDER Customer_ID ASC
    ```
- Alternative syntax:
    ```
    SELECT MyTable.* FROM Saving  ORDER BY Customer_ID ASC
    ```
- With grouping:
    ```
    SELECT Customer_ID, SUM (Balance) AS Total FROM MyTable
       GROUP BY Customer_ID ORDER BY Customer_ID
    ```

- With HAVING:

  ```
  SELECT Customer_ID FROM MyTable
     GROUP BY Customer_ID HAVING COUNT > 1 ORDER BY Customer_ID
  ```

- With COMPUTE:

  ```
  SELECT Customer_ID, Balance FROM MyTable
     ORDER BY Customer_ID COMPUTE AVG(Balance) BY Customer_ID
  ```

Joins and Subqueries

A join allows you to combine data from two or more tables. The join itself defines to SQL Server the actual technique used to process records of one table against the other table to produce a resultset. A subquery, which is similar to a join, can refer to data from more than one table. A subquery is a SELECT statement nested inside another SELECT statement. Subqueries can also be used in insert, delete, and update operations. A statement that includes a subquery operates on rows from one table, based on how it evaluates the nested SELECT statement. Where a join can blend information from multiple tables, a subquery used a nested query's results to act as a condition for the processing of the outer SELECT statement. The subquery can refer to the same table as the outer query or to a different table altogether. In Transact-SQL, a subquery that returns a single value can be used anywhere an expression is allowed.

The following sections examine the many variations of joins and the different syntax rules that are applied to develop a join. Comparisons are made between the use of a join and the use of a subquery. There are essentially three different styles of joins: inner, outer, and cross; there are also numerous variations that can be applied.

Many Transact-SQL statements that include a subquery can be alternatively formulated as joins. A self-join is a good example of a join type that can be performed either way. Other queries can be formulated by using only a subquery. There is essentially no performance difference between utilizing joins and using subqueries; often, the selection of one over the other comes down to a personal preference or the ease of implementation in a particular application. When existence checks must be performed, a join outperforms a subquery. Using a subqueries can often saves steps.

SQL Standard Syntax

In most implementations, it is recommended that the conditions for a join be designated in the FROM portion of a statement (although is also possible to specify these conditions in a WHERE clause). WHERE and HAVING clauses are often used to supply further conditions to reduce the number of records in the resulting joined resultset.

In the following set of examples, several different forms of SELECT statements and joins are provided. Three base tables are provided and the full content is displayed (see Figure 3.1 and Figure 3.2) as a point of reference. You can determine the actual results, based on the different types of joins and SELECT clauses.

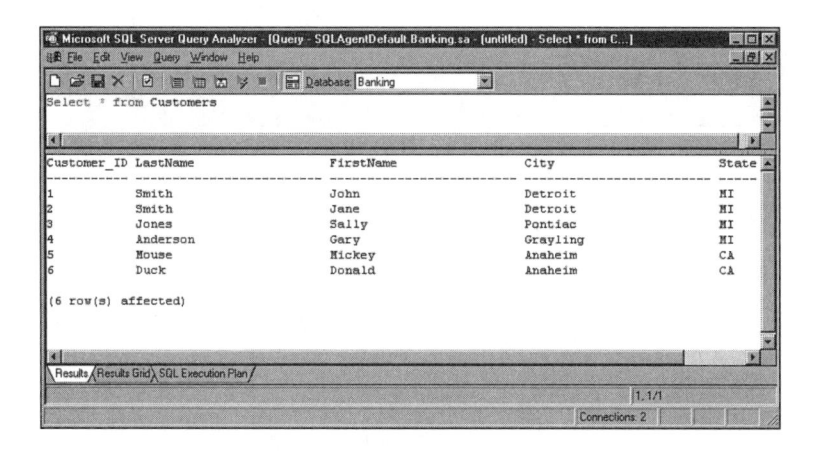

FIGURE 3.1
All customers in the table.

Inner Joins

Inner joins, which also include equi-joins and natural joins, use a comparison operator to match rows from two tables, based on the values in common columns from each table. An *equi-join* is a join in which the column values that are compared to each other are equal. An equi-join produces redundant column information because the join column is specified twice. A natural join displays the column information just once and eliminates the redundant data produced by an equi-join. The most common form of join is used to provide a temporary link between two tables. In doing so, fields from both tables can be provided in the output, as shown in Figure 3.3.

94 CHAPTER 3 Creating Data Services

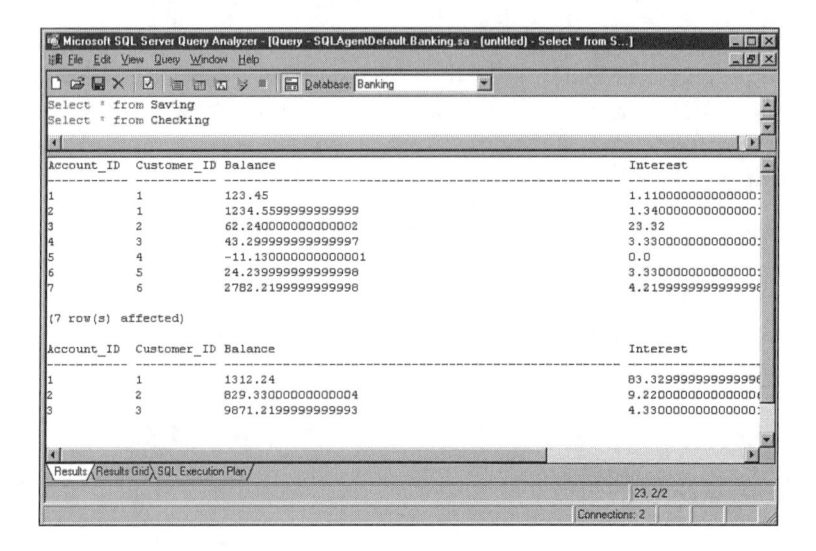

```
Select * from Saving
Select * from Checking

Account_ID   Customer_ID   Balance                          Interest
----------   -----------   -------                          --------
1            1             123.45                           1.1100000000000001
2            1             1234.5599999999999               1.3400000000000001
3            2             62.240000000000002               23.32
4            3             43.299999999999997               3.3300000000000001
5            4             -11.130000000000001              0.0
6            5             24.299999999999998               3.3300000000000001
7            6             2782.2199999999998               4.2199999999999998

(7 row(s) affected)

Account_ID   Customer_ID   Balance                          Interest
----------   -----------   -------                          --------
1            1             1312.24                          83.329999999999998
2            2             829.33000000000004               9.2200000000000006
3            3             9871.2199999999993               4.3300000000000001
```

FIGURE 3.2
All related bank accounts.

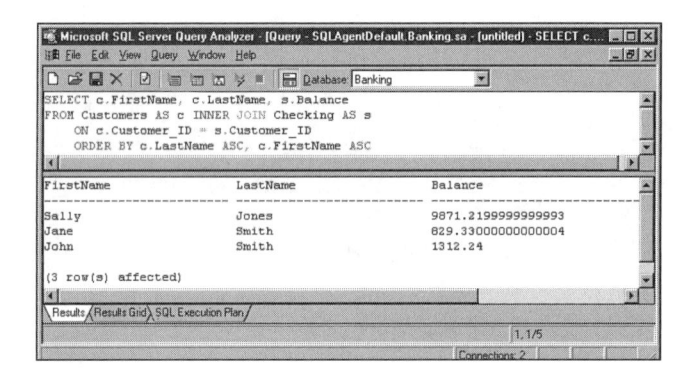

```
SELECT c.FirstName, c.LastName, s.Balance
FROM Customers AS c INNER JOIN Checking AS s
    ON c.Customer_ID = s.Customer_ID
    ORDER BY c.LastName ASC, c.FirstName ASC

FirstName                LastName                 Balance
---------                --------                 -------
Sally                    Jones                    9871.2199999999993
Jane                     Smith                    829.33000000000004
John                     Smith                    1312.24

(3 row(s) affected)
```

FIGURE 3.3
The balances of all customer checking accounts.

Outer Joins

An outer join returns all rows from at least one of the tables or views; depending on whether left, right, or full is specified. The WHERE and HAVING clauses can eliminate some of the resulting rows in the resultset. All rows are retrieved from the left table referenced with a left outer join and from the right table referenced in a right outer join. All rows from both tables are returned in a full outer join. Note that a NULL result is possible because not all records from one table have a match in the other (see Figure 3.4).

SQL Standard Syntax

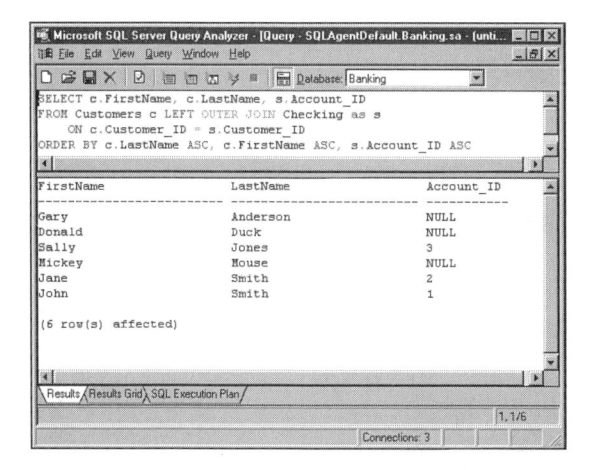

```
Microsoft SQL Server Query Analyzer - [Query - SQLAgentDefault.Banking.sa - (unti...
File Edit View Query Window Help

Database: Banking

SELECT c.FirstName, c.LastName, s.Account_ID
FROM Customers c LEFT OUTER JOIN Checking as s
    ON c.Customer_ID = s.Customer_ID
ORDER BY c.LastName ASC, c.FirstName ASC, s.Account_ID ASC

FirstName                  LastName                   Account_ID
-----------------------    -----------------------    -----------
Gary                       Anderson                   NULL
Donald                     Duck                       NULL
Sally                      Jones                      3
Mickey                     Mouse                      NULL
Jane                       Smith                      2
John                       Smith                      1

(6 row(s) affected)
```

FIGURE 3.4
All customers showing the account ID for those who have checking accounts.

Often, a right outer join produces results that are similar to those of an inner join when two tables have a one-to-one or a one-to-many relationship. (See Figure 3.5 and compare the output to Figure 3.3.)

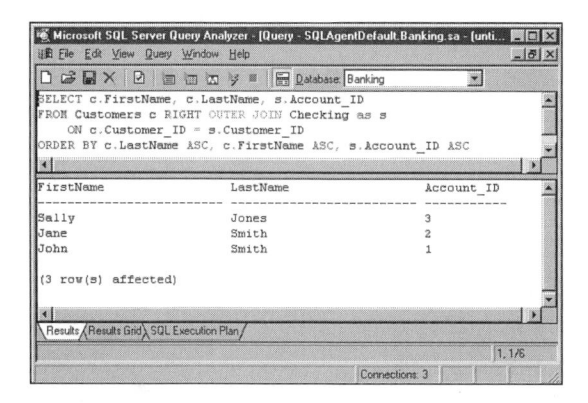

```
Microsoft SQL Server Query Analyzer - [Query - SQLAgentDefault.Banking.sa - (unti...
File Edit View Query Window Help

Database: Banking

SELECT c.FirstName, c.LastName, s.Account_ID
FROM Customers c RIGHT OUTER JOIN Checking as s
    ON c.Customer_ID = s.Customer_ID
ORDER BY c.LastName ASC, c.FirstName ASC, s.Account_ID ASC

FirstName                  LastName                   Account_ID
-----------------------    -----------------------    -----------
Sally                      Jones                      3
Jane                       Smith                      2
John                       Smith                      1

(3 row(s) affected)
```

FIGURE 3.5
Account IDs of customers with checking accounts.

Cross-Joins

A *cross-join* is often referred to as an *unrestricted join* because it does not have a WHERE clause. If a WHERE clause is added to the cross-join, the result will be similar to that of an inner join. A cross-join produces the

Cartesian product of the tables involved in the join. A *Cartesian product* is a resultset that includes a larger number of rows because it is made up of the product of the two tables (the number of rows in the first table multiplied by the number of rows in the second table). (See Figure 3.6.)

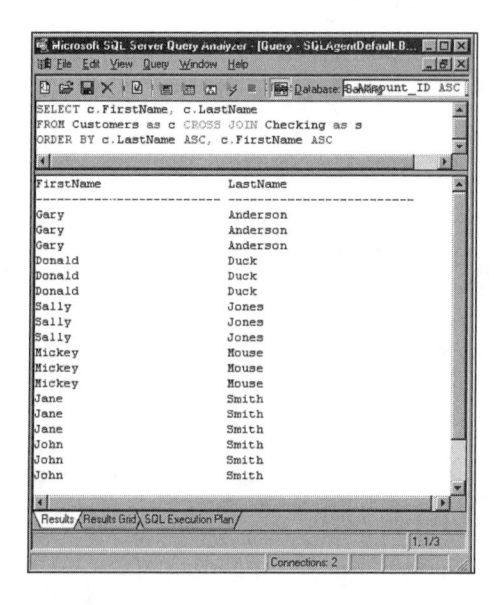

FIGURE 3.6
Customers cross-joined with checking.

Subqueries

A *subquery*, sometimes called an *inner query*, is a SELECT statement nested inside of a SELECT, INSERT, UPDATE, or DELETE statement; or inside of another subquery. A subquery that is nested in an outer SELECT statement is a regular SELECT statement with a regular FROM clause, and can optionally have WHERE, GROUP BY, or HAVING clauses. The SELECT statement itself is always enclosed in parentheses. A subquery SELECT statement cannot include an ORDER BY, COMPUTE, or FOR BROWSE clause because it solely provides a condition for the outer query. A TOP clause can be included, in which case the ORDER BY clause is permissible.

A subquery can be nested inside a WHERE or HAVING clause with up to 32 levels of nesting. If a table appears only in a subquery and not in the outer query, the columns from that table cannot be included in the output.

Statements that include a subquery usually take one of these formats:

- `WHERE expression [NOT] IN (subquery)`
- `WHERE expression comparison operator [ANY ¦ ALL] (subquery)`
- `WHERE [NOT] EXISTS (subquery)`

There are three basic implementations of a subquery. A subquery can operate on a list utilized with IN (see Figure 3.7), on those that a comparison operator modified by ANY, or on those that a comparison operator modified by ALL. These can be introduced with an unmodified comparison operator and must return a single value or pin conjunction with existence tests using the EXISTS or NOT EXISTS keyword.

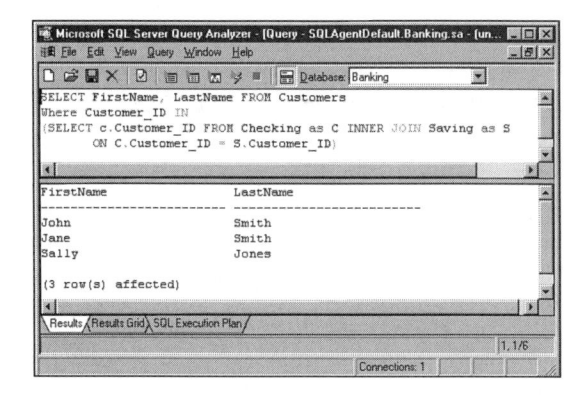

FIGURE 3.7
All customers with both checking and savings accounts.

Aliases

An *alias* is a name given for reference purposes to a table using the AS keyword. The use of an alias is necessary in some instances, such as a self-join, but it may be used simply to make coding easier to accomplish in any instance when a statement involves more than one table. Many of the previous examples used aliases to make the entry of code easier to perform. Many statements in which the subquery and the outer query refer to the same table can be stated as self-joins. The use of an outer and inner query does not require aliases because there are two separate SELECT statements. Table aliases are required in a self-join because the table that is being joined to it appears in two different roles. Aliases can also be used in nested queries that refer to the same table in an inner and outer query.

Aliases may also be used in a correlated subquery, which is a repeating subquery. Many queries can be evaluated by executing the subquery once, and substituting the resulting value or values into the where clause of the outer query. In queries that include a correlated subquery, the subquery depends on the outer query for its values. This means that the subquery is executed repeatedly, one time for each row that is selected by the outer query. Because the inner query is dependant on values in the outer query, it is necessary to substitute a value from the outer query into the inner query, and then perform the inner query to test the validity of each record. This process continues for each record.

IN or NOT IN

These are represented conditions that can be used as evaluation criteria for a subquery. IN determines whether a given value matches any value in a list developed by an inner query. Conversely, NOT IN determines whether a value is absent from the inner query's resultset.

INSERT, UPDATE, or DELETE

In the same way that a SELECT operation uses subqueries and joins, the UPDATE, INSERT, and DELETE operations also take advantage of the features of joins and subqueries. You can use a subquery to delete all rows from one table that don't have the corresponding records in another table. In the same manner, you can use subqueries and joins to supply conditions for updating and deleting records.

Comparison Operators

Comparison operators are used with character, numeric, or date data; they can be used in the WHERE or HAVING clause of a query. Comparison operators evaluate to a Boolean data type; they return TRUE or FALSE, based on the outcome of the tested condition.

Valid comparison operators are as follows:

- \> (greater than)
- < (less than)
- = (equals)
- <= (less than or equal to)
- \>= (greater than or equal to)

- != (not equal to)
- <> (not equal to)
- !< (not less than)
- !> (not greater than)

Comparison operators can also be used in program logic to test for conditions. Anyone with access to the actual data can use comparison operators in additional queries. Queries also use string comparisons to compare the value in a local variable, cursor, or column with a constant.

Logical operators may also be utilized as follows:

- AND (TRUE if both Boolean expressions are TRUE)
- OR (TRUE if either Boolean expression is TRUE)
- NOT (Reverses the value of any Boolean operator)
- BETWEEN (TRUE if evaluated between a range)
- LIKE (TRUE if the operator matches a pattern)
- SOME (TRUE if some of a set of comparisons is TRUE)
- ANY (TRUE if any one of a set of comparisons is TRUE)
- ALL (TRUE if all of a set of comparisons is TRUE)

EXISTS or NOT EXISTS

Subqueries use EXISTS and NOT EXISTS tests to find out whether there is an intersection or difference between two sets.

- EXISTS (TRUE if all elements belong to both sets)
- NOT EXISTS (TRUE if elements are contained only in the first set)

UNION

UNION combines the results of two or more queries into a single resultset that consists of all the rows belonging to all queries in the union. If you use the UNION form with the keyword ALL, the resultset incorporates all rows into the results, including duplicates. If the ALL keyword is not specified, duplicate rows are removed in the resultset. You can look at a UNION operation as being simply the combination of two or more SELECT operations.

The SQL syntax for a UNION is provided for reference, as follows:

```
select statement
UNION [ALL]

select statement
[UNION [ALL] select statement][,...n]
```

An example of a UNION of three tables:

```
SELECT FirstName, LastName FROM Customers
UNION SELECT FirstName, LastName FROM Vendors
UNION SELECT FirstName, LastName FROM Employees
```

Transact-SQL Scripts

A *script* is a series of Transact-SQL statements that are stored in a file. The file can be used as input to SQL Server Query Analyzer or to the osql and isql utilities. The utilities can then execute the SQL statements that are stored in the file.

Transact-SQL scripts have one or more batches that end with GO to identify the end of a batch. If a Transact-SQL script does not have any GO statements, it is executed as a single batch.

Transact-SQL scripts can be used to keep a permanent copy of the steps used to create and populate the databases. They can be used to transfer the statements from one computer to another and can help to quickly educate new employees by enabling them to understand the coding that has taken place.

You can generate Transact-SQL scripts to create the jobs that you define. With job scripting, you can control the versions of job-creation source code, and you can migrate jobs from test into production. You can also script alerts and operators.

Control of Flow

Transact-SQL provides control-of-flow language that controls the flow of execution of Transact-SQL statements, statement blocks, and stored procedures. Control-of-flow language allows the developer to implement specific logic within scripts and procedures. These words can be used in ad hoc Transact-SQL statements, in batches, and in stored procedures. If not implemented, by default, SQL Server will process all Transact-SQL statements in a sequential manner. Control-of-flow language permits statements to be connected, related to each other, and made interdependent by using programming-like constructs.

BEGIN...END
The BEGIN...END statement is used to define a block of Transact-SQL statements that can be executed together. It's used most commonly with conditional operations to perform more than a single command, based on the result of a condition that normally defaults to a single command.

GOTO
Contrary to popular opinion, sometimes you cannot structure code in any other way except to use a GOTO (my college professor will want to string me up for this sentence). In some instances, you must use a GOTO operation to send execution to another point within a script to avoid having to make extensive changes to existing code. GOTO is also helpful when you need to break out of deeply nested control-of-flow statements.

The GOTO statement alters the flow of execution to a label. The use of GOTO should be limited because it creates difficulty in trying to track the execution of code for debugging purposes, creating what is commonly referred to as *spaghetti code* (because it goes all over the place). If possible, try to develop a more structured style by using statement blocks and conditional elements. GOTO statements can be nested.

Define the label:
```
label:
```

Alter the execution flow by going to the label:
```
GOTO label
```

IF...ELSE
The IF...ELSE statement specifies criteria for the execution of a statement or block of statements. The IF statement can be compounded, which is similar to the constructs used in other languages. An experienced developer in any language should be quite comfortable with the SQL syntax form of this operation, as follows:
```
IF Boolean expression
{sql statement | statement block}
[ELSE
{sql statement | statement block}]
```

RETURN

The RETURN statement exits unconditionally from a query or procedure. It can be used to exit from a procedure, batch, or statement block. The RETURN statement provides feedback in the form of a non-null integer expression to any calling procedure.

The return status value can be included in subsequent statements within the script that executed the current procedure, but it must be entered in the following form:

    EXECUTE @return status variable = procedure name

SQL Server reserves 0 to indicate the successful completion of a procedure and negative values from −1 through −99 to indicate different reasons for failure. If more than one error occurs during execution, the status with the highest absolute value is returned. User-defined return values always take precedence over those supplied by SQL Server. User-defined return status values should not conflict with those reserved by SQL Server. If no user-defined return value is provided, the SQL Server value is used. The values 0 through −14 are currently used by SQL Server and are the representations, as shown in Table 3.3.

TABLE 3.3

SQL SERVER RESERVED RETURN VALUES

Value	Explanation
0	Procedure executed successfully.
−1	Object is missing.
−2	Data type error occurred.
−3	Process was chosen as deadlock victim.
−4	Permission error occurred.
−5	Syntax error occurred.
−6	Miscellaneous user error occurred.
−7	Resource error, such as out of space.
−8	Nonfatal internal problem was encountered.
−9	System limit was reached.
−10	Fatal internal inconsistency occurred.
−11	Fatal internal inconsistency occurred.

SQL Standard Syntax

Value	Explanation
–12	Table or index is corrupt.
–13	Database is corrupt.
–14	Hardware error occurred.

NOTE: Unless documented otherwise, all system stored procedures return a value of 0, which indicates success; a nonzero value indicates failure.

The RETURN operation is often combined with conditional expressions, with alternative values being used based on the conditions provided. The basic form of the RETURN statement in SQL syntax is provided as a singular command, as follows:

```
RETURN [(integer expression)]
```

WAITFOR

The WAITFOR statement suspends the execution connection until a specified time interval has passed or until a specific time of day. The WAITFOR statement is specified with either the DELAY clause or the TIME clause, depending on which functionality you want. The WAITFOR statement can use a delay of up to 24 hours. The following example compares a delay of two seconds (using DELAY) with a specific instruction to wait until 22:00 (using TIME).

```
WAITFOR DELAY '00:00:02'
WAITFOR TIME '22:00'
```

The disadvantage of the WAITFOR statement is that the connection from the application remains suspended until the WAITFOR statement completes. Therefore, it should be used sparingly and only when the procedure needs to suspend processing for some relatively limited amount of time. Using SQL Agent or SQL-DMO to schedule a task is a better method of executing an action at a specific time of day.

WHILE

WHILE sets a condition for the repeated execution of an SQL statement or statement block. The statements are executed repeatedly, as long as the specified condition is true. The execution of statements in the WHILE loop can be controlled from inside the loop by using BREAK and CONTINUE keywords. The outline for an SQL syntax of a conditional WHILE block is provided in the following listing. The BREAK and CONTINUE options are usually part of an internal conditional expression that is used within a statement block.

```
WHILE Boolean expression
{sql statement ¦ statement block}
[BREAK]
{sql statement ¦ statement block}
[CONTINUE]
```

BREAK

The BREAK statement exits the innermost WHILE loop. Any statements following the END keyword are executed. BREAK is often, but not always, activated by an IF test.

CONTINUE

CONTINUE restarts a WHILE loop. Any statements after the CONTINUE keyword are ignored. CONTINUE is often, but not always, activated by an IF test. CONTINUE is used to retest the condition and begin execution at the top of the loop.

CASE

The CASE keyword evaluates a list of conditions and returns one of multiple possible result expressions. This is similar to using a series of IF...ELSE statements that are compounded together for mutual exclusion. In general, a CASE statement is more efficient and easier to code in any situation that involves more than three possible conditions. A simple CASE function compares an expression to a set of simple expressions to determine the result, whereas a searched CASE function evaluates a set of Boolean expressions to determine the result. All WHEN operations are evaluated in turn, with only the first matching or TRUE response being executed. If no WHEN clause is executed and there is an ELSE clause, then it is executed. The two possible SQL CASE operations are provided in the following syntax descriptions:

A simple CASE function:

```
CASE input expression
WHEN when expression THEN result expression
[,...n]
[ELSE else result expression]
END
```

A searched CASE function:

```
CASE
WHEN Boolean expression THEN result expression
[,...n]
[ELSE else result expression]
END
```

Comments

Comments, also known as remarks, can be inserted on a separate line, placed at the end of a Transact-SQL command line, or placed within a Transact-SQL statement. Comments are most commonly used to document code, but can also be used as a debugging tool to temporarily disable parts of Transact-SQL statements and the batches being diagnosed. There are two commenting techniques available in SQL Server: line comments and block comments. A line comment uses − (double hyphens). A comment block uses /* ... */ (forward slash-asterisk character pairs), which allows you to place larger comments into a script.

When the utilities read the characters GO in the first two bytes of a line, they send all the code since the last GO statement to the server as one batch. If a GO occurs at the start of a line between the /* and */ delimiters, then an unmatched comment delimiter will be sent with each batch, and they will trigger syntax errors.

An example syntax:

```
— text of comment
```

or

```
/* text of comment
   more text of comment
   more text of comment */
```

DECLARE

Variables are declared in the body of a batch or procedure with the DECLARE statement, and given or assigned values with either a SET or SELECT statement. Cursor variables can be declared with this statement and used with other cursor-related statements. After declaration, all variables are initialized as NULL. A variable cannot be of text, *n*text, or image data type. The DECLARE statement, as indicated in the following SQL syntax, can be used to declare normal or CURSOR type variables. Variables and their respective data types are given a little later in the chapter. The following example illustrates the SQL syntax for the DECLARE statement:

```
DECLARE
{{@local variable    data type}¦ {cursor variable name    CURSOR}}
↪[, ...n]
```

PRINT

The PRINT keyword returns a user-defined message of up to 1,024 characters to the client's message handler. To print a user-defined error message with an error number that can be returned by @@ERROR, use RAISERROR instead of PRINT. Printing can be performed by using straight text, through a variable, through the return value of a function, or by using the concatenation of any of these options.

```
PRINT 'any ASCII text' | @local variable | @@function | string
➥expression
```

EXECUTE

EXECUTE executes a system procedure, a user-defined stored procedure, or an extended stored procedure. It also supports the execution of a character string within a Transact-SQL batch. If the first three characters of the procedure name are sp_, SQL Server searches the master database for the procedure. If no qualified procedure name is provided, SQL Server searches for the procedure as if the owner name were dbo. A stored procedure can be executed directly by referring to its name or it can be executed through the use of a string variable that contains a CREATE PROCEDURE statement, as shown in the following SQL syntax descriptions.

Execute a stored procedure:

```
[[EXEC[UTE]]
{[@return status =] procedure name [;number] | @procedure name
➥variable}
[[@parameter =] {value | @variable} [OUTPUT] | [DEFAULT]] [,...n]
[WITH RECOMPILE]
```

Execute a character string:

```
EXEC[UTE] ({@string variable | [N]'Transact-SQL string'} [+...n])
```

Important issues regarding the appropriate use of the SELECT statement with the COMPUTE clause are as follows:

- *Nesting* occurs when one stored procedure calls another. This is also referred to as *stacking*. SQL Server limits the number of nested stack calls to 16. If the nesting level is exceeded, then the entire set of called stored procedures will fail.

- Remote stored procedures and extended stored procedures are not within the scope of a transaction (unless they are issued within a BEGIN DISTRIBUTED TRANSACTION statement or used with various configuration options); commands executed through calls to them cannot be rolled back.

- If you execute a procedure that passes in a cursor variable with a cursor allocated to it, an error occurs.

- You do not have to specify the EXECUTE keyword when executing stored procedures if the statement is the first one in a batch.

- Statements inside the EXECUTE statement are not compiled until the EXECUTE statement is executed.

You must have execute permissions for a stored procedure that is used. These permissions default to the owner of the stored procedure. The owner of the stored procedure can transfer these permissions to other users. Permissions to use the statement within the execute string are checked at the time execute is encountered, even if the EXECUTE statement is included within a stored procedure. When a stored procedure is run that executes a string, permissions are checked in the context of the user who executes the procedure, not in the context of the user who created the procedure. If a user owns two stored procedures in which the first procedure calls the second, however, then execute permission checking is not performed for the second stored procedure.

The following examples illustrate the use of the EXECUTE statement with a variety of options. An execute operation has a lot of flexibility and many different syntax options. For further examples of its use, see the examples section for the EXECUTE statement in SQL Server Books Online. Further information on related commands (such as joins) will be found later in this book.

- A simple execute that passes a single parameter to a stored procedure:
    ```
    EXEC MyProcedure MyTable
    ```

- The variable can be explicitly named in the execution:
    ```
    EXEC MyProcedure @tablename = MyTable
    ```

- An execute with a remote stored procedure:
    ```
    DECLARE @retstat int
    EXECUTE @retstat = SQLSERVER.pubs.dbo.checkcontract '409-56-4008'
    ```

- An execute with an extended stored procedure:
    ```
    USE master
    EXECUTE xp_cmdshell 'dir *.exe'
    ```

Variables

A Transact-SQL variable holds a data value. After the variable is declared, or defined, one Transact-SQL statement in a batch can set the variable to a value and a later statement in the batch can get the value from the variable. A variable can also be used as a parameter. A parameter is used to pass data between a stored procedure and the batch or script that executes it. Parameters can be either input or output. (See "DECLARE" for information on declaring variables.) Values can be placed into a variable by using a SET statement or as a result of a Transact-SQL select operation:

```
SET @MyVariable = 123456

@MyVariable = SELECT Customer_ID WHERE LastName = 'Smith' AND
➥FirstName = 'John'
```

Local variables are declared starting with @. Global Variables are declared starting with @@. SQL Server variables and data types are provided in Table 3.4 and the synonyms for SQL-92 in Table 3.5.

TABLE 3.4

SQL SERVER DATA TYPES

Type	Description
bit	Integer data with either a 1 or 0 value.
int	Integer data from -2^{31} ($-2,147,483,648$) through $2^{31}-1$ ($2,147,483,647$).
smallint	Integer data from 2^{15} ($-32,768$) through $2^{15}-1$ ($32,767$).
tinyint	Integer data from 0 through 255.
decimal	Fixed precision and scale numeric data from $-10^{38}-1$ through $10^{38}-1$.
numeric	A synonym for decimal.
money	Monetary data values from -2^{63} $-922,337,203,685,477.5808$) through $2^{6}-1$ (+922,337,203,685,477.5807), with accuracy to one ten-thousandth of a monetary unit.
smallmoney	Monetary data values from $-214,748.3648$ through $+214,748.3647$, with accuracy to one ten-thousandth of a monetary unit.
float	Floating precision number data from $-1.79E + 308$ through $1.79E + 308$.
real	Floating precision number data from $-3.40E + 38$ through $3.40E + 38$.
datetime	Date/time data from January 1, 1753 to December 31, 9999, with an accuracy of three-hundredths of a second, or 3.33 milliseconds.

Type	Description
smalldatetime	Date/time data from January 1, 1900 through June 6, 2079, with an accuracy of one minute.
cursor	A reference to a cursor.
timestamp	A database-wide unique number.
uniqueidentifier	A globally unique identifier (GUID).
char	Fixed-length, non-Unicode character data with a maximum length of 8,000 characters.
varchar	Variable-length, non-Unicode data with a maximum of 8,000 characters.
text	Variable-length, non-Unicode data with a maximum length of 2^3–1 (2,147,483,647) characters.
nchar	Fixed-length, Unicode data with a maximum length of 4,000 characters.
nvarchar	Variable-length, Unicode data with a maximum length of 4,000 characters. sysname is a system-supplied user-defined data type that is a synonym for nvarchar(128) and is used to reference database object names.
*n*text	Variable-length, Unicode data with a maximum length of 2^3–1 (1,073,741,823) characters.
binary	Fixed-length, binary data with a maximum length of 8,000 bytes.
varbinary	Variable-length, binary data with a maximum length of 8,000 bytes.
image	Variable-length, binary data with a maximum length of 2^3–1 (2,147,483,647) bytes.

TABLE 3.5
SQL-92 Data Type Equivalencies

SQL-92 Type	SQL Server Equivalent
binary varying	varbinary
char varying	varchar
character	char
character	char
character	char
character varying	varchar
dec	decimal
double precision	float

continues

TABLE 3.5 continued

SQL-92 Type	SQL Server Equivalent
float[ ] for n = 1–7	real
float[ ] for n = 8–15	float
integer	int
national character	nchar
national char	nchar
numeric	decimal
national text	ntext
national char varying	nvarchar
national character varying	nvarchar

Functions

Functions are used in SQL Server queries, reports, and many Transact-SQL statements to return information. Most functions take input parameters and return a value. The difference between a function and a procedure is that a function must return a value; a procedure only returns a value when it is set up as a function operation whose return value is used for the purpose of further processing. Functions can be used almost anywhere a variable can because, like variables, a function represents a value. The Transact-SQL programming language provides three types of functions: rowset functions that are used like table references; aggregate functions that operate on a collection of values but return a single, summarizing value; and scalar functions that operate on a single value, and then return a single value. Scalar functions can be used wherever an expression is valid.

Rowset Functions

The Transact-SQL programming language provides for four rowset functions. These functions return an object that can be used in place of a table reference in any SQL statement that uses a table reference. The four rowset functions—OPENQUERY, ContainsTable, OPENROWSET, and FreeTextTable—are discussed at the end of this chapter.

Aggregate Functions

Aggregate functions perform a calculation on a set of values and return a single value. With the exception of the COUNT function, aggregate functions ignore null values; COUNT includes null values to provide a total value for the number of rows that meet the criteria of the SELECT statement. Aggregate functions are often used with GROUP BY clauses. Transact-SQL programming language provides for the following aggregate functions and their respective returned values:

TABLE 3.6
SQL SERVER AGGREGATE FUNCTIONS

Function	Usage
AVG	Average of the values in a group
MIN	Lowest of the values in a group
COUNT	Number of rows in a group that meet the criteria
SUM	Total of the values in a group
MAX	Highest of the values in a group
VAR	Statistical variance of all values in the given expression
VARP	Statistical variance for the population for all values in the given expression
STDEV	Statistical standard deviation of all values in the given expression
STDEVP	Statistical standard deviation for the population for all values in the given expression

Scalar Functions

Scalar functions represent the largest number of functions and perform a number of tasks. The following sections divide the scalar functions into the categories in which each are usually utilized. All scalar functions are included to provide for a complete reference. Some of the more important functions will be discussed in greater detail later in the book.

> **NOTE** Even though you will not run into all functions in the exam, quite often the functions are included as incorrect answers for other questions. Knowing what each of the functions is really used for will help you to not select them if they pop up in an unrelated question.

There are a considerable number of scalar functions that are available in SQL Server. The following list defines each category of function, and Table 3.7 provides further information about each function.

- **Configuration functions.** Return information about the current configuration.
- **Cursor functions.** Return information about cursors.
- **Date and Time functions.** Perform operations on a date and time input value; and return a string, numeric, or date and time value.
- **Mathematical functions.** Perform calculations based on input values provided as parameters to the function, and return a numeric value.
- **Metadata functions.** Return information about the database and database objects.
- **Security functions.** Return information about users and roles.
- **String functions.** Perform operations on a string-input value, and return a string or numeric value.
- **System functions.** Perform operations; return information about values, objects, and settings of SQL Server.
- **System Statistical functions.** Return statistical information about the system.
- **Text and Image functions.** Perform operations on a text or image-input values or column, and return information about the value.

TABLE 3.7

SQL SERVER SCALAR FUNCTIONS

Function	Description
Configuration Functions	
@@CONNECTIONS	Number of connections or attempted connections since the Server started.
@@OPTIONS	Information about current SET options.
@@DATEFIRST	Current value of the SET DATEFIRST parameter, which indicates the specified first day of each week: 1 for Monday, 2 for Tuesday, and so on (up to 7 for Sunday).

SQL Standard Syntax 113

Function	*Description*
@@NESTLEVEL	Nesting level of the current stored procedure execution.
@@DBTS	Current timestamp data type for the current database.
@@REMSERVER	Name of the remote database server as it appears in the login record.
@@LANGUAGE	Name of the language currently in use.
@@SPID	Server process ID of the current user process.
@@LANGID	Local language ID of the language currently in use.
@@SERVERNAME	Name of the local server running SQL Server.
@@LOCK_TIMEOUT	Current lock timeout setting, in milliseconds, for the current session.
@@SERVICENAME	Name of the registry key under which SQL Server is running.
@@MAX_CONNECTIONS	Maximum number of simultaneous user connections allowed on a Server. The number returned is not necessarily the number that is currently configured.
@@TEXTSIZE	Current value of the TEXTSIZE option of the SET statement, which specifies the maximum length, in bytes, of text or image data that a SELECT statement returns.
@@MAX_PRECISION	Level of precision used by decimal and numeric data types, as currently set in the server.
@@VERSION	Date, version, and processor type for the current installation of Microsoft SQL Server.
Cursor Functions	
@@CURSOR_ROWS	Number of qualifying rows in the last cursor opened on the connection.
@@FETCH_STATUS	Status of the last cursor FETCH statement issued against any cursor currently opened by the connection.
CURSOR_STATUS	Allows the caller of a stored procedure to determine whether or not the procedure returned a cursor and result set for a given parameter.
Date and Time Functions	
DATEADD	A new datetime value, based on adding an interval to a specified date.
DAY	Integer that represents the day part of the specified date.
DATEDIFF	Number of *datepart* "boundaries" crossed between two specified dates.

continues

TABLE 3.7 continued

Function	Description
GETDATE	Current system date and time in the Server's standard internal format for datetime values.
DATENAME	A character string that represents the specified date part.
MONTH	An integer that represents the month part of a specified date.
DATEPART	An integer that represents the date part of the specified date.
YEAR	An integer that represents the year part of a specified date.
Mathematical Functions	
ABS	Absolute, positive value of the given expression.
LOG10	Base-10 logarithm of the given float expression.
ACOS	Angle (in radians). Also called arc cosine.
PI	Constant value of `PI`.
ASIN	Angle (in radians). Also called arcsine.
POWER	Value of the given expression to the specified power.
ATAN	Angle (in radians). Also called arctangent.
RADIANS	Radians given a numeric in degrees. The result of the RADIANS function is the same data type as the given *numeric expression*.
ATN2	Angle (in radians), also called arc tangent, whose tangent is between the two given float expressions.
RAND	Random float value between zero and one; given some *seed* value of int, smallint, or tinyint data type.
CEILING	Smallest integer greater than or equal to the given numeric expression.
ROUND	Numeric expression, rounded to the specified length or precision.
COS	Trigonometric cosine of the given angle (in radians) in the given expression.
SIGN	Positive (+1), zero, or negative (−1) sign of the given expression.
COT	Trigonometric cotangent of the specified angle (in radians) in the given float expression.
SIN	Trigonometric sine of the given angle (in radians) in an approximate numeric (float) expression.

Function	*Description*
DEGREES	Given an angle in radians, returns the corresponding angle in degrees.
SQUARE	Square of the given expression.
EXP	Exponential value of the given float expression.
SQRT	Square root of the given expression.
FLOOR	Largest integer that is less than or equal to the given numeric expression.
TAN	Tangent of the input expression.
LOG	Natural logarithm of the given float expression.

Metadata Functions

Function	Description
COL_LENGTH	Defined length of a column.
FILEPROPERTY	Specified file name property value when given a file name and property name.
COL_NAME	Name of a database column when given the corresponding table identification number and column identification number.
FULLTEXTCATALOGPROPERTY	Information about full-text catalog properties.
COLUMNPROPERTY	Information about a column or procedure parameter.
FULLTEXTSERVICEPROPERTY	Full-Text Service-level properties.
DATABASEPROPERTY	Named database property value when given a database and property name.
INDEX_COL	Indexed column name.
DB_ID	Database identification number.
INDEXPROPERTY	Named index property value when given a table identification number, index name, and property name.
DB_NAME	Database name.
OBJECT_ID	Database object identification number.
FILE_ID	File identification number (file ID) for the given logical file name in the current database.
OBJECT_NAME	Database object name.
FILEGROUPPROPERTY	Specified filegroup property value when given a filegroup and property name.
OBJECTPROPERTY	Information about objects in the current database.
FILEGROUP_NAME	Filegroup name for the given filegroup identification number (ID).

continues

TABLE 3.7 continued

Function	Description
@@PROCID	Stored procedure ID of the current procedure.
FILEGROUP_ID	Filegroup identification number (ID) for the given filegroup name.
TYPEPROPERTY	Information about a data type.
FILE_NAME	Logical file name for the given file identification number (ID).
Security Functions	
IS_MEMBER	Indicates whether the current user is a member of the specified NT group or SQL Server role.
SUSER_SID	Security identification number (SID) for the user's login name.
IS_SRVROLEMEMBER	Indicates whether the current user login is a member of the specified server role.
SUSER_SNAME	Login identification name from a user's security identification number (SID).
SUSER_ID	User's login identification number. The SUSER_ID system function is included in SQL Server 7 for backward compatibility. Use SUSER_SID instead.
USER_ID	User's database identification number.
SUSER_NAME	User's login identification name. The SUSER_NAME system function is included in SQL Server 7 for backward compatibility only. Use SUSER_SNAME instead.
USER	Allows a system-supplied value for the current user's database username to be inserted into a table when no default value is specified.
String Functions	
ASCII	ASCII code value, an integer of the leftmost character of a character expression.
REPLICATE	Repeats a character expression a specified number of times.
CHAR	A string function that converts an int ASCII code to a character.
REVERSE	Reverse of a character expression.
CHARINDEX	Starting position of the specified *pattern* in an expression.
RIGHT	Part of a character string, starting *integer expression* characters from the right.

Function	*Description*
DIFFERENCE	Difference between the SOUNDEX values of two character expressions as an integer.
RTRIM	Character string after removing all trailing blanks.
LEFT	Number of characters from the left of the specified character string.
SOUNDEX	Four-character (SOUNDEX) code to evaluate the similarity of two strings.
LEN	Number of characters, rather than the number of bytes, of the given string expression, excluding trailing blanks.
SPACE	String of repeated spaces.
LOWER	Character expression after converting uppercase character data to lowercase.
STR	Character data converted from numeric data.
LTRIM	Character expression after removing leading blanks.
STUFF	Deletes *length* characters from the first *character expression* at *start* and inserts the second *character expression* into the first *character expression* at *start*.
NCHAR	Unicode character with the given integer code, as defined by the Unicode standard.
SUBSTRING	Part of a character, binary, text, or image expression.
PATINDEX	Starting position of the first occurrence of a pattern in a specified expression (or zeros if the pattern is not found) on all valid text and character data types.
UNICODE	Integer value, as defined by the Unicode standard, for the first character of the input expression.
REPLACE	Replaces all occurrences of the second given string expression in the first string expression with a third expression.
UPPER	Character expression with lowercase character data converted to uppercase.
QUOTENAME	Unicode string with the delimiters added to make the input string a valid SQL Server delimited identifier.
System Functions	
APP_NAME	Program name for the current session if the program has set one.
IDENT_SEED	Seed value (returned as numeric(@@maxprecision,0)), specified during the creation of an identity column in a table or a view that has an identity column.

continues

TABLE 3.7 continued

Function	Description
CASE	Evaluates a list of conditions and returns one of multiple possible result expressions.
ISDATE	Checks a variable or column with varchar data type for valid date format. The function returns 1 when the variable or column contains a valid date; otherwise, it returns 0.
CAST and CONVERT	Explicitly converts an expression of one data type to another. CAST is a synonym for CONVERT.
ISNULL	Checks a variable or column to see if it contains a NULL value.
COALESCE	First non-null expression among its arguments.
ISNUMERIC	1 when the input expression evaluates to a valid integer, floating-point number, money or decimal type; 0 otherwise. A return of 1 guarantees that the input string expression can be converted to one of these numeric types.
CURRENT_TIMESTAMP	Current date and time. This function is equivalent to GETDATE().
NEWID	Creates a unique value of type uniqueidentifier.
CURRENT_USER	Current user. This function is equivalent to USER_NAME().
NULLIF	Null value if the two specified expressions are equivalent.
DATALENGTH	Number of bytes used to represent any expression.
PARSENAME	Specified part of an object name. Parts of an object that can be retrieved are the object name, owner name, database name, and server name.
@@ERROR	Error number for the last Transact-SQL statement executed.
PERMISSIONS	Value containing a bitmap that indicates the statement, object, or column permissions for the current user.
FORMATMESSAGE	Constructs a message from an existing message in sysmessages. The functionality of FORMATMESSAGE resembles that of the RAISERROR statement. RAISERROR prints the message immediately, whereas FORMATMESSAGE returns the edited message for further processing.
@@ROWCOUNT	Number of rows affected by the last statement.
GETANSINULL	Default nullability for the database for this session.
SESSION_USER	Allows a system-supplied value for the current session's username to be inserted into a table when no default value is specified. Also allows the username to be used in queries, error messages, and so on.

Function	Description
HOST_ID	Workstation identification number.
STATS_DATE	Date that the statistics for the specified index were last updated.
HOST_NAME	Workstation name.
SYSTEM_USER	Allows a system-supplied value for the current system username to be inserted into a table when no default value is specified.
@@IDENTITY	Last-inserted identity value.
@@TRANCOUNT	Number of active transactions for the current user.
IDENT_INCR	Increment value (returned as numeric (@@maxprecision,0)), specified during the creation of an identity column in a table or view that has an identity column.
USER_NAME	User's database username given an identification number.

System Statistical Functions

Function	Description
@@TIMETICKS	Number of microseconds per tick.
@@PACKET_ERRORS	Number of network packet errors that occurred on SQL Server connections since the last time SQL Server started.
@@PACK_SENT	Number of output packets written to the network by SQL Server since it last started.
@@PACK_RECEIVED	Number of input packets read from the network by SQL Server since it last started.
@@CPU_BUSY	Time in milliseconds (based on the resolution of the system timer) that the CPU has spent doing work since SQL Server last started.
@@IDLE	Time in milliseconds (based on the resolution of the system timer) that SQL Server has been idle since it last started.
@@IO_BUSY	Time in milliseconds (based on the resolution of the system timer) that SQL Server has spent doing input and output operations since it last started.
@@TOTAL_ERRORS	Number of disk read/write errors encountered by SQL Server since it last started.
@@TOTAL_READ	Number of disk reads (not cache reads) by SQL Server since it last started.
@@TOTAL_WRITE	Number of disk writes by SQL Server since it last started.

continues

TABLE 3.7 continued

Function	Description
Text and Image Functions	
PATINDEX	Starting position of the first occurrence of a pattern in a specified expression (or zeros, if the pattern is not found) on all valid text and character data types.
TEXTVALID	A text, *n*text, or image function that checks whether a given text pointer is valid.
TEXTPTR	Text-pointer value in varbinary format. The text pointer is checked to ensure that it points to the first text page.

Error-Handling Methods

There are many techniques of handling errors within scripts. In many situations, SQL Server returns error codes that are specific to the type of errors that occur. (For a list of native error numbers, see the error column of the sysmessages system table in the master database in SQL Server.) These errors can be diagnosed to determine the specific type of problem, and then your script can take appropriate action. You can set up your own return codes to indicate the success or failure of your process to any calling procedure. When checking errors using @@ERROR, you simply provide the SQL Server error number and the action to take. This is usually performed in conjunction with an IF operation, as shown in the following example:

```
IF @@ERROR = 547
PRINT 'A check constraint violation occurred'
```

Errors raised in SQL Server include information that can be used as an aid for diagnosing the problem. Information provided includes a unique error number, a message string that provides the cause of the error, a severity code to indicate how serious the error is, a state code referencing the point the error occurred, the procedure name where the error occurred, and the line number within the procedure. All of the SQL Server errors are stored in the system table. In addition to the system messages, user-defined errors that are stored in sysmessages and master.dbo.sysmessages can be created. The RAISERROR statement can then be used to raise these user-defined errors, if necessary.

You can log errors in the server error log and the event log by using the LOG option. This option is required for messages with a severity level of 19 through 25, and only members of the sysadmin fixed database role can issue it. You can select the NOWAIT option to send messages immediately to the client. The SETERROR option sets @@error value to the *message id* or 50,000, regardless of the severity level. An example:

```
RAISEERROR (101, 1, 2) WITH SETERROR
```

Views

A *view* is a set of columns and rows that take on the appearance of a table. A view is maintained in a virtual fashion and does not actually store data. The rows and columns of data come from underlying tables and are produced by a query. A view is usually used to provide some standard look at a table or tables that has conditions applied to limit the rows and columns seen. A view can also be used as a method of simplifying administrations by supplying a limited look at a table, providing permissions on the view, and not requiring more granular permissions needed on the table. A view can restrict a user to specific columns or rows; join columns from multiple tables, presenting them to the user as if it was a singular table; or provide aggregate information instead of providing the details of the data. A view can also be created based on a separate view.

Designing Views

Many situations lend themselves to the implementation of a view. A view can be used to focus on specific data, providing the data that most interests the user and applies directly to their duties, and can be presented without providing any unnecessary information. A view can simplify data manipulation so the inexperienced users can easily manage the data from many tables; without the need to know anything about joins, unions, and other SQL processes. A view can customize data, providing data in different formats by using different levels of detail for separate users. A view can export data, taking data from multiple sources and allowing it to be exported to other computers for use as a single table.

Creating Views

A view can be created through the Enterprise Manager or by using the SQL statement CREATE VIEW. The description of the SQL syntax format for the CREATE VIEW operation is as follows:

```
CREATE VIEW view name [(column [, ...n])] [WITH ENCRYPTION]
    AS select statement [WITH CHECK OPTION]
```

A view cannot include ORDER BY, COMPUTE, or COMPUTE BY clauses; nor can it utilize the INTO keyword or reference a temporary table. A view can reference up to 1,024 columns.

The name of the view is stored in the sysobjects table. Information about the columns defined is added to the syscolumns table. Information about dependencies is added to the sysdepends table. In addition, the text of the CREATE VIEW statement is added to the syscomments table. The execution plan for a view is updated and recompiled each time the view is accessed.

You must have CREATE VIEW permission to use this statement. These permissions default to the members of the db_owner and db_ddladmin fixed database roles. Members of the db_owner or sysadmin database roles can transfer these permissions to other users.

Using Views

Views can be used in Transact-SQL wherever tables can be implemented. A view can be implemented that will allow the user access to a read-only copy of the data, insert new records into a table, delete from a table, change the existing data within a table, or use a view as a mechanism for generating a report.

Altering Views

A view can be altered by using the Enterprise Manager or the SQL statement ALTER VIEW, as shown in the following SQL syntax description:

```
ALTER VIEW view name [(column [, ...n])] [WITH ENCRYPTION]
    AS select statement [WITH CHECK OPTION]
```

When modifying a view, SQL Server takes an exclusive schema lock on the view.

You must have ALTER VIEW permissions on the view you are changing. These permissions default to members of the db_owner and db_ddladmin fixed database roles, and to the view owner. These permissions are not transferable.

Modifying Data

Views can be used within UPDATE, DELETE, and INSERT operations in the same manner you would use a table. The columns listed in the UPDATE or INSERT statement must belong to a single base table within the view definition. They must not include the aggregate functions: AVG, COUNT, SUM, MIN, and

MAX. They must not include a GROUP BY clause or be formulated using the UNION, DISTINCT, or TOP clauses. Additionally, to delete data in a view, only one table can be listed in the FROM clause and the table must be updateable.

Querying Data

Because a view can be essentially substituted for a table anywhere, you can easily query the contents of a view through the Enterprise Manager or by using a standard SELECT statement.

Stored Procedures

A *stored procedure* is a set of Transact-SQL statements that are compiled into a single execution plan. Stored procedures can be set up to return data or simply to perform a task. SQL Server stored procedures can return data by using output parameters, which can return either data or a cursor variables. Stored procedures can implement an integer return code. Multiple resultsets can be generated by each procedure through the implementation of select operations. A global cursor can be referenced so that data can be seen outside the stored procedure.

Stored procedures are usually used to supply the statements and logic needed to accomplish a commonly performed task. Once the stored procedure is created, it can be repeatedly called to take advantage of the functionality it supplies. Coding business logic into a single stored procedure also offers a single point of control to ensure that business rules are correctly enforced. In most instances, stored procedures improve performance. A stored procedure is a way to precompile an execution plan. In earlier versions of SQL Server, executing a stored procedure was more efficient than executing an SQL statement because SQL Server did not have to compile an execution plan; it simply used the stored plan for the procedure. SQL Server version 7 retains execution plans, even for statements that are not in a stored procedure. So, the difference in performance is not as great as in previous versions.

Using stored procedures is also an excellent technique for providing code protection. They can also shield users from needing to know the details of the tables in the database, which provides a more secure environment. If a set of stored procedures supports all of the business functions that users need to perform, users never need to access the tables directly; they can just execute the stored procedures that model the business processes with which they are familiar.

SQL Server also supports temporary stored procedures that, like temporary tables, are automatically dropped when you disconnect. Temporary stored procedures are stored in tempdb. Temporary stored procedures can be used in the case when an application builds dynamic Transact-SQL statements that are executed several times. This prevents the need to recompile these statements each time they are used, although this is not as important as in previous releases of SQL Server.

Creating the Procedure

You can create stored procedures by using the CREATE PROCEDURE statement, the Enterprise Manager, or the Create Stored Procedures Wizard. You can create a stored procedure only in the current database. With the exception of CREATE statements, any number and type of SQL statements can be included in stored procedures. The following SQL syntax description shows the options that can be provided when creating stored procedures by using CREATE PROCEDURE:

```
CREATE PROC[EDURE] procedure name[;number][{@parameter data type}
    [VARYING][= default][OUTPUT]] [,…n] [WITH {RECOMPILE ¦ ENCRYPTION
        ¦ RECOMPILE, ENCRYPTION}][FOR REPLICATION] AS sql statement
    [...n]
```

Important issues with regard to stored procedures are as follows:

- CREATE PROCEDURE statements cannot be combined with other SQL statements in a single batch.

- The CREATE PROCEDURE definition itself can include any number and type of SQL statement (except for the CREATE DEFAULT, CREATE PROCEDURE, CREATE RULE, CREATE VIEW, and CREATE TRIGGER statements, which cannot be used anywhere within a stored procedure).

- When you execute a procedure that calls another procedure, the called procedure can access all objects created by the first procedure, including temporary tables.

- If you execute a remote stored procedure that makes changes on a remote Microsoft SQL Server, those changes cannot be rolled back. Remote stored procedures do not take part in transactions.

- Private and public temporary stored procedures, similar to temporary tables, can be created with the # (local) and ## (global) prefixes added to the procedure name.

- A maximum of 255 parameters can be included in a stored procedure.

- When supplying parameters in the form *@parameter = value*, you can supply them in any order.

- You can omit a parameter for which a default has been supplied.

- Supplying one parameter in the form *@parameter = value* mandates that all subsequent parameters also be identified in this manner.

- Although you can omit parameters for which defaults are supplied, you cannot skip any parameters. If no defaults are provided, all parameters must be given.

You must have create procedure permissions to use CREATE PROCEDURE. These permissions default to the database owner. The database owner can transfer these permissions to other users.

Executing the Procedure

To call a stored procedure, use the EXECUTE statement, or the PREPARE and EXECUTE statements. Once created, a stored procedure can be repeatedly executed when needed.

Performing Calculations

There are many mathematical operations that can be performed by using an array of arithmetic functions, combined with standard mathematical operators. Mathematical functions perform mathematical operations on numeric expressions and return the results of the operation. Any of the standard data types can be used in arithmetic functions, except where specific numeric types are called for. Some of the functions work only on integers, whereas some others require other specific types.

There are some considerations and error-handling measures that must be considered when performing mathematical operations. A floating-point underflow error occurs when the float or real result of a mathematical function is too small to display. A result of 0.0 is returned and no error message is displayed. A domain error can occur when the value provided in the mathematical function is not a valid value. A range error can occur when the value specified is outside of the allowable values. Examples of these errors follow.

- Domain error:

  SQRT(-1)

- Arithmetic Overflow error:

  POWER(10.0, 400)

- Value of 0.0 (floating point underflow):

  POWER(10.0, -400)

Implementation of the SET ARITHABORT ON terminates a query and aborts a user-defined transaction. This setting overrides SET ANSI_WARNINGS, which aborts the command. SET ARITHIGNORE ON causes no warning message to be displayed, and is overridden by both SET ARITHABORT ON and SET ANSI_WARNINGS.

The assignment operator, similar to other programming languages, uses the "=", equal, set a variable to the result of an arithmetic expression. An example:

SET @MyVariable = 1

SQL Server uses a standard set of arithmetic operators to perform mathematical operations. The following list defines this set of operators:

- + (Add)
- - (Subtract)
- * (Multiply)
- / (Divide)
- % (Modulo(Remainder))

There is also a full set of unary operators, which perform an operation on only one numeric expression:

- + (Indicates Positive)
- - (Indicates Negative)
- ~ (Bitwise NOT)

> **NOTE** + and - can be used on any real number, whereas ~ can be used only on integers.

For more complex operations, you can use bitwise operators to perform bit manipulations between two integer expressions. ANDing combines bits so that 1 AND 1 will give 1. ORing combines bits so that 1 OR 0 will give 1, 0 OR 1 will give 1, and 1 OR 1 will give 1. Exclusive ORing (XOR) produces results similar to ORing (except that 1 XOR 1 will give 0).

- & (Bitwise AND)
- | (Bitwise OR)
- ^ (Bitwise Exclusive OR)

The operands for bitwise operators can be integer or binary types, except that both operands cannot be binary types.

When a complex operation is to be performed that involves many functions and operators, particular precautions must be taken to ensure that the operations are performed in appropriate order. The order of execution can drastically affect the resulting value. The following list shows the order of execution from first to last:

1. + (Positive) − (Negative) ~ (Bitwise NOT)
2. * (Multiply) / (Division) % (Modulo)
3. + (Add) (+ Concatenate) - (Subtract)
4. = > < >= <= <> != !> !< (Comparisons)
5. ^ (Exclusive OR) & (AND) | (OR)
6. NOT
7. AND
8. ALL SOME ANY BETWEEN IN LIKE OR
9. = (Assignment)

Input and Output Parameters

All procedure parameters can receive input values when the program that called the stored procedure executes the procedure. If you specify the OUTPUT keyword for a parameter in the procedure definition, the procedure can return the parameter's current value to the calling program when the procedure exits. The calling program must also use the OUTPUT keyword when executing the procedure in order to save the parameter's value in a variable that can be used in the calling program.

An example:

```
CREATE PROCEDURE MyProcedure
@MyInputParameter varchar(20),
@MyOutputParameter int OUTPUT AS
SELECT @MyOutputParameter = MyTableColumn FROM MyTable
```

Input values can also be specified for OUTPUT parameters when the procedure is executed. This allows the procedure to receive a value from the calling program, change it or perform operations with it, and then return the new value to the calling program. In the previous example, the @MyInputParameter variable can be assigned a value prior to executing the procedure. The @MyOutputParameter variable contains the parameter's value in the body of the procedure, and the value of the @MyOutputParameter variable is returned to the calling program when the procedure exits. This procedure is often referred to as a "pass-by-reference capability" because the procedure can alter the value and pass the altered value back from the procedure call.

If you specify OUTPUT for a parameter when you execute a procedure and the parameter is not defined by using OUTPUT in the stored procedure, you get an error message. You can execute a procedure with OUTPUT parameters and not specify OUTPUT when executing the procedure. An error is not returned, but you cannot use the output value in the calling program.

RAISERROR

You use a RAISERROR procedure whenever you want to identify an error situation. *Raising* an error is the process of signaling that an error has occurred. With RAISERROR, the error will be raised back to the calling process, which can then take corrective or alternate action. You can also use a RAISEERROR function to simulate user-defined errors when debugging an implementation. Raising an error sets the system flag to record that an error has occurred. The client can either retrieve an entry from the sysmessages table or build a message dynamically with user-specified severity and state information. Use the RAISERROR statement, as described in the following SQL syntax, to identify that an error has occurred:

```
RAISERROR ({message id ¦ message string}{, severity, state}[,
↪argument [,…n]])[WITH option]
```

User-defined error message are stored in the sysmessages table and should be defined with a unique error ID greater than 50,000. Ad hoc messages raise error 50,000 when no specific message id is used. The maximum value for the ID is 2,147,483,647, which gives you the freedom to define messages that are applicable to the implementation. In most companies, categories of error messages are defined in ranges and are utilized on a system-wide scale to allow for some degree of standardization and organization for the sysmessages table. The message string in an ad hoc message has as many as 8,000 characters. The format for the message string is as follows:

    % [[flag] [width] [precision] [{h ¦ l}]] type

The *flag* represents a code that determines the spacing and justification of the error message. A – (minus sign) is used to provide a left-justified message within the field width; whereas the + (plus sign) is provided for signing the output for positive/negative identification. A 0 (zero) provides zero padding to the minimum width. If 0 and – are both indicated, then the 0 is ignored. When using hexadecimal types, you can implement a # (number/pound sign), but if it is used with standard numeric types, the format is ignored. A blank space provides space padding for a signed, positive value (it is ignored if included with the plus format).

The types being used are indicated through a single character identifier for the types, as shown in Table 3.8.

TABLE 3.8

SINGLE CHARACTER TYPE IDENTIFIERS

Identifier	*Type*
d or I	Signed integer
o	Unsigned octal
p	Pointer
s	String
u	Unsigned integer
x or X	Unsigned hexadecimal

> **NOTE** Float, double, and single character types are not supported.

Any user can use severity levels from 0 through 18. Only members of the sysadmin fixed database role use severity levels 19 through 25. For severity levels 19 through 25, the WITH LOG option is required. Severity levels 20 through 25 are considered fatal. If a fatal severity level is encountered, the client connection is terminated after receiving the message, and the error is logged in the error log and the event log.

Three system stored procedures are used to interact with the sysmessages table. `sp_addmessage` adds user-defined error messages, `sp_dropmessage` deletes messages, and `sp_altermessage` changes the state of a message. The SQL syntax for these stored procedures and their available options are as follows:

```
sp_addmessage {number, severity, 'message'} [, 'language'] [, 'with
 log'] [, 'replace']

sp_dropmessage [@message number =] message number[, [@language =]
 'language']

sp_altermessage {message number} [, 'write to log'] [, 'value']
```

Recompilation

Optimization through the recompilation of stored procedures automatically occurs in SQL Server after system restart at the next procedure access, when a database is changed or if an underlying table used by the procedure changes. You can force recompilation without needing to restart the server by using the `sp_recompile` system stored procedure, as identified by the following SQL syntax description:

```
sp_recompile [@object name =] 'table'
```

Triggers

Triggers are really just a special kind of stored procedure. As the name indicates, a trigger is "fired," based on an activity performed on a table. A trigger fires when an UPDATE, INSERT, or DELETE operation is performed against the table for which it was defined. Triggers are usually used to enforce business rules or enforce referential integrity when data is modified. Triggers are not as efficient as constraints, defaults, and rules, because a trigger fires only after the statement that caused the trigger completes its operation. Therefore, a trigger should not be used where other mechanisms provide the necessary functionality. Unlike previous versions of SQL Server, which only permitted three triggers (one each of insert, update and delete operations), SQL Server 7 can include multiple triggers for each of these operations or one trigger can be used on any number of separate operations. Triggers can be nested to 32 levels; that is, a trigger can force another trigger to execute, and so on, for a maximum of 31 times.

Creating Triggers

You use the CREATE TRIGGER statement to create a trigger. Referential integrity can be defined with foreign key constraints (by using the FOREIGN KEY keywords) in the CREATE TABLE statement. If constraints exist on the trigger table, they are checked prior to trigger execution. If either primary or foreign key constraints are violated, the trigger is not executed (fired). Microsoft SQL Server allows the creation of multiple triggers for any given INSERT, UPDATE, or DELETE statement. The format of the CREATE TRIGGER operation is provided in the following SQL syntax description:

```
CREATE TRIGGER trigger name ON table [WITH ENCRYPTION]
{ {FOR {[,] [DELETE] [,] [INSERT] [,] [UPDATE] }[WITH APPEND] [NOT
➥FOR REPLICATION]
      AS sql statement [ ...n] }
  ¦ {FOR {[,] [INSERT] [,] [UPDATE]} [WITH APPEND] [NOT FOR
➥REPLICATION] AS
         { IF UPDATE (column) [{AND ¦ OR} UPDATE (column)] [ ...n]
            ¦ IF (COLUMNS_UPDATED() {bitwise operator} updated
➥bitmask)
            { comparison operator} column bitmask [...] }sql statement [
➥...n] } }
```

There are two temporary tables used in these operations. The deleted and inserted temporary tables are used when DELETE and INSERT operations are being performed. Although you can reference either table during a trigger, the deleted table will not have any records during an input trigger—only the inserted table contains data. Of course, the reverse is also true. There is no "updated" table to hold updates. The UPDATE operation is a DELETE followed by an INSERT, and it interacts with both temporary tables. The truncation of a table does not execute a delete table.

Although SQL Server provides declarative referential integrity (DRI) when you create a table, DRI does not provide cross-database referential integrity. To enforce referential integrity, use primary and foreign key constraints.

The creation of a trigger must be the first statement in the batch. The implementation of a trigger is limited to a single table, although it can reference many tables. Any option set inside a trigger remains in effect for the duration, but it then returns to its setting prior to the trigger execution. You cannot create a trigger on a view.

An example:

```
CREATE TRIGGER MyInsertTrigger
ON MyTable FOR INSERT
AS
EXEC master..xp_sendmail 'Administrator', 'My text message for mail'
```

To create a trigger, you must have CREATE TRIGGER permissions for the table. These permissions default to the owner of the table and cannot be transferred to others

Implementing Rules

Rules perform some of the same functions that a check constraint achieves. A constraint is preferred as a technique to restrict the values in a column. Constraints are also more concise than rules because only one rule can be applied to a column, but multiple constraints can be applied. Rules are provided for backward compatibility and may not be utilized in future versions of SQL Server. To create a rule, you can use the CREATE RULE statement, as identified by the following SQL syntax description:

```
CREATE RULE rule AS condition expression
```

When creating a rule, it does not apply to the data already in the database at the time of creation. After creating a rule, execute sp_bindrule to bind the rule to a column or to a user-defined data type. If the rule is not compatible with the column to which it has been bound, SQL Server returns an error message. It is necessary to drop a rule before creating a new one with the same name. A rule must be unbound by using sp_unbindrule before it is dropped.

You must have CREATE RULE permissions, which default to the members of the db_owner fixed database role. These permissions may be transferred to other users.

Cascading Updates and Deletes

You can use a trigger to enforce referential integrity through the deletion of related rows in other tables, based on a delete trigger. In a similar fashion, if an update will affect the related tables of a one-to-many relationship, you can have the update trigger perform the necessary table to the records effected.

Summarizing Data

Summarizing data on a small scale involves the use of aggregate functions, as defined earlier; and providing for additional options and groupings by using a select operation that can produce computed results, grouped together and ordered for more concise viewing, or to produce more informative results. On a larger scale, the summarization of data can be used in data warehousing by using aggregate produced from the current operational data. A data warehouse typically stores data in different levels of summarization. The summary data maintained will depend on the data requirements of the implementation.

> **NOTE** Although data warehousing is beyond the scope of this book, the capabilities of the new features implemented with SQL Server 7 lead to easier implementation of very large databases. New MOC courses and exams will be released soon to deal with the handling of data warehouses. Database implementers who rely on Microsoft products and certifications should definitely consider broadening their scope of knowledge to extend to data warehousing.

For the purpose of presenting summarization techniques, this book covers the scope of aggregate functions and other options as they relate to a SELECT statement. These features include using aggregate functions, implementing joins and unions, and using SELECT statement options.

Creating Resultsets

As previously discussed, the creation of resultsets involves the often complex formulation of SELECT statements and properly handling all of the appropriate options of a SELECT operation. The next several sections look more closely at the optional clauses used with SELECT.

TOP *n* PERCENT

The TOP clause is used to limit the number of rows returned in the result set:

- Top 50 rows in a resultset:

    TOP 50

- Top 25 percent:

    TOP 25 PERCENT

The rows can be returned in a specific order if an appropriate ORDER BY clause is used. The other technique that is sometimes used to produce a limited number of rows in a resultset is to set the ROWCOUNT by using the following syntax:

    SET ROWCOUNT *n*

By setting the ROWCOUNT, you limit the number of rows prior to ordering, which usually does not produce the desired result. The ROWCOUNT affects any future rowset until the ROWCOUNT is set to 0, which turns it off and allows all rows to be listed again.

GROUP BY

Grouping is a standard form that ensures better readability of data and provides more useful information from the data. You use the GROUP BY statement to provide for grouping functionality with or without the ALL operand, as defined by the following SQL syntax:

    GROUP BY [ALL] *group by list*

Grouping partitions the resultset into groups, based on the values in the columns of the *group by list*. If you specify that you want to include all groups produced by grouping, even if they do not meet the conditions of the select, then you must use the ALL keyword.

Any nonaggregate columns specified in a grouping must be included in the GROUP BY clause. You cannot select a column and then not include it because SQL Server would not be able to produce the output in a grouped fashion with a column that is not to be grouped. A comparison of the GROUP BY and GROUP BY ALL operations are shown in the Figure 3.8 and Figure 3.9.

HAVING

The HAVING clause is most commonly implemented with a grouping and provides the search conditions for a resultset that is similar to that of the implementation of a SELECT with WHERE (see Figure 3.10). The SQL syntax for the having operation is as follows:

```
HAVING <search conditions>
```

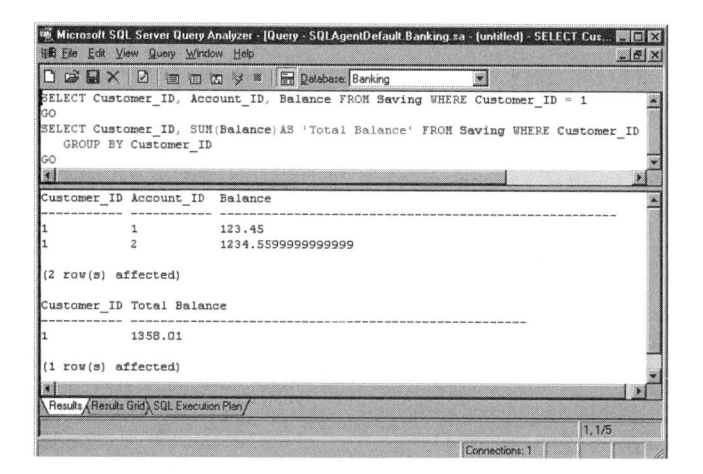

FIGURE 3.8
Group By operation.

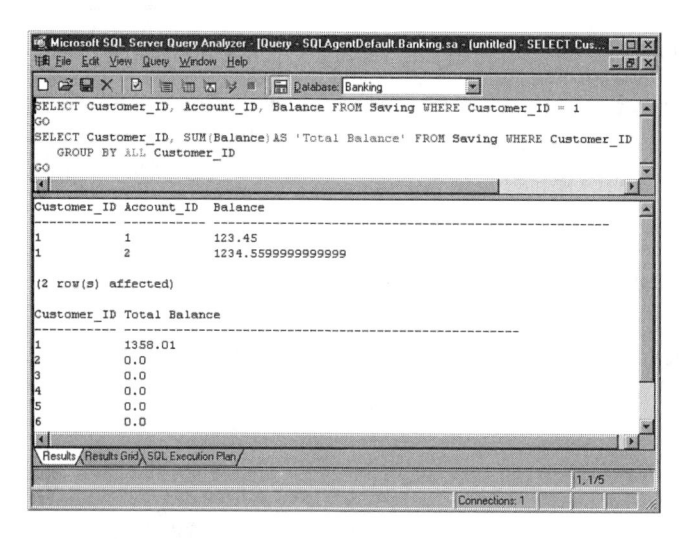

FIGURE 3.9
Group By All operation.

136 CHAPTER 3 Creating Data Services

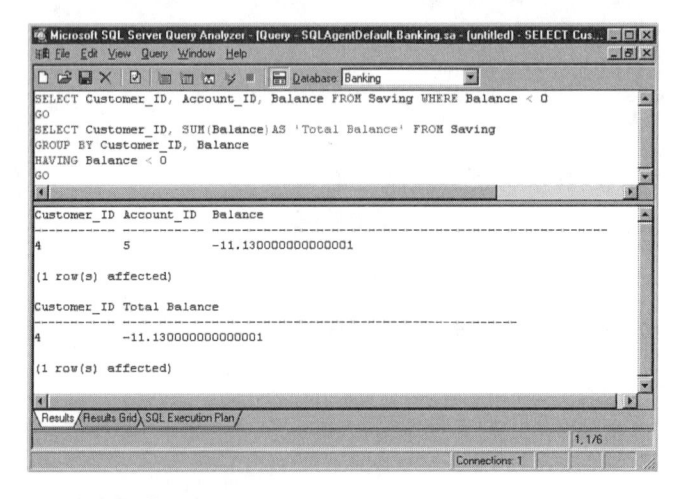

FIGURE 3.10
Total balance provided limited by HAVING.

COMPUTE BY

The computation of summary rows can be performed by using the two variations of the previous SQL syntax description, which give slightly different results. By using computations, you can see both detail and summary rows with one SELECT procedure. The summary values that are generated by a simple COMPUTE appear as separate result sets in the query results (see Figure 3.11), where the COMPUTE BY provides two resultsets for each group that qualifies for the SELECT (see Figure 3.12). The first resultset for each group has the set of detail rows that contain the select list information for that group. The second resultset for each group has one row that contains the subtotals of the aggregate functions. The SQL syntax for the COMPUTE operation is as follows:

```
COMPUTE { { AVG ¦ COUNT ¦ MAX ¦ MIN ¦ SUM } (expression) } [,…n]
➥[ BY expression [,…n]
```

CUBE

The CUBE keyword specifies that, in addition to the usual aggregate rows provided by a grouping, *super-aggregate* rows are introduced into the result set (see Figure 3.13). A super-aggregate row is a summary row that is generated by grouping on a subset of the *expressions* in the grouping.

The null values being bound to the grouping and the grouping are applied to all other operands. The null value in this case represents all the values in a particular column.

SQL Standard Syntax

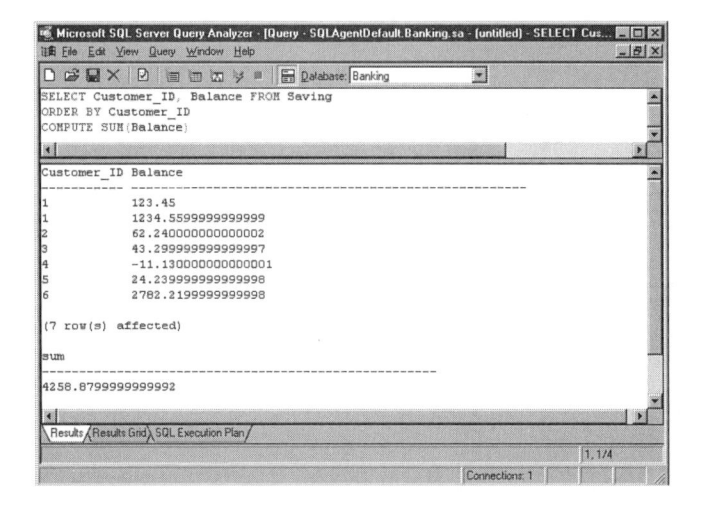

FIGURE 3.11
Total balance of all accounts using COMPUTE SUM.

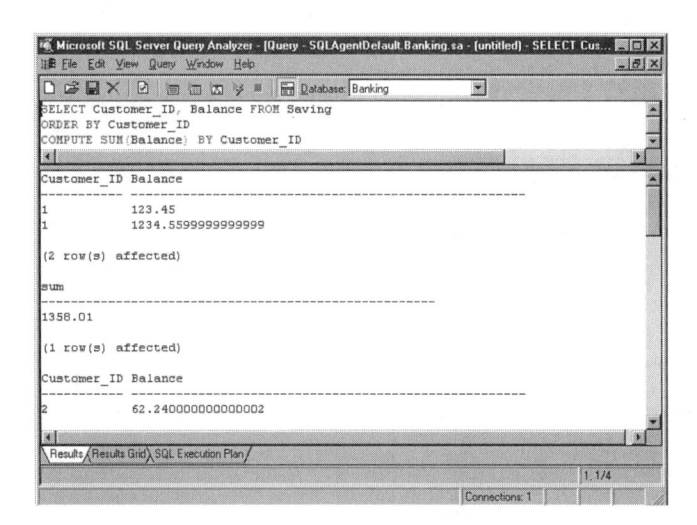

FIGURE 3.12
Total balance of each account group using COMPUTE BY SUM.

ROLLUP

The use of the ROLLUP keyword is similar to the use of CUBE, but a rollup provides information in the form of a running total for the column (see Figure 3.14).

138 CHAPTER 3 Creating Data Services

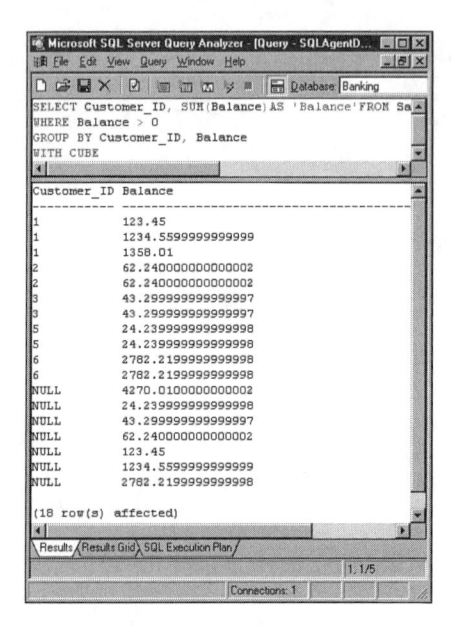

FIGURE 3.13
Total balances using CUBE.

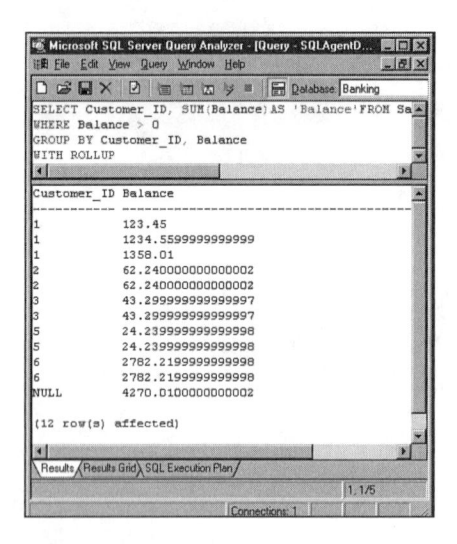

FIGURE 3.14
Running total balances using ROLLUP.

The ROLLUP operator creates groupings by moving in only one direction, from right to left, along the list of columns in the GROUP BY clause. It then applies the aggregate function to these groupings. The CUBE operator creates all combinations of groupings from the list of columns in the GROUP BY clause.

Session Level Configuration

The SET statement alters the current session. SET statements are grouped into a number of categories. (We already considered a number of these statements throughout the chapter and will be looking at more in future chapters.) A complete listing of the SET operations are provided in Table 3.9.

> **NOTE** For the purpose of the exam, knowing what each of these operations does is probably sufficient. In a production environment, however, knowing how to use the appropriate settings is an important aspect of appropriate implementation.

TABLE 3.9

SET OPERATIONS

Set Statement	Description
Date and Time Statements	
SET DATEFIRST	First day of the week to a number from 1 through 7. The U.S. English default is 7 (Sunday).
SET DATEFORMAT	Order of the date parts (month/day/year) for entering datetime or smalldatetime data.
Locking Statements	
SET DEADLOCK_PRIORITY	Controls how this session reacts to a deadlock situation.
SET LOCK_TIMEOUT	Specifies the number of milliseconds that a statement waits for a lock to be released.

continues

TABLE 3.9 continued

Set Statement	Description
Miscellaneous Statements	
SET CONCAT_NULL_YIELDS_NULL	Controls whether or not concatenation results are treated as null or empty string values.
SET LANGUAGE	Specifies the language environment. The session language determines the datetime formats and system messages.
SET CURSOR_CLOSE_ON_COMMIT	Controls whether or not a cursor is closed when a transaction is committed.
SET OFFSETS	Returns to DB-Library applications the offset of specified keywords in Transact-SQL statements.
SET DISABLE_DEF_CNST_CHK	In SQL Server version 6.x, specified interim deferred violation checking and was used for efficiency purposes. Now built into SQL Server 7.
SET PROCID	Returns the identification number of the stored procedure to DB-Library applications before sending the result sets generated by that stored procedure.
SET FIPS_FLAGGER	The checking for compliance with the FIPS 127-2 standard, which is based on the SQL-92 standard.
SET QUOTED_IDENTIFIER	Causes SQL Server to follow the SQL-92 rules regarding quotation mark delimiting identifiers and literal strings. Identifiers delimited by double quotation marks can be either Transact-SQL reserved keywords or can contain characters not normally allowed by the Transact-SQL syntax rules for identifiers.
SET IDENTITY_INSERT	Allows explicit values to be inserted into the identity column of a table.
Query Execution Statements	
SET ARITHABORT	Terminates a query when an overflow or divide-by-zero error occurs during query execution.
SET NUMERIC_ROUNDABORT	Specifies the level of error reporting that is generated when rounding in an expression causes a loss of precision.
SET ARITHIGNORE	Controls whether error messages are returned from overflow or divide-by-zero errors during a query.

SQL Standard Syntax 141

Set Statement	Description
SET PARSEONLY	Checks the syntax of each Transact-SQL statement and returns any error messages without compiling or executing the statement.
SET FMTONLY	Returns only metadata to the client.
SET QUERY_GOVERNOR_COST_LIMIT	Overrides the currently configured value for the connection.
SET NOCOUNT	Stops the message that indicates the number of rows affected by a Transact-SQL statement from being returned as part of the results.
SET ROWCOUNT	Causes SQL Server to stop processing the query after the specified number of rows is returned.
SET NOEXEC	Compiles each query, but does not execute it.
SET TEXTSIZE	Specifies the size of text and ntext data returned with a SELECT statement.

SQL-92 Settings Statements

SET ANSI_DEFAULTS	Controls a group of SQL Server settings that collectively specify SQL-92 standard behavior.
SET ANSI_NULLS	Specifies SQL-92-compliant behavior of the comparison operators EQUAL and NOT EQUAL (<>) when used with null values.
SET ANSI_NULL_DFLT_OFF	Alters the session's behavior to override the default nullability of new columns when the ANSI null default setting for the database is true.
SET ANSI_PADDING	Controls how new columns handle the storing of trailing blanks in char, varchar, binary, and varbinary data.
SET ANSI_NULL_DFLT_ON	Alters the session's behavior to override the default nullability of new columns when the ANSI null default option for the database is false.
SET ANSI_WARNINGS	Specifies SQL-92 standard behavior for several error conditions.

Statistics Statements

SET FORCEPLAN	Makes the SQL Server optimizer process join in the same order as tables appear in the FROM clause of a SELECT statement only.
SET STATISTICS IO	Causes SQL Server to display information regarding the amount of disk activity generated by Transact-SQL statements.

continues

142 CHAPTER 3 Creating Data Services

TABLE 3.9 continued

Set Statement	Description
SET SHOWPLAN_ALL	Causes SQL Server to not execute Transact-SQL statements. Instead, SQL Server returns detailed information about how the statements are executed and estimates the resource requirements for the statements.
SET STATISTICS TIME	Displays the number of milliseconds that are required to parse, compile, and execute each statement.
SET SHOWPLAN_TEXT	Causes SQL Server to not execute Transact-SQL statements. Instead, SQL Server returns detailed information about how the statements are executed.
Transactions Statements	
SET IMPLICIT_TRANSACTIONS	Sets implicit transaction mode for the connection.
SET TRANSACTION ISOLATION LEVEL	Controls the default transaction locking behavior for all SQL Server SELECT statements issued by a connection.
SET REMOTE_PROC_TRANSACTIONS	Specifies that when a local transaction is active, a Transact-SQL distributed transaction managed by the Microsoft Distributed Transaction Manager (MS DTC) starts when a remote stored procedure call is executed.
SET XACT_ABORT	Specifies whether SQL Server automatically rolls back the current transaction if a Transact-SQL statement raises a runtime error.

All statements are set to execute at run-time except for SET FIPS_FLAGGER, SET OFFSETS, SET PARSEONLY, and SET QUOTED_IDENTIFIER. These statements are all set at parse-time. If a SET statement is set in a stored procedure, the setting lasts only for the duration of the procedure.

Accessing Data

Accessing and changing data in SQL Server is accomplished by using an application or utility to send requests to SQL Server. You can use SQL Server Enterprise Manager, SQL Server Query Analyzer, or the osql utility; start working with the data in SQL Server. Applications and utilities use a database API to send commands to SQL Server and retrieve the results of those commands. The commands sent to SQL Server are Transact-SQL statements. Transact-SQL statements are built by using the SQL language defined in the Transact-SQL Reference.

Other applications, such as SQL Server Enterprise Manager, use an object model that increases efficiency. In this case, the objects use Transact-SQL. Mastering the SELECT statement is the first step in becoming fluent in Transact-SQL. Understanding the objects within a database and the server itself puts you further on your way.

> **NOTE** Additional elements used in Transact-SQL statements, as discussed throughout this chapter, are used on a day-to-day basis as database implementors. The next chapter continues to look at the underlying techniques of database implementation, but if you can work with a large percentage of the material in this chapter, you are probably ready to take the certification exam.

To complete this chapter, we look at the data sources in an Enterprise environment and some of the statements that are used to work with these sources.

Static/Dynamic Sources

Static sources represent resultsets that are returned by hard-coded SQL statements, either within stored procedures or by using an interface SQL Query tool. Dynamic data sources are used when you build and execute Transact-SQL statements on the fly within your procedure. As defined earlier in this chapter, the performance improvements in SQL Server 7 optimize static and dynamic statements, which provides greater performance.

Remote Stored Procedures

To set up a remote server to allow the use of remote stored procedures:

1. Run the following code on the first server running SQL Server:
   ```
   EXEC sp_addserver MyServer1, local
   EXEC sp_addserver MyServer2
   EXEC sp_configure 'remote access', 1
   RECONFIGURE
   GO
   ```

2. Stop and restart the first SQL Server.

3. Run the following code on the second SQL Server (make sure that you are logging in by using SQL Server authentication):

```
EXEC sp_addserver MyServer2, local
EXEC sp_addserver MyServer1
EXEC sp_configure 'remote access', 1
RECONFIGURE
GO
EXEC sp_addremotelogin MyServer1, sa, sa
EXEC sp_remoteoption MyServer1, sa, sa, trusted, true
GO
```

4. Stop and restart the second SQL Server.

5. Using the SA login, execute a stored procedure on the second SQL Server from the first SQL Server.

To execute a remote stored procedures:

```
DECLARE @MyReturnVariable int
➥EXECUTE @MyReturnVariable = MyServer2.MyTable.dbo.MyProcedure
'12345'
```

Linked Servers

A linked server configuration allows SQL Server to execute commands against OLE DB data sources on different servers. Linked servers offer the advantage of remote server access with the capability to issue distributed queries, updates, commands, and transactions on heterogeneous data sources.

A linked server definition specifies an OLE DB provider DLL (which must be on the same computer as SQL Server is installed) and an OLE DB data source. OLE DB providers exist for a wide variety of files and file formats, including text files, spreadsheet data, and the results of full-text content searches. A linked server can be used to handle distributed queries.

Similar to using remote servers, you must set up a linked server and register the connection information with SQL Server. After accommodating the linked server, you can use a logical friendly name to access the data source. You create a linked server definition by using sp_addlinkedserver. To view information about the linked servers, use sp_linkedservers. Use sp_dropserver to remove a linked server as well as a remote server. Use a fully qualified name to access the linked server.

OPENROWSET

This method is an alternative to accessing tables in a linked server and is performed as a one-time operation of connecting and accessing remote data. The function can be referenced in the FROM clause of a query as if it were a table name. You can also reference OPENROWSET as the target table of an insert, delete or update operation. The options for the uses of OPENROWSET are similar to those used in providing any database connection, as identified in the following SQL syntax description:

```
OPENROWSET('provider name' {'datasource'; 'user id'; 'password' |
➥'provider string'},
   {[catalog.][schema.]object | 'query'})
```

OPENROWSET permissions are determined by the permissions of *user id* being passed to the OLE DB provider.

An example of OPENROWSET with SELECT and the SQL Server OLE DB Provider:

```
SELECT MyCon.* FROM OPENROWSET('SQLOLEDB','MyDB';'sa';'MyPass',
  'SELECT * FROM MyTable.dbo.Customers ORDER BY LastName, FirstName')
AS MyCon
```

OPENQUERY

Executes a pass-through query on a previously linked server. The OPENQUERY function can be referenced in the FROM clause of a query as if it were a table name. You can also reference OPENQUERY as a target table of an insert, delete, or update operation. A simple operation that is performed by using a base level of SQL syntax:

```
OPENQUERY(linked server, 'query')
```

An example:

```
SELECT * FROM OPENQUERY(MyServer, 'Select LastName, Customer_ID,
➥FROM MyDB.MyTable')
```

CONTAINSTABLE

The CONTAINSTABLE clause is used within the SELECT statement to return a table of zero, or one or more rows for those columns that contain character-based data types for matches to single words and phrases. Proximity or weighted match qualifiers can be used to identify non-precise matches. CONTAINSTABLE can be referenced in the FROM clause of a SELECT statement as if it were a regular table name.

Queries using CONTAINSTABLE specify contains-type full-text queries that return a relevance ranking value for each row. The CONTAINSTABLE function uses the same search conditions as the CONTAINS predicate. The CONTAINS predicate is discussed in detail later in this book, within the topic of full-text queries. For more information on the use of CONTAINSTABLE, refer to SQL Server Books Online.

FREETEXTTABLE

The FREETEXTTABLE clause is used within the SELECT statement to return a table of zero, or one or more rows for columns similar to the fashion of the CONTAINSTABLE clause mentioned previously. Character-based data types for values that match the meaning but not the exact wording of the text in the specified *freetext_string*, FREETEXTTABLE can be referenced in the FROM clause of a SELECT statement like a regular table name.

Queries using FREETEXTTABLE also specify freetext-type full-text queries that return a relevance ranking value for each row.

PUTTING IT ALL TOGETHER

You will find a considerable number of examples of sample SQL code on the exam. It is important to become comfortable with looking at a complete stored procedure or a block of code that performs several actions. Several of the exam questions will ask you to quickly debug code to note errors, omissions, and base functionality.

This section specifically addresses some aspects of writing complete statement blocks, with the purpose of getting used to seeing structures similar to what you will find on the exam.

Example: Conditional Error Check

The first example has a routine that attempts to make deletions to a table. The deletions take place within the scope of a transaction; if errors occur, the transaction is rolled back. If no errors occur, the transaction is committed. You should note that COMMIT TRANS and ROLLBACK are included within statement blocks. It is only possible for one of these statements to be executed, based on whether or not errors are found.

```
Use Pubs
GO
DECLARE @deleteerror int
BEGIN TRAN
 DELETE authors
  WHERE au_id = '409-56-7088'
SELECT @deleteerror = @@ERROR
IF @deleteerror = 0
 BEGIN
  PRINT "The author information has been deleted"
  COMMIT TRAN -- Within block executed if no errors occur
 END
ELSE
 BEGIN
  PRINT "An error occurred during execution of the DELETE"
  ROLLBACK TRAN - Within block executed if errors were found
 END
```

Example: Referential Integrity

The next example looks at creating a trigger that will cascade the deletions of the primary record in a one-to-many relationship back through all secondary records in the related table. In creating a deletion trigger, keep in mind that when a trigger executes another operation, it can cause other actions to take place. If there were a foreign key restraint in place, this trigger would not execute properly and the restraint would cause the initial DELETE operation to fail. If the desired operation is a cascading DELETE, then you must first remove the FOREIGN KEY constraint.

```
Use Pubs
GO
CREATE TRIGGER CascadeDelete
 ON Stores
 FOR DELETE - Trigger will only fire if no FOREIGN KEY constraint or
 ↦no secondary records in Discounts table anyway
 AS
 DELETE FROM Discounts
  WHERE Store_ID IN (SELECT * FROM deleted)
```

WHAT IS IMPORTANT TO KNOW

The following bullets summarize the chapter and accentuate the key concepts to memorize for the exam:

- Dynamic and Static SQL can both be optimized of SQL Server engine through procedure cache and execution plans.

- All cursors provide different functionality with separate advantages and disadvantages. Often, the selection of the correct cursor is the primary factor for improving implementation performance.

- Cursors, variables, and stored procedures all provide options for global and local scope that determine the usability and visibility of these objects to external operations.

- INSERT adds additional records to a table and makes use of the "inserted" temporary table to hold new values until they are placed into the table. DELETE performs similar activities while implementing activity against the "deleted" temporary table. UPDATE interacts with both tables because it is really the combination of a DELETE and INSERT operation.

- There are many different styles of joins (each producing a different resultset). Subqueries can produce the same results. Unions also combine information from multiple resultsets and produce similar resultsets, providing the appearance to the user of a single set.

- Control-of-flow provides an SQL programmer with much of the same logic and structured programming elements that are available in other languages.

- Views provide a method of controlling what the user sees, how they see it, and the operations they can perform without the need for the full administration of table-level permissions.

- Stored procedures provide for the full implementations of Transact-SQL operations that are performed frequently to be saved and optimized for future use.

- Stored procedures that provide for parameter usage can be fully optimized.

- Triggers are stored procedures that will automatically execute, based on the insert, update and delete procedures. Unlike previous versions of SQL Server, you can have multiple triggers of each type and a single trigger can be applied to many types.
- You can create and fire your own error in procedures by defining error numbers above 50,000 and using the RAISEERROR method to signify that the error has occurred.
- Remote servers are those that are running SQL Server; linked servers are OLE-DB, running any compatible database environment.
- The SELECT statement, with all of its selection of clauses, will make up 50 percent of the exam. Master it from as many different perspectives as possible.

OBJECTIVES

- Create and manage files, filegroups, and transaction logs that define a database.
- Create tables that enforce data integrity and referential integrity.
  - Choose the appropriate data types.
  - Create user-defined data types.
  - Define columns as NULL or NOT NULL.
  - Define columns to generate values by using the IDENTITY property, the uniqueidentifier data type, and the NEWID function.
  - Implement constraints.
- Create and maintain indexes.
  - Choose an indexing strategy that optimizes performance.
  - Given a situation, choose the appropriate type of index to create.
  - Choose the column or columns to index.
  - Choose the appropriate index characteristics (specifically, FILLFACTOR, DROP_EXISTING, and PAD INDEX).
- Populate the database with data from an external data source. Methods include bulk copy program and Data Transformation Services (DTS).
- Implement full-text search.

CHAPTER 4

Creating a Physical Database

Maintaining the Physical Implementation

In this chapter, the second of two that deal with the use of SQL syntax, we further explore the aspects of the physical design and implementation of a database. We concentrate on those aspects that pertain more to the maintenance of the physical implementation than to those of the physical design. Data, system, and referential integrity; indexing techniques; and bulk copying of data and full-text search implementation are discussed.

File Management

The file format in SQL Server 7 is significantly different from previous versions. In previous versions, all database objects were stored in a device file that carried a .DAT extension. With the release of SQL Server 7, device management is no longer necessary. Although some forms of device files still remain, the movement away from the device file is a significant benefit to database administration. The terminology for devices is still being maintained for use with backup operations. For the actual storage of database objects, however, some management of the new file organization techniques is necessary.

Some of the modifications to the system provide for easier file management. For example, it is now possible to create all files that are needed for a database by using a single statement. The CREATE DATABASE statement initializes all files, and creates the database and logs in a single step. A database consists of two or more files, with each file being used only for a single database. This eliminates a lot of the confusion related to device management found in previous versions. A single file cannot be shared by multiple databases, so competition for device space is no longer a concern. Also, a separate file for the database and its log is mandated, again creating a much more straightforward technique for handling database management.

A big sigh of relief will no doubt be heard from any administrators and implementers concerned about expanding data and log information beyond the limits of the devices. Although it was possible to design an implementation to automatically grow these device files in previous versions, it was not an easy task and it required careful implementation or constant monitoring by an administrator. SQL Server 7 allows database files to expand automatically, eliminating the need for additional administration. Filegroups are also now supported. (Filegroups are similar to user-defined segments, for those users who are familiar with earlier versions of SQL Server). For further discussion of filegroups, see the section, "Creating Filegroups," later this chapter.

Overall, file-maintenance issues have lessened, but they are not completely eliminated. The following sections deal with the basics of file, log, and filegroup creation. Other maintenance issues are discussed in detail later in this chapter.

Creating Database Files

Database files are now created in a singular statement, along with the creation of a database. A database must contain at least two files: one to store data and the second to store the log. A third type of file can also be used to provide for multiple data or multiple log files.

The primary data file also has some header information in it, which provides SQL Server with necessary information about a database. The primary data file always carries an .MDF extension. A secondary data file can be created to hold data, allowing the data and/or log to span more than one file. The secondary file(s) is created by using an .NDF extension. The log file holds the information needed to recover a database in the event of a failure. A log file carries an .LDF extension.

> **NOTE** DISK INIT and DISK REINIT are completely removed from SQL Server 7, which may have ramifications if the scripts containing these statements are in production use.

Use the CREATE DATABASE statement to create a new database and the files used to store the database. Alternatively, this statement can be used to attach a database from the files of a previously created database. The SQL syntax description for the CREATE DATABASE statements is as follows:

```
CREATE DATABASE database name [ ON [PRIMARY] [ <file specification>
➥[,...n] ] [, <filegroup> [,...n] ] ]
    [ LOG ON { <file specification> } ] [ FOR LOAD ¦ FOR ATTACH ]
```

```
<file specification> ::= ( [ NAME = logical file name, ] FILENAME
= 'os file name' [, SIZE = size]
   [, MAXSIZE = { max size | UNLIMITED } ] [, FILEGROWTH = growth
increment] ) [,...n]
   <filegroup> ::= FILEGROUP filegroup name <file specification>
[,...n]
```

> **NOTE** The restoration process can create database files, eliminating the need for specifying the FOR LOAD option that is provided for backward-compatibility purposes only. If you use the FOR LOAD option, SQL Server sets the DBO USE ONLY option.

Important issues concerning the appropriate uses of the CREATE DATABASE statement are as follows:

- The default growth increment measure is MB, but it can also be specified with a KB or % suffix. When % is specified, the growth increment size is the specified percentage of the size of the file at the time the increment occurs. The default value if FILEGROWTH is not specified is 10% and the minimum value is 64K. The size specified is rounded to the nearest 64K.

- Similar to previous versions of SQL Server, a database is first created as a copy of the model database and its catalog. The database is then filled with empty pages. Any user-defined objects in the model database are copied to the newly created databases. You can substantially reduce administration by adding the objects that would normally be added in all your databases to the model database.

- The minimum size for a log file is 512K.

- Each database has a single owner—the owner is the user who creates the database. The database owner can be changed through sp_changedbowner.

- The master database should be backed up after a user database is created.

- When the SIZE parameter is not specified for a secondary file or log file, SQL Server makes the file 1MB.

You must have CREATE DATABASE permission, which defaults to the system administrator. Although the system administrator can grant this permission to other users, the creation of databases should be limited to as few users as possible. Loss of security and control over disk usage can result if too many users have creation privileges.

The following examples illustrate the use of the CREATE DATABASE statement with a variety of options. For further examples of its use, see SQL Server books online. Further information on the related options will be discussed in detail later in this chapter.

An example of creating a database that specifies the data and log files is as follows:

```
CREATE DATABASE Shareholders
ON
( NAME = Shares_data,
FILENAME = 'c:\mssql7\data\share.mdf',
SIZE = 20,
MAXSIZE = 50,
FILEGROWTH = 5 )
LOG ON
( NAME = 'Shares_log',
FILENAME = 'c:\mssql7\data\share.ldf',
SIZE = 10MB,
MAXSIZE = 25MB,
FILEGROWTH = 5MB )
```

An example of creating a database that specifies multiple data and log files is as follows:

```
CREATE DATABASE Branches
ON
PRIMARY ( NAME = Branch_P_data,
FILENAME = 'c:\mssql7\data\branchP.mdf',
SIZE = 20MB,
MAXSIZE = 70,
FILEGROWTH = 2),
( NAME = Branch_S_data,
FILENAME = 'c:\mssql7\data\branchS.ndf',
SIZE = 20MB,
MAXSIZE = 70,
FILEGROWTH = 2),
LOG ON
( NAME = Branch_Log1,
FILENAME = 'c:\mssql7\data\branch1.ldf',
SIZE = 10MB,
MAXSIZE = 30,
FILEGROWTH = 2),
( NAME = Branch_Log2,
FILENAME = 'c:\mssql7\data\branch2.ldf',
```

```
SIZE = 10MB,
MAXSIZE = 30,
FILEGROWTH = 2)
```

Create a simple database:

```
CREATE DATABASE Suppliers
ON
( NAME = Suppliers_data,
FILENAME = 'c:\mssql7\data\suppliers.mdf',
SIZE = 5,
MAXSIZE = 15,
FILEGROWTH = 2 )
```

Create a database without specifying files:

```
CREATE DATABASE Supplies
```

Create a database without specifying size:

```
CREATE DATABASE Personnel
ON
( NAME = personnel_data,
FILENAME = 'c:\mssql7\data\personn.mdf' )
```

Creating Filegroups

In most database scenarios, you do not implement more than one data file and one log file. Sometimes, however, you may wish to implement a filegroup. Filegroups are used to allow a group of files to be handled as a singular unit, so they make implementations that require multiple files easier to accommodate. By using a filegroup, SQL Server provides an administrative mechanism of grouping files within a database. You may want to implement filegroups to spread data across more than one logical disk partition or physical disk drive. In some cases, this provides for increased performance—as long as the hardware is sufficient to optimize reading and writing to multiple drives concurrently.

> **NOTE** Filegroups cannot be created independently of database files.

You can create a filegroup when a database is created, or you can add them in later when more files are needed or desired. Once a filegroup is assigned to a database, you cannot move files to a different filegroup.

Therefore, a file cannot be a member of more than one filegroup. SQL Server 7 provides for a lot of flexibility in the implementation of filegroups. Tables, indexes, text, ntext, and image data can be associated with a specific filegroup, allocating all pages to one specific group. Filegroups can contain only data files; log files cannot be part of a filegroup. A filegroup can be added to an existing database by using the ALTER DATABASE statement, discussed in the next section.

Managing Database Files

By default, SQL Server allows data files to increase in size as needed for data storage. Thus, a file can grow to the point where all disk space is exhausted. You can specify that a file is not to grow beyond its creation size or implement a maximum size for file growth. Use the MAXSIZE option of the CREATE DATABASE or ALTER DATABASE statements to indicate the largest size that a file can grow to.

After a database and associated files are created and the implementation is complete, it is necessary to maintain the system by periodically applying several commands. You can increase or reduce the size of a database and its files as needed. Backups have to be implemented on a regular basis and the periodic restoration of databases and files may be required. Database options and attributes need to be changed and updated, based on operations that must be performed on the database objects, files, or to the server itself. It may also be necessary to delete databases and their respective files when they are no longer required.

BACKUP and RESTORE were discussed in Chapter 3, "Creating Data Services." Remember that it is not recommended to use the older DUMP and LOAD statements, although they are supplied for backward-compatibility. In future versions of SQL Server, you may not be able to use the DUMP and LOAD statements at all. Even if they remain available, the more up-to-date BACKUP and RESTORE statements should be used because Microsoft created them for this purpose. The remaining maintenance topics, related to periodic maintenance, are discussed in the following four sections: altering a database, shrinking databases, database deletions and files, and database parameters, respectively.

Altering a Database

The process of altering a database and its files by changing file definitions or adjusting file-size settings may need to be periodically performed as part of regular maintenance activities. You use the ALTER DATABASE statement to perform these types of activities. You cannot reduce the size settings with this statement (see the section, "Shrinking a Database and Files," later in this chapter). With the ALTER DATABASE statement, you can change a database by adding a data file, log file, or filegroup; remove a file or filegroup (as long as it is empty); set READONLY or READWRITE access; or change the default filegroup. You can also use ALTER DATABASE to modify the file name for files in the tempdb database. When tempdb is modified, changes do not take effect until the server is stopped and restarted. The SQL syntax description for ALTER DATABASE is as follows:

```
ALTER DATABASE database
   { ADD FILE <file specification> [,...n] [TO FILEGROUP filegroup
➥name]
        ¦ ADD LOG FILE <file specification> [,...n] ¦ REMOVE FILE
➥logical file name
        ¦ ADD FILEGROUP filegroup name ¦ REMOVE FILEGROUP filegroup
➥name
        ¦ MODIFY FILE <file specification> ¦ MODIFY FILEGROUP
➥filegroup name filegroup property }
   <file specification> ::=
   (NAME = 'logical file name' [, FILENAME = 'os file name' ]
➥[, SIZE = size] [, MAXSIZE = { max size ¦
       UNLIMITED } ] [, FILEGROWTH = growth increment] )
```

You must have ALTER DATABASE permissions to change a database. These permissions default to the database owner, as long as the owner has CREATE DATABASE permissions. Permissions for altering a database cannot be transferred to other users. The system administrator also has permissions to alter databases.

The following examples illustrate the use of the ALTER DATABASE statement with a variety of options. For further examples of its use, see SQL Server books online.

Add a file to a database:

```
ALTER DATABASE Shareholders
ADD FILE
( NAME = 'Shares_data2',
  FILENAME = 'c:\mssql7\data\share.ndf',
  SIZE = 15MB,
  MAXSIZE = 50MB,
  FILEGROWTH = 2MB )
```

Remove a file from a database:
```
ALTER DATABASE Shareholders
REMOVE FILE Shares_data2
```

Modify a file:
```
ALTER DATABASE Shareholders
MODIFY FILE
(NAME = 'Shares_data',
SIZE = 30MB)
```

Shrinking a Database and Files

You can shrink each file within a database to remove unused pages (this applies to both data and log files). It is possible to shrink a database file manually, as a group, or individually. You use the DBCC statement with the SHRINKDATABASE or SHRINKFILE parameters (DBCC parameters are shown in the "Fast Facts Review" section later in this book). You can set the database to automatically shrink at periodic intervals by using the sp_dboption system stored procedure (discussed in the "Database Parameters" section that follows).

> **NOTE** DBCC (database consistency checker) has some 30 or more parameters. Each has a number of different options, many of which will be on the exam. The DBCC operations that relate to database implementation are discussed in full in this and the following chapter, and reviewed again in the "Fast Facts Review" chapter, later in this book.

Use DBCC SHRINKDATABASE to shrink the size of the data files in the specified database. The SQL syntax description that follows provides the basis for the options you can include in database shrinking:

```
DBCC SHRINKDATABASE (database name [, target percent] [, {NOTRUNCATE
➥| TRUNCATEONLY}])
```

Important issues about the appropriate use of the DBCC SHRINKDATABASE statement are as follows:

- The default setting is for TRUNCATEONLY, freeing all unused space to the operating system. NOTRUNCATE must be used if this is not desired and if free space is to be maintained in the database files.

- The initial size of the files in a database when it was created is also the minimum size. You must use the ALTER DATABASE statement to change the minimum file size. You can also use DBCC SHRINKFILE to select a specific file to be shrunk.

- The target percentage, which is used to leave some blank pages in the database files, has no effect if the resulting percentage is evaluated to a figure larger than the current size.

- The database can never be shrunk down to a size smaller than that of the model database.

- Log files are shrunk in a deferred operation. A log file is reset when the log is truncated.

- A database to be shrunk does not have to be placed into single user mode; other users can continue to access a database while the shrinking is taking place. This is also true of the system databases.

If you use the DBCC SHRINKDATABASE statement with no parameters except a database name, a resultset is returned that indicates the database ID, file ID, current size, minimum size, used pages, and estimated pages. You also receive similar feedback after any other DBCC SHRINKDATABASE operation.

The use of the DBCC SHRINKDATABASE statement is limited to the members of the db_owner or sysadmin database roles and cannot be transferred to other users.

The following example illustrates the use of the DBCC SHRINKDATABASE statement. For further examples of its use see SQL Server books online. To decrease size, leaving 5% free space:

```
DBCC SHRINKDATABASE (MyDatabase, 5)
```

DBCC SHRINKFILE

You can selectively choose a specific file and shrink its size. You use the DBCC SHRINKFILE statement as you use DBCC SHRINKDATABASE. The only significant difference is that it is applied against a singular file, not against the entire database. The SQL syntax description for DBCC SHRINKFILE is as follows:

```
DBCC SHRINKFILE ({file name | file id }
    {[, target size] [, {EMPTYFILE | NOTRUNCATE | TRUNCATEONLY}]})
```

Important issues regarding the appropriate uses of the DBCC SHRINKDATABASE statement are as follows:

- See the listing of issues specified under DBCC SHRINKDATABASE.

- The EMPTYFILE option can be used to move data from the specified file to other files in the same filegroup. No further use of this file is made to store data. The file can then be dropped by using ALTER DATABASE.

- Use the DBCC SHRINKFILE statement to reduce the size of a file to a size smaller than its original size. The minimum file size then reflects the newly specified size.

- To remove any data that may be in a file, execute DBCC SHRINKFILE('*file name*', EMPTYFILE) before executing ALTER DATABASE.

DBCC SHRINKFILE permissions default to members of the db_owner or sysadmin database roles. These permissions are not transferable to other users. The example that follows illustrates the shrinking of a singular file.

Shrink a file to 5 MB:

```
DBCC SHRINKFILE (MyDataFile, 5)
```

Database Parameters

When considering database-maintenance issues, you might have to sometimes adjust the settings for a database to perform updates and other operations. There are a number of statements that interact with database settings to allow work to be accommodated. Database parameters essentially fall into three categories: accessibility, configuration, and informational. A number of commands are used to access these parameters. This section discusses the three categories and the applicable statements used.

Accessibility Parameters

A number of database settings affect the accessibility of the database to users. These settings are designed to protect the integrity of the data while performing tasks against the database. At times, a database may need to be set to READONLY or be placed OFFLINE completely. At other times, the data has to be accessible in a READWRITE environment, but be limited to interactions by the database owner, system administrator, or a single user at a time. The statements used to effect these settings are CREATE DATABASE, ALTER DATABASE, and sp_dboption.

162 CHAPTER 4 Creating a Physical Database

The CREATE DATABASE and ALTER DATABASE, discussed in previous sections, can be used to set up FOR LOAD or FOR ATTACH in the database settings, and READ-ONLY or READWRITE on files and filegroups. The system stored procedure sp_dboption can be used to set a number of different options against the entire database. The stored procedure sp_dboption is to databases what sp_configure is to the server itself. Use the sp_dboption procedure (its syntax description is as follows) to set dbo use only, offline, read only, select into/bulkcopy, or single user:

```
sp_dboption ['database'] [, 'option name'] [, 'value']
```

To display the list of available database options, execute sp_dboption with no parameters. To list all of the configured options for a particular database, execute sp_helpdb.

The following list contains the options set by sp_dboption. A description of the options is given during the pertinent area of discussion in the next few sections of this chapter.

- Autoclose
- Autoshrink
- ANSI null default
- ANSI nulls
- ANSI warnings
- Concat null yields null
- Cursor close on commit
- Dbo use only
- Default to local cursor
- Merge publish
- Offline
- Published
- Quoted identifier
- Read only
- Recursive triggers
- Select into/bulkcopy

- Single user
- Subscribed
- Torn page detection
- Trunc. log on chkpt.

The only option you can set for the master database is to truncate the log on checkpoints. The database owner or system administrator can set or turn off particular database options for all new databases by applying sp_dboption against the model database.

> **NOTE** sp_dboption should not be used on either the master or tempdb databases.

Execute permissions to display the list of options only (without changing them), for the sp_dboption stored procedure default to all users. Execute permissions that allow the stored procedure to change options default to the system administrator and the database owner.

Set a database to read-only:

    EXEC sp_dboption 'pubs', 'read only', 'TRUE'

Turn off a read-only option:

    EXEC sp_dboption 'pubs', 'read only', 'FALSE'

Setting a database with the FOR LOAD option is provided for backward-compatibility. It has slightly different implications in SQL Server 7, when compared to previous versions of SQL Server. It is not necessary to set the FOR LOAD option when restoring a database because the RESTORE statement can recreate the files needed as part of the restore operation. Setting FOR LOAD turns on the DBO USE ONLY setting and marks the database as loading.

The FOR ATTACH option indicates that you are attaching a database from an existing set of files. There must be a file-specification entry that specifies the first primary file. The only other file-specification entries needed are those for any files that have a different path from when the database was first created or last attached. The database being attached must be created by using the same code page and sort order as the SQL Server. Use the system stored procedure sp_attach_db, instead of using CREATE DATABASE FOR ATTACH. Use CREATE DATABASE FOR ATTACH only when you must specify more than 16 file specifications.

The DBO USE ONLY option sets a database for use only by a member of the db_owner database role. Active users of the database can continue to access the database without disruption or notification. No new users are allowed and those existing users who disconnect or change database context are not allowed continued access to the database.

OFFLINE indicates that the database is closed, shut down cleanly, and marked offline. Use this option when a database is to be distributed on removable media. A database that is offline cannot be modified. To create a removable media database, you use the sp_create_removable and sp_certify_removeable system stored procedures. To create and check removable databases, use the sp_detach_db and sp_attach_db system stored procedures to detach the removable database from a server and reattach the database to another server.

READ ONLY indicates that users can retrieve data from the database, but cannot modify the data. Because a read-only database does not allow data modifications, automatic recovery is skipped at system startup.

> **NOTE** When specifying a new value for the READ ONLY option, no one can be using the database unless the database in use is the master database. In addition, only the system administrator can use the master if the READ ONLY option is being set.

SELECT INTO/BULK COPY allows a database to accept non-logged operations. A non-logged operation is one in which changes may be made to data without the changes being reflected in the transaction log. The statements that perform non-logged operations include UPDATETEXT, WRITETEXT, and SELECT INTO. The BULK COPY command, prompt utility (bcp), or BULK INSERT statement are also non-logged operations that perform bulk table loads. You cannot issue the BACKUP LOG statement after a non-logged process is performed—you must use BACKUP DATABASE to perform a backup.

The SINGLE USER option restricts database access to a single user. Any single user who accesses the database when single user is set to TRUE can continue to use the database, but restrictions are in place to prevent access to other users at the same time. A new user can access this database only if all other users have disconnected or switched to another database. With this option set, the truncate log on checkpoint option is not supported.

> **NOTE** If the AUTOCLOSE, AUTOSHRINK, DBO USE ONLY, READ ONLY, SINGLE USER, SELECT INTO/BULK COPY, or TORN PAGE DETECTION settings changed since the last full database backup, these settings must be reset before restoring the database.

Configuration Parameters

Maintenance tasks often involve the setup or alteration of a database configuration. Maintenance can include altering database and file sizes, changing the options related to ANSI support (handling of character and NULL defaults), indicating replication options, or other activities that relate to the way the database reacts in certain situations.

Use the CREATE DATABASE and ALTER DATABASE commands to identify files, filegroups, and their sizes. You can also use these commands to indicate the original file sizes (SIZE), maximum obtainable sizes (MAXSIZE), and the rate in which future growth will occur (FILEGROWTH). If you do not specify a maximum size, UNLIMITED becomes the default, allowing the database files to grow to the entire space available on the hard drive. Other configuration changes are performed through the sp_dboption stored procedure.

As explained earlier in this chapter, the sp_dboption stored procedure allows for the alteration of database parameters just as the sp_configure stored procedure allows for the changing of server options. We already discussed sp_dboption's use in controlling the access to the database; this section concentrates on some of the most important configuration parameters.

The files and filegroups that are used by a database often have to be increased or shrunk. They can now be performed automatically by configuring sp_dboption with the AUTOSHRINK parameter. Using this facility, sp_dboption sets the server to automatically shrink a database when an excessive amount of free pages is in the database. The actual shrinking occurs in the background and should not affect user activity. When the database is set to shrink automatically, shrinking occurs whenever a significant amount of free space is available in the database. The percentage of free space to be removed cannot be configured through sp_dboption, however. SQL Server always removes as much free space as possible. The only way to configure the amount of free space to be removed, such as only 25 percent of the current free space in the database, is to use the property page within the Enterprise Manager to shrink the database.

You can configure a database to automatically close after the last user exits. This allows for the freeing of resources, but it may affect performance if databases are frequently opened and closed during the day. Use db_option with the AUTOCLOSE parameter to make resources available after the completion of the last user access.

Several parameters relate to the handling of ANSI standard handling, NULL content, and the use of NULL content with character concatenation. The ANSI NULL CONTENT option allows the database owner to control the database default nullability. When not explicitly defined, a user-defined data type or a column definition uses the default setting for nullability. SQL Server defaults to NOT NULL. If you set this option to TRUE, you change the database default to NULL, in effect. With this setting, all user-defined data types or columns that are not explicitly defined as NOT NULL during a CREATE TABLE or ALTER TABLE statement default to allowing null values. Columns that are defined with constraints follow constraint rules, regardless of this setting. The ANSI NULL setting indicates that all comparisons to a null value evaluate to NULL. The ANSI warnings setting indicates that errors or warnings are issued when conditions such as "divide by zero" occur. The final setting, CONCAT NULL YIELDS NULL, determines the results of the combining of strings (concatenation). If you join a charter string with a character variable or field that has NULL content, the result is NULL if this option is selected.

When you work with an Enterprise environment in SQL Server, you sometimes may want to enable or disable the replication settings for a database. (Replication is discussed in full later in this book.) If you implement some form of replication, there are three possible db_option parameters that can be used. You use the MERGE PUBLISH parameter to indicate that a database can be used for merge-replication publications. In a standard replication scenario, use PUBLISHED to permit a table of a database to be published for replication; use SUBSCRIBED so that a database can be subscribed for publication.

There are a few remaining configuration options left to discuss. Other database activity may require the use of the db_option parameter to indicate how the database will handle cursor activity, recursive trigger situations (one trigger causing another trigger to fire), checkpoint operations, and interaction with the transaction log if a checkpoint occurs.

Two parameters allow you to fine-tune the handling of cursors. The CURSOR CLOSE ON COMMIT parameter, when set, indicates that any open cursor is to be closed when a transaction is committed. This is in compliance with the SQL-92 standard. The setting is off by default; a cursor remains open across transaction boundaries and only closes when the connection is closed or when the cursor is explicitly closed. The DEFAULT TO LOCAL CURSOR parameter, if set, indicates that all cursors are local to the particular batch, stored procedure, or trigger in which the cursor was created. You must use output parameters and provide for cursor variables to have a cursor be available outside the batch, stored procedure, or trigger. If a cursor is passed back in an OUTPUT parameter, the cursor is closed and all resources are freed up when the last cursor variable referencing the cursor is closed or goes out of scope.

A recursive trigger can occur if an UPDATE, INSERT, or DELETE process is performed; which in itself performs another UPDATE, INSERT, or DELETE operation. The second UPDATE, INSERT, or DELETE operation can cause the original trigger to fire again. (This can happen in the case of cascading updates and/or deletes, as defined earlier with regard to maintaining referential integrity.) The RECURSIVE TRIGGER parameter of the db_option stored procedure, when set, allows a trigger to fire recursively. If recursive trigger firing is not desired, you can turn this option off.

The last configuration parameter pertains to the action that is performed against the transaction log when a checkpoint is executed. A checkpoint flushes the cache and ensures that all committed transactions are actually written to the database. At this point, the transaction log is marked so that SQL Server has a reference point for where an accurate accounting of the saved data can be made in the log. If the log is left alone, many "dead-wood" transactions are left in the log, unnecessarily taking up space. (The only time you might want this to occur is if you are use a standby server.) To flush the dead transactions from the log, issue db_option with the trunc. log on chkpt. parameter set to true.

Informational Parameters

These final parameters provide important information about the database and its files. The stored procedure sp_helpdb provides most of this information (discussed in the following paragraphs), but one parameter of sp_dboption also provides important information. The TORN PAGE DETECTION parameter, when on, allows SQL Server to detect incomplete operations caused by power failures or other system outages that may cause data-page errors. SQL Server marks the pages of the data and checks the validity of the marker when it is read back at a later time. If a page was written incorrectly, a restore operation needs to be performed. To ensure against data loss in the event of some crashes, you can implement a UPS battery-pack or battery-backed disk caches. If you have a battery-backed disk cache implemented, you need not set torn page detection.

You can use the stored procedure sp_helpdb to report information about a database, or about all databases if no database name is supplied (see Figure 4.1). The results that display after executing sp_helpdb provide you with the name, size, owner, ID, creation date, and status information about the database. Figure 4.2 shows the report for the Pubs database.

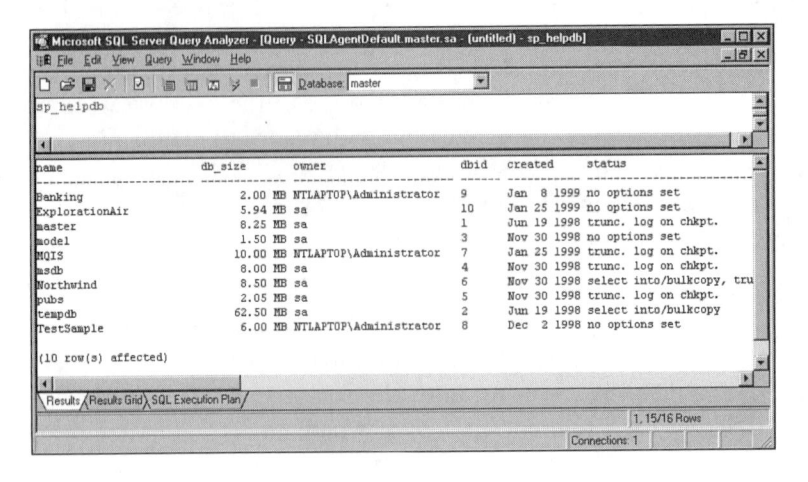

FIGURE 4.1
Use sp_helpdb to report on all databases.

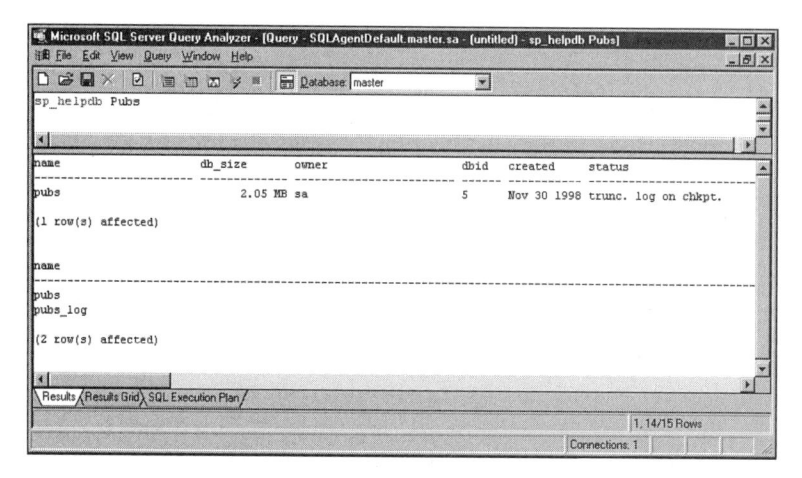

FIGURE 4.2
Use sp_helpdb to report on a single database (Pubs).

Managing Log Files

Logs are used to record the transactions that occur against a database. A log can be explicitly created; if it is not, a single log file is automatically created with a system-generated name and a size that is 25 percent of the sum of the sizes of all the data files for the database. Use the CREATE DATABASE and ALTER DATABASE statements to create or alter options for log files. Maintaining log files is much easier with the release of SQL Server 7 because the files are dynamically controlled by SQL Server. Although management tasks can be performed, regular backups and periodic restores (if needed) are usually the only required maintenance tasks.

MAINTAINING INTEGRITY

Although data and referential integrity was covered in Chapter 3, in this chapter, we revisit and complete the discussion of both of these topics—playing particular attention to the control of data prior to its entry in the physical database.

Data and Referential Integrity

Data integrity reflects the old programming acronym *GIGO* (Garbage In gives Garbage Out). If the data going into the database is incorrect, trying to obtain meaningful results in the output is all but impossible. Referential integrity, when applied correctly, ensures and protects data in related tables. It should not be possible to delete invoices if payments are still outstanding, nor should it be possible to allow a credit purchase to a customer who is not on file. Referential integrity protects against these types of problems.

The following sections discuss integrity from the perspective of the data itself. Selecting the correct storage framework for the data, as well as the integration between data elements, is discussed in an attempt to gain better control over the accuracy of data in a database.

Data Type Selection

Selecting the appropriate type of data is the first step for setting up the validity of the data to be entered into a database. Each data type has size limitations (see Table 3.4 in Chapter 3). System data types and user-defined data types (discussed in the next section) can be used to enforce data integrity. Data that is entered or changed must conform to the data type that was specified in the initial definition of a table. Try not to blend too many data types into a character format. Although it is true that a character data type supports almost all input, accuracy can be lost in the conversion process between data types when you perform calculations.

Be careful when you choose the appropriate data type to hold dates and times. A *datetime* data type helps enforce data integrity because it accepts only a valid date between January 1, 1753, and December 31, 9999, as input. (Can we see a Y10K problem here?). The date and time can be accurate to $1/300^{th}$ of a second, or 3.33 milliseconds. SQL Server rejects all values that it cannot recognize as dates between 1753 and 9999. A *smalldatetime* data type accepts the input of dates from January 1, 1900, through June 6, 2079, with accuracy to the minute.

> **NOTE** A *timestamp* data type is not used to store dates, *per se*. You can have only one column per table as a timestamp type; if present, it holds values that represent the date and time that the record was added or last updated.

Other integrity-related considerations when selecting data types are related to selecting the appropriate size for a character field and the correct numeric type to hold numbers. When you select character fields, sizing a field or using a varchar can have performance implications. If you select a numeric field with too low a limit, it can result in incorrect calculations.

Some considerations for the selecting character-related data types are as follow:

- Use char when the data entries in a column are non-Unicode (one byte per character) and are expected to be consistently close to the same size.

- Use varchar when the data entries in a column are non-Unicode (one byte per character), but are expected to vary considerably in size.

- Use nchar and nvarchar for the same reasons on Unicode (two bytes per character) data.

Some considerations for selecting a numeric-related data type are as follows:

- A return code from a stored procedure must always be an integer type.

- The precision—the number of digits a number can contain—varies between types. (See Table 4.1.)

- Precision can be altered for a "decimal" or "numeric" data type. The defined setting also affects the scale of a number (precision: number of digits; scale: number of digits to the right of the decimal).

TABLE 4.1

VARIABLE TYPES AND THEIR RESPECTIVE PRECISION

Type	Precision
tinyint	3
smallint	5
int	10
smallmoney	10

continues

TABLE 4.1 continued

Type	Precision
money	19
real	38
float	308

User-Defined Data Types

User-defined data types are always defined in terms of a base system data type. They provide a way to apply a name to a data structure that will use a data type in a consistent manner. The name provided is more descriptive of the types of values to be held. This can make it easier for a programmer or database administrator to understand the intended use of anything defined with the named data type. User-defined data types can be used when tables must store the same type of data in a column; you must ensure that the data matches the same type, length, and nullability.

To create a user-defined data type, you must supply three parameters: the name that the data type will be known as, the system data type upon which the new data type is based, and the data type's *nullability* (whether it allows null values or not). If you do not define the nullability, it will be assigned, based on the ANSI null default setting.

> **NOTE** You can define a user-defined data type in the model database. If done, every newly created database will also have that type definition.

To create a user-defined data type, use the sp_addtype stored procedure and supply the necessary parameters. The SQL syntax description is as follows:

    sp_addtype {type}, [, system data type] [, 'null type']

The sp_addtype stored procedure adds a reference to the systypes system table for the user-defined data type. In the following example, a user-defined data type is created for Social Security numbers, not allowing NULL content.

    sp_addtype ssn, 'VARCHAR(11)', 'NOT NULL'

NULL and NOT NULL

A value of NULL indicates the value is not known; this is different from a space, empty, blank, or zero value. NULL is also different from a zero-length string (represented by side-by-side quotes). NULL is never equal to NULL in a comparison; you must use an IS NULL or IS NOT NULL (SQL-92 syntax) in a comparison operation when determining NULL data content. A NULL value shows up as (NULL) in any resultset that contains NULL data. If you wish to place NULL data into a field or variable, you may do so by using the NULL keyword. Transact-SQL also offers an extension for NULL processing. If the option ANSI_NULLS is set to off, comparisons between NULLs, such as NULL = NULL, evaluate to TRUE. Comparisons between NULL and any data value evaluate to FALSE. Columns can either accept or reject NULL values. If a column definition contains the NOT NULL clause, you cannot insert rows that have a NULL value.

Generated Values

Many columns can be defined in tables, so that SQL Server generates the values for the columns. In some cases, you may want records to be incrementally numbered (an IDENTITY column), counting records by one or some other increment. You may require a column to be identified as holding a GUID (globally unique identifier); this identifier is needed in some forms of replication and also has other purposes. You may wish to create a column whose value is determined through a computed column expression. The next few sections take a look at IDENTITY columns, columns defined as the uniqueidentifier data type, and computed columns (as well as the way the three columns are used in a database implementation). Default values can also be specified as column values; when implemented, they are used if no input value is received when a row is created.

IDENTITY

An IDENTITY column is used in a field to provide an automatically incrementing value. IDENTITY columns are often used for a table's PRIMARY KEY, so each record in a table has a unique identifying number. An IDENTITY is automatically generated as new records are added. No value is inputted for an IDENTITY column; a starting value referred to as the *seed* and an increment for each additional record is provided with the field definition instead. The only real drawback of this type of usage is that it leaves gaps in the numerical sequence in a table where deletions can occur. An existing gap can be filled in the IDENTITY column by using the SET IDENTITY_INSERT ON statement prior to entering a record that has the value to fill the gap.

A DBCC parameter, CHECKIDENT, is available to check the current IDENTITY value and compare it with the maximum value in the IDENTITY column. If necessary, DBCC CHECKIDENT corrects the current IDENTITY value for a column. The current IDENTITY value is not corrected, however, if the IDENTITY column was created with the NOT FOR REPLICATION clause. To have DBCC implement corrections, you must not use the NORESEED option. Doing this reports on the value of the IDENTITY and what it should be, but does not make any alterations.

An IDENTITY column can be easily identified, as shown for the Account_ID in Figure 4.3.

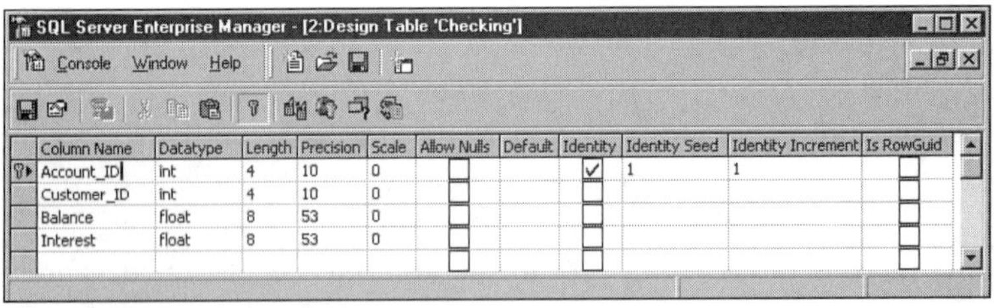

FIGURE 4.3
Account_ID is shown as the PRIMARY KEY. It's set up as an IDENTITY column.

You can indicate an IDENTITY column as you create a table by using the SQL CREATE TABLE statement. When performed in this manner, SQL Server uses the NOT FOR REPLICATION option of CREATE TABLE. This option is set to negate the automatic incrementing of an IDENTITY column, and it allows inserts to be performed through the replication process, without altering the IDENTITY value of the inserted rows. The SQL syntax description for the CREATE TABLE statement is as follows:

```
CREATE TABLE table name ( { <column definition>¦ column name AS
↪computed column expression
            ¦ <table constraint> } [, ...n] )
[ON {filegroup ¦ DEFAULT} ] [TEXTIMAGE_ON {filegroup ¦ DEFAULT} ]
<column definition> ::= { column name - data type }
[ NULL ¦ NOT NULL ] [ IDENTITY [(seed, increment ) [NOT FOR
↪REPLICATION] ] ] [ ROWGUIDCOL ]
[ <column constraint> ::=
```

```
[CONSTRAINT constraint name]
{ { PRIMARY KEY ¦ UNIQUE } [CLUSTERED ¦ NONCLUSTERED]
   [WITH [FILLFACTOR = fillfactor] ] [ON {filegroup ¦ DEFAULT} ] ¦
➥[FOREIGN KEY]
   REFERENCES reference table [ ( reference column ) ] [NOT FOR
➥REPLICATION]
       ¦ DEFAULT constant expression   ¦ CHECK [NOT FOR REPLICATION]
➥(logical expression) } ] [ ...n]
<table constraint> ::= [CONSTRAINT constraint name]
{ [ { PRIMARY KEY ¦ UNIQUE } [ CLUSTERED ¦ NONCLUSTERED] {
➥( column[,...n] ) }
   [ WITH [FILLFACTOR = fillfactor] ] [ON {filegroup ¦ DEFAULT} ] ]
   ¦ FOREIGN KEY [(column[,...n])] REFERENCES reference table
➥[(reference column[,...n])]
   [NOT FOR REPLICATION] ¦ CHECK [NOT FOR REPLICATION] (search
➥conditions) }
```

The IDENTITY property of a column can be assigned as a tinyint, smallint, int, decimal(p,0), or numeric(p,0) data type. Only one IDENTITY column can be created per table. You must specify both the seed (starting value) and an increment, or neither. If you specify neither, the default is (1,1).

> **NOTE** By the numbers, SQL Server can have as many as two billion tables per database and 1,024 columns per table. The number of rows and total size of the table are limited only by the available storage. The maximum number of bytes per row is 8,092. If you create tables with varchar, nvarchar, or varbinary columns whose total defined width exceeds 8,092 bytes, the table is created, but a warning message appears. If you try to insert more than 8,092 bytes into such a row, or update a row so that its total row size exceeds 8,092 bytes, you see an error message and the statement fails. Each table can contain up to 249 NONCLUSTERED indexes and one CLUSTERED index.

The following example provides the CREATE TABLE statement, which includes the definition of a PRIMARY KEY, an IDENTITY column, and a second column with a NOT NULL constraint, providing a complete table definition:

```
CREATE TABLE MyTable
(MyTable_Id smallint IDENTITY (1,1) PRIMARY KEY CLUSTERED,
MyColumn2 varchar (25) NOT NULL DEFAULT 'Column content yet to be
➥inputted')
```

Further information about the appropriate use of the CREATE TABLE statement is provided throughout this chapter. The previous example was provided to show only the use of a basic table creation with an IDENTITY column set for the PRIMARY KEY.

Unique Identifiers

A globally unique identifier (GUID) represents a 16-byte binary value. A GUID is a binary number that is guaranteed to be unique. The main use for a GUID is when you assign an identifier that must be unique in a network that has many computers at many sites. The uniqueidentifier data type does not automatically generate new GUIDs, so set a DEFAULT to NEWID() if this type of functionality is desired. The value for a GUID column can be inserted by using the NEWID function (discussed in the next section of this chapter); by calling an API function or method that returns a GUID; or by converting from a string constant in the form xxxxxxxx-xxxx-xxxx-xxxx-xxxxxxxxxxxx, where each "x" is a hexadecimal digit. A GUID is also used by the operating system to refer to classes. Classes use a GUID to indicate the uniqueness of an object. To see an example of a class GUID (see Figure 4.4), you can look in the Registry under HKEY_CLASSES_ROOT under the CLSID key.

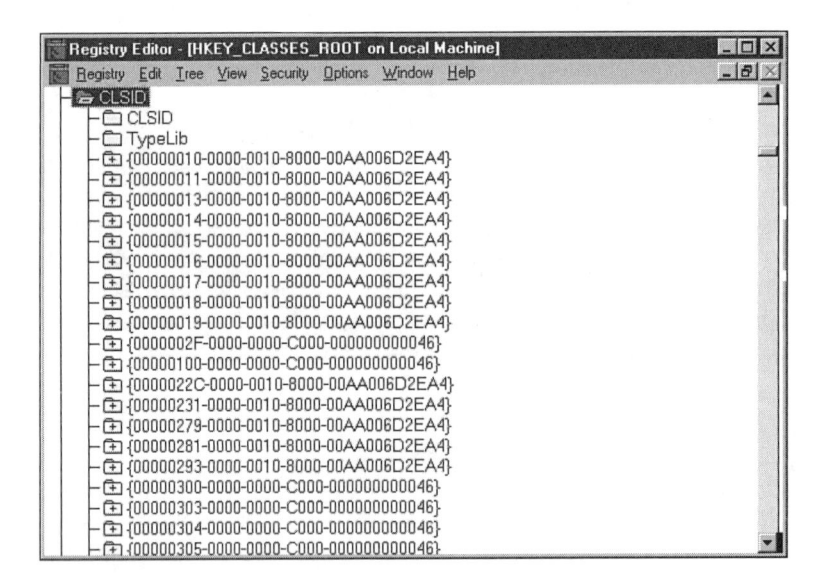

FIGURE 4.4
Registry classes using globally unique identifiers.

A uniqueidentifier is not typically defined as a constant because it is very difficult to ensure that the uniqueidentifier created is actually unique. You can, however, create a uniqueidentifier constant in a character string format ('6F9619FF-8B86-D011-B42D-00C04FC964FF') or in a binary format

(0xff19966f868b11d0b42d00c04fc964ff). In a table, a GUID can be used as a mechanism to uniquely define each row of the table through the use of ROWGUIDCOL.

Although it is possible for a table to have multiple uniqueidentifier columns, only one uniqueidentifier column may be specified with the ROWGUIDCOL property. This row property does not do anything to enforce uniqueness—the uniqueness must be enforced through the use of a PRIMARY KEY or similar mechanism. The ROWGUIDCOL in SQL Server is most commonly used in the replication process. The main advantage of the uniqueidentifier data type is that the values that are generated by using the NEWID function or the API GUID functions are guaranteed to be unique. The ROWGUIDCOL is a keyword, indicating that the new column is globally unique and can only be defined to a uniqueidentifier data type.

The uniqueidentifier data type does have several disadvantages that need to be considered before you use it in any implementation. First, the values are long, cryptic, and hard for users to key correctly (they are almost impossible to remember because of their complexity). Next, the values are randomly generated with no mechanism for establishing a pattern that has more meaning. There is no way to sequence a uniqueidentifier. At 16 bytes per value, a uniqueidentifier data type is very large when compared to other data types. This negatively affects the performance of indexes built by using uniqueidentifiers. You should consider using the IDENTITY property when global uniqueness is not necessary or when an incremental value is desired.

When using a GUID in coding comparison operations, consider that associating the bit patterns of the two values does not perform the comparison. The only operations allowed are the equality comparison operators (= and <>), and the IS NULL and IS NOT NULL operators. All column constraints and properties, except IDENTITY, are allowed on the uniqueidentifier data type.

The following code segment uses the uniqueidentifier data type in a column with a DEFAULT using NEWID() to fill the content of each new record with a GUID in the column:

```
CREATE TABLE Globally_Unique_Data
(MyGUID uniqueidentifier
CONSTRAINT GUID_Default
DEFAULT NEWID(),
Employee_Name varchar(60),
CONSTRAINT GUID_PK PRIMARY KEY (MyGUID))
```

NEWID

The NEWID function is a Transact-SQL statement that operates like the application API functions that generate GUIDs. New uniqueidentifier values are derived from the identification number of the network card plus a unique number derived from the CPU clock. Each network card already has a unique identification number assigned to it. Network card manufacturers guarantee that no other network card in the next 100 years will have the same number. The uniqueidentifier returned by NEWID() is generated by using the network card on the server, which differs somewhat from the API functions that are generated by using a GUID that uses the network card on the client machine.

Computed Column Expressions

It is possible to create a column within a table whose value is derived by using an expression. A computed column is not stored in the table as traditional column data. A computed column is computed from an expression that uses other column values in the same table. The defined expression can contain any non-computed column name, constant, function, and/or variable in any combination. The expression cannot be a subquery. A computed column cannot be used as a key column in an index or as part of any PRIMARY KEY, UNIQUE, FOREIGN KEY, or DEFAULT definition. Also, a computed column cannot be the target of an INSERT or UPDATE statement.

In the following example, an expression is used to compute the AvgBalance column as the average of the balances for each day of the week:

```
CREATE TABLE MyTable
( MonBalance float, TueBalance float, WedBalance float, ThuBalance
➥float, FriBalance float,
  AvgBalance AS (MonBalance + TueBalance + WedBalance + ThuBalance +
➥FriBalance) / 5 )
```

Using Default Values

The DEFAULT keyword specifies a value to be provided when a value is not explicitly supplied during an insert operation. You cannot supply a default value for timestamp or IDENTITY columns, but all other columns are permitted. The only values permitted with the use of DEFAULT are a literal value (such as a character string), a system function (such as NEWID), a NULL value, or a mathematical expression.

A DEFAULT can be created in conjunction with a table creation by using CREATE TABLE, or you can create a default object by using CREATE DEFAULT and use the sp_bindefault stored procedure that is provided for backward-compatibility purposes. The SQL syntax description for sp_bindefault is as follows:

```
sp_bindefault [@default name =] 'default', [@object name =] 'object
➥name' [, [@futureonly =] 'futureonly flag']
```

The FUTUREONLY parameter is issued if you want to keep the existing columns of a user-defined data type from inheriting the new default. It is not used when binding a default to a column. If the FUTUREONLY flag has a NULL value, the new default is bound to any columns of the user-defined data type that currently have no default or that are using the existing default of the user data type. You must first use the CREATE DEFAULT statement to create the default. You can then execute sp_bindefault to bind to a column or user-defined data type. An existing column of the user-defined data type inherits the new default. Any newly added columns of the user-defined data type always inherit the default once it is bound.

> **NOTE** A DEFAULT must be compatible with the data type of the column. If the default is not compatible with the column to which you have bound it, SQL Server returns an error message when it tries to insert the default value (not when you bind it).

You cannot bind a default to a column that already has a DEFAULT definition. When you bind a default to a column, information is added to the syscolumns system table. When you bind a default to a user-defined data type, information is added to the systypes table.

Constraint Implementation

A constraint is actually any number of separate types of parameters that enforce data and referential integrity within a table or individual column. A constraint is implemented as a PRIMARY KEY, UNIQUE, FOREIGN KEY, or CHECK. (PRIMARY and FOREIGN KEY constraints are discussed in the Indexes section, later in this chapter.) Previous topics concerned the concepts of UNIQUE and CHECK constraints; we complete the discussion of these items in the next sections, which deal with each type of constraint and usage considerations.

Constraints offer a way to automatically enforce the integrity of a database. Constraints allow for the definition of rules regarding the values allowed in columns, and are considered to be the standard techniques for enforcing integrity. Constraints are preferred over triggers, rules, and defaults; they are also used by the query optimizer to improve performance in selectivity estimation, cost calculations, and query rewriting.

There are five separate classifications of constraints. The NOT NULL constraint specifies that the column does not accept NULL values. The CHECK constraint enforces limits on values that can be placed in a column. The UNIQUE constraint enforces the uniqueness of the values in a set of columns. A PRIMARY KEY constraint identifies the column or set of columns whose values uniquely identify a row in a table. A FOREIGN KEY constraint identifies the relationships between tables. Each constraint is discussed in its own section in the following paragraphs within this topic (and is discussed further in the following topic that deals with index maintenance).

Constraints can be classified as column constraints or table constraints. A *column constraint* is specified as part of a column definition and applies only to that column. A *table constraint* is declared independently from a column definition and can apply to more than one column in a table. A table constraint must be used when more than one column is to be included in a constraint.

NOT NULL Constraints

A NOT NULL constraint indicates that a column must have a non-NULL value entered to it with any given insert operation. A column is never permitted to have a value that evaluates to NULL or "unknown."

FOREIGN KEY Constraints

A FOREIGN KEY constraint defines a relationship between two tables. A foreign key in one table points to a PRIMARY KEY in another table. You cannot insert a new row into a table where a foreign key constraint has been defined, if there is no matching PRIMARY KEY with that value in the related table. You cannot delete a row from a referenced table whose PRIMARY KEY has a value that matches the foreign key in the table where the constraint is defined. This allows the database implementation to maintain referential integrity between the two related tables. FOREIGN KEYs will be discussed further in the section, "Index Maintenance."

PRIMARY KEY Constraints

No two rows in a table can have the same PRIMARY KEY value. This is necessary to maintain referential integrity and to allow for faster searching through table contents. A PRIMARY KEY is not permitted to have a NULL value, whether it is in the entire column or in one of the columns that make up a composite key. Each table should have a PRIMARY KEY, although SQL Server makes no such mandate. PRIMARY KEYs are discussed further in the section, "Index Maintenance."

UNIQUE Constraints

A UNIQUE constraint establishes a one-of-a-kind value within a table. No two rows in the table are allowed to have the same non-null values for the columns in a UNIQUE constraint. PRIMARY KEYs also enforce uniqueness, but PRIMARY KEYs do not allow null values. A UNIQUE constraint is preferred over a unique index, unless the index is really used to search capabilities in related applications. You should always avoid unnecessary index creation to produce efficient table updates. A column does not have to be the PRIMARY KEY for you to use a UNIQUE constraint, even though multiple columns in this respect would not abide to complete normalization rules. UNIQUE constraints can be referenced by a FOREIGN KEY constraint. When a UNIQUE constraint is created, SQL Server creates a unique index.

CHECK Constraints

A CHECK constraint limits the possible values that can be entered into columns. A CHECK constraint specifies a Boolean search condition that evaluates to TRUE or FALSE. Any value entered for the column that does not evaluate to TRUE is rejected. Multiple CHECK constraints can be defined for each column.

Index Maintenance

Indexes are used in a number of different instances within a table design. With a primary implementation of indexing, you also include indexes whenever a column might be used as a target for a search condition (such as a ZIP code, a person's name, and possibly a phone number). By placing an index on such a column, you increase the speed in which a search can be completed.

The secondary purpose for an index is to place data into a specified order for the purposes of producing a report. A consideration between when to use an index and when to use the ORDER BY operation often depends on the size of the recordset, the volatility of a table, and whether or not an index is also used in searching. Remember that an index requires constant updating whenever inserts are made, even if the index is not currently being used. The more indexes placed on a table, the slower the insert operations are performed (not to mention that the space used by the databases increases significantly with any indexes added). For these reasons, the use of indexes should be scrutinized carefully and kept to a minimum.

The following sections provide a comparison of CLUSTERED and NONCLUSTERED indexes, their impact on the system, considerations for PRIMARY KEY creations and FOREIGN KEY allocations, and a look at how UNIQUE constraints interact for the creation of UNIQUE indexes. Creation, maintenance, removal, selection criteria, and architecture are all explored within this far-reaching topic.

Creating Indexes

As shown earlier, indexes are created automatically with PRIMARY and UNIQUE constraints. If you need to create an index that is independent of a constraint, you can use the CREATE INDEX statement, which creates an index on a given table. This statement can be used to either change the physical ordering of a table or provide a logical ordering of table data to increase query efficiency. Only the table owner can create indexes on that table. The SQL syntax for the CREATE INDEX statement is as follows:

```
CREATE [UNIQUE] [CLUSTERED | NONCLUSTERED] INDEX index name ON table
➥(column [, ...n])
    [WITH [PAD_INDEX] [[,] FILLFACTOR = fillfactor] [[,]
➥IGNORE_DUP_KEY] [[,] DROP_EXISTING]
    [[,] STATISTICS_NORECOMPUTE] ] [ON filegroup]
```

If you use the STATISTICS_NORECOMPUTE option to specify that out-of-date index statistics are not automatically recomputed, you can restore the automatic statistics updating by executing UDPATE STATISTICS without the NORECOMPUTE option. Disabling the automatic recomputation of distribution statistics may prevent the SQL Server optimizer from picking optimal execution plans for queries involving the table.

When you create indexes by using the CREATE INDEX statement, the space is allocated to tables and indexes in increments of one extent at a time.

A single extent is eight pages and each page is 8K. Each time an extent is filled, another is allocated. Indexes that are on very small or empty tables use single-page allocations until eight pages are added to the index, and they then switch to extent allocations. For a report on the amount of space that is allocated and used by an index, use the sp_spaceused stored procedure.

> **NOTE** The maximum allowable index size is 900 bytes. This does not permit the use of large char, varchar, binary, and varbinary columns that are greater than 900 bytes; or nchar or nvarchar columns greater than 450 characters (remember that Unicode data is two bytes per character).

When the CREATE INDEX statement is performed within the context of an explicit transaction, allocation locks are taken by SQL Server and held until the transaction is committed. Large index creations may consume enormous amounts of memory simply to obtain these locks. Index creation can fail if lock space is exhausted. It is possible to create an index on a temporary table. To display a report on an object's indexes, execute the sp_helpindex stored procedure.

> **NOTE** Using the CREATE INDEX statement during a database or transaction log backup causes the BACKUP statement to abort—thus, the backup operation fails.

Indexing Strategies

There are two basic strategies for index creation, which parallel the SQL Server index architecture. Indexes are created as either CLUSTERED or NON-CLUSTERED and both CLUSTERED and NONCLUSTERED indexes can be created as a natural or unique index. Because a CLUSTERED index causes the data to be physically re-sorted into the index sequence, only one CLUSTERED index can exist on a table. (It is best to think of a CLUSTERED index as a clustering of the data.) A NONCLUSTERED index provides a series of pointers to the physical data and works in the same manner as the index at the back of a book (the pointers are collected into the sequence of the index, without physically changing the order of the data).

PRIMARY KEY is a constraint that enforces entity integrity for a given column or columns through a unique index. Only one PRIMARY KEY constraint can be created per table. A PRIMARY KEY is usually defined as a CLUSTERED index. In fact, this is the default situation within SQL Server, in which the default for a UNIQUE index created by a constraint defaults to a NONCLUSTERED index.

During the creation process of a CLUSTERED index, a significant amount of space is used. In fact, SQL Server requires approximately 1.2 times the size of the data to create a CLUSTERED index because all of the data is duplicated, with the old data deleted after the index creation is complete.

To select an appropriate indexing strategy that is both efficient and improves the performance of a database application, you want to increase the speed of your queries and resulting searches. To do this, you need to understand how the SQL Server index architecture handles a variety of maintenance issues, which is no singular, easy task. In the upcoming sections, the various issues—with their related statements and parameters—are discussed in an attempt to develop this understanding.

In the next two sections, CLUSTERED and NONCLUSTERED indexes are compared and contrasted to allow for the further development of index architecture.

CLUSTERED Indexes

A CLUSTERED index is organized so that the order of the index is the same as the order of the data. In a partial sense, the storage of the data is the storage of the index. CLUSTERED indexes are automatically created with PRIMARY KEY constraints, so if your table already has a PRIMARY KEY constraint, you cannot create additional CLUSTERED indexes. If your desire is to have a CLUSTERED index that is not the PRIMARY KEY, you must explicitly create the PRIMARY KEY as NONCLUSTERED and the desired alternate key as CLUSTERED.

SQL Server stores information about CLUSTERED indexes in the sysindexes system table. Occasionally, this table can contain incorrect information. The DBCC UPDATEUSAGE statement reports and corrects inaccuracies in the sysindexes table that may result in incorrect space usage reports by the sp_spaceused system stored procedure. The sysindexes table, which is stored in each database, contains one row for each index and table in the database. The sysindexes table contains information about the table in which the index belongs, and information that defines the index itself.

The information stored in sysindexes is shown in Table 4.2.

TABLE 4.2

CONTENT OF SYSINDEXES SYSTEM TABLE

Column Name	Data Type	Description
id	int	ID of table
status	int	Internal system-status
first	binary(6)	Pointer to the first or root page
indid	smallint	Identifier for CLUSTERED or NONCLUSTERED
root	binary(6)	Pointer to the root page or last page
minlen	smallint	Minimum size of a row
keycnt	smallint	Number of keys
groupid	smallint	Filegroup ID on which the object was created
dpages	int	Count of index or data pages used
reserved	int	Pages allocated for all indexes and table data, for text or image data, and for the index
used	int	Pages used for all index and table data, for text or image data, and for the index.
rowcnt	binary(8)	Data-level rowcount or 0
rowmodctr	int	Total of inserts, deletes, or updates since last statistics update
soid	tinyint	Sort order ID that the index was created with, or 0
csid	tinyint	Character set ID that index was created with, or 0
xmaxlen	smallint	Maximum size of a row
maxirow	smallint	Maximum size of a nonleaf index row
OrigFillFactor	tinyint	Original fillfactor value used
reserved1	tinyint	Reserved
reserved2	int	Reserved
FirstIAM	binary(6)	Reserved
impid	smallint	Reserved. Index implementation flag
lockflags	smallint	Constraint of granularity
pgmodctr	int	Tracks the number of pages changed in an index

continues

TABLE 4.2 continued

Column Name	Data Type	Description
keys	varbinary(512)	List of the column IDs that make up the index
name	sysname	Name of table or index
statblob	image	Statistics BLOB
maxlen	int	Reserved
rows	int	Data-level rowcount

SQL Server stores indexes in a binary tree structure (see Figure 4.5), with the index key values at the top of the structure. This is identified as a *root node*. Each index page is referred to as a *node*. The tree contains pointers to the previous node and next node in sequence within a page header, with the remainder of the page used to store the index rows. At the bottom of the structure, you find the leaf nodes that hold the actual data. From the root node, an index points to other index pages, which are referred to as *intermediate level nodes*. Each index row contains a key value, and a pointer to either another index page or a data row. At the end of the chain in a CLUSTERED index, the index points to the leaf node that actually contains the data.

In a CLUSTERED index, the root points to the top of the CLUSTERED index. To find the desired data, SQL Server navigates down the index to find the row corresponding to a CLUSTERED index key. To find a range of data pages, SQL Server navigates through the index to find the starting key value in the range, and then scans through the data pages by using the previous or next pointers. This allows SQL Server to quickly isolate the page with the specified value, and it then searches the page for the record or records with the specified value.

In many implementations, CLUSTERED indexes are used with columns that are frequently accessed in a GROUP BY clause. If a CLUSTERED index is created using values that are not unique, SQL Server adds a unique four-byte identifier to those data rows with duplicate clustering key columns. These additional bytes are not part of the user-defined table schema and do not appear in the result set of any query performed against the table. If the non-unique index is later dropped, the unique identifier is no longer added to new rows. The server uses fixed-disk addresses as row locators instead.

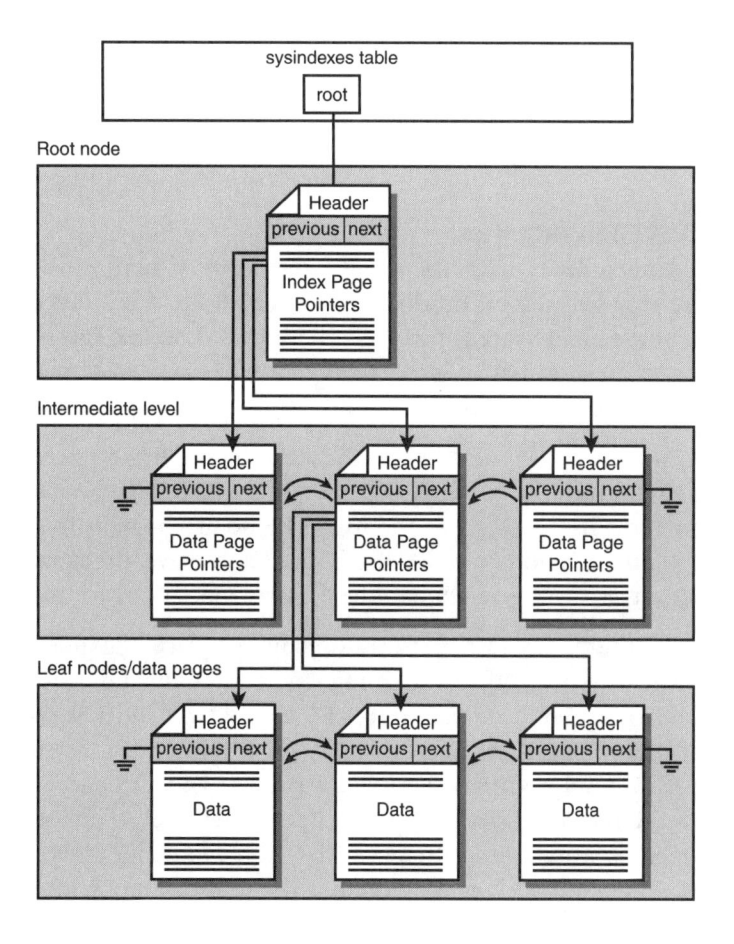

FIGURE 4.5
CLUSTERED index storage architecture, using binary trees.

> **NOTE** The data rows with additional four-byte unique identifiers still retain the unique identifier values after the dropping of an index, although the values are not used. Only recreating a unique CLUSTERED index removes previously added unique identifier values.

The CLUSTERED index dictates the placement of newly inserted rows. If a table does not have a CLUSTERED index, newly inserted rows are no longer placed at the end of the table, as in previous versions. SQL Server 7 keeps track of available space on each page, allowing the INSERT statements to be made in the first page with space. This eliminates the potential hotspot at the end of the table and allows the space that is freed by DELETE statements to be reused.

NONCLUSTERED Indexes

NONCLUSTERED indexes have the same binary tree structure as CLUSTERED indexes, with two significant differences (see Figure 4.6). The data rows are not sorted and stored based on the index. The leaf layer of a NONCLUSTERED index consists of index rows that have NONCLUSTERED key values and pointers to the data row.

In SQL Server 7, the index rows in the leaf level use two types of pointers to data pages. If the table does not have a CLUSTERED index, the NONCLUSTERED leaf row contains a pointer to the row. The pointer is built from the file ID, page number, and row ID. If the table does have a CLUSTERED index, the NONCLUSTERED leaf rows contain the CLUSTERED index key for the row.

The data for a NONCLUSTERED index is stored in one place; the index is stored in another, with pointers to the storage location of the index items in the data. The lowest level, or leaf node, of a NONCLUSTERED index is the storage location of an entry. A NONCLUSTERED index, in contrast to a CLUSTERED index, has an extra level between the index structure and the data itself. The items in the index are stored in the order of the index. The information in the table is stored in a different order. You can define a separate NONCLUSTERED index for each of the columns that are commonly used to find the data in the table.

Index Selection

There are many separate criteria to select the forms of indexing that you need to use in any implementation. Most database implementations use some degree of all index forms. PRIMARY and FOREIGN KEYS, UNIQUE and NONUNIQUE indexing, and CLUSTERED and NONCLUSTERED indexes all have an appropriate place in an implementation. In the following paragraphs, a guideline is provided for where and how each type of index might be used.

Try to avoid choosing large columns (number of bytes) as the keys to CLUSTERED indexes if a table also has NONCLUSTERED indexes. This also holds true for PRIMARY KEYS, which are often one and the same. Because the CLUSTERED values are maintained in every NONCLUSTERED index and PRIMARY KEY references are maintained in every foreign key, selecting the appropriate field to use as a key often saves a considerable amount of storage space. Short indexes with fewer bytes are, in general, more efficient than larger ones. It is important to make the clustering key, in particular, as small as possible. If a large CLUSTERED index key is defined, any NONCLUSTERED indexes that are defined on the same table are significantly larger because the NONCLUSTERED index entries contain the clustering key.

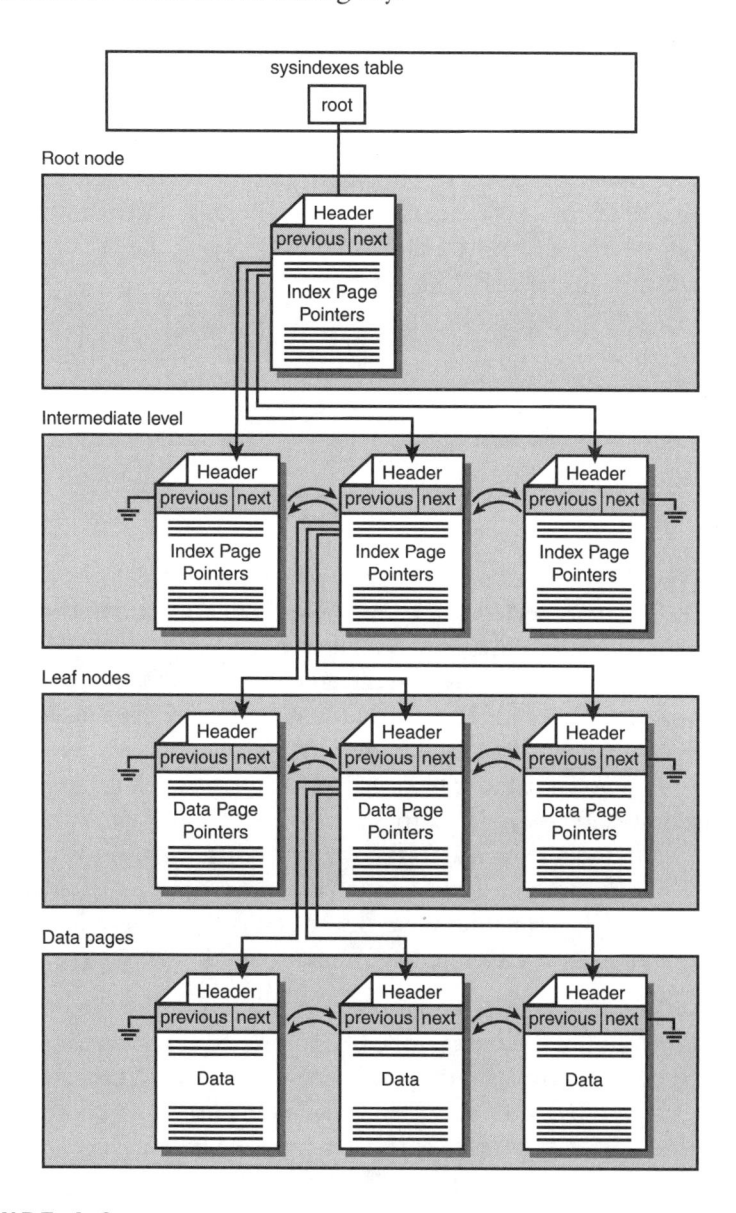

FIGURE 4.6
CLUSTERED index storage architecture, using binary trees.

Using a CLUSTERED index is advantageous when many rows with contiguous values are being retrieved. Once the row with the first key value is found, rows with subsequent indexed values are guaranteed to be physically adjacent to the first. If there is a column that is used frequently to sort the data retrieved from a table, it can be advantageous to cluster the table on that column and save the cost of a sort on each query. CLUSTERED indexes are also very efficient at finding a specific record when the key value is unique.

A CLUSTERED index creates an object in which the physical order of rows is the same as the indexed order of the rows, and the bottom leaf level of the CLUSTERED index contains the actual data rows. Because NONCLUSTERED indexes are rebuilt when a CLUSTERED index is created, create the CLUSTERED index before creating any NONCLUSTERED indexes.

> **NOTE** Because the leaf level of a CLUSTERED index and its data pages are the same by definition, creating a CLUSTERED index and using the ON *filegroup* clause effectively moves a table from the file on which the table was created to the new filegroup.

When SQL Server searches for data based on a NONCLUSTERED index, it searches the index for the specified value to obtain the location of the rows of data, and then retrieves the data directly from its storage locations. This makes NONNONCLUSTERED indexes the optimal choice for exact match query implementations. A NONCLUSTERED index creates an object that specifies the logical ordering of a table. The leaf level of a NONNONCLUSTERED index contains references to row index entries. That is, each index entry contains an indexed value and a reference to the row with that value. If the table does not have a CLUSTERED index, the reference is the row's disk address. If the table does have a CLUSTERED index, the reference is the search key in the CLUSTERED index. Each table can have as many as 249 NONCLUSTERED indexes.

A FOREIGN KEY constraint provides referential integrity for the data in the column or columns. These constraints require that each value in the column exist in the corresponding referenced column. When you design these relationships, it is important that you ensure appropriate table makeup because FOREIGN KEY constraints can only reference columns that are PRIMARY or UNIQUE constraints.

A UNIQUE index can be explicitly created, or it is created automatically when a UNIQUE or PRIMARY KEY constraint is defined. During this creation process and the checking of UNIQUE indexes, it is the only time that a NULL is considered to be equal to another NULL. If an attempt is made to enter data for which there is a UNIQUE index and the IGNORE_DUP_KEY option is specified, only the rows violating the UNIQUE index fail. Thus, instead of rolling back all of the data from an INSERT operation, only the problematic data is ignored.

Column Selection

When selecting the columns that are to be used in an index, consider the columns likely to be needed for queries and in other search conditions that use a WHERE clause. By indexing the columns needed for these operations, you improve the overall performance and response to their operations. A computed column cannot be used as a key column or as part of any PRIMARY KEY, UNIQUE, FOREIGN KEY, or CHECK constraint definition.

Composite indexes are used when two or more columns are best searched as a unit (such as in a person's name), or if many queries reference only columns in the index. You can include up to 16 columns of the same table or 900 bytes in a composite index.

> **NOTE** Columns consisting of the ntext, text, image, bit data types, or computed columns cannot be specified as columns for an index. Although composite indexes of two or more columns can be used as an index expression, SQL Server built-in functions such as UPPER cannot be used in the index expression.

Index Characteristics

Each style of index has different characteristics, many of which have already been discussed. Index information can be stored with the data causing the data order to change; or it can be kept separate from the data, as with the index in the back of a book. Indexes can allow for table relationships to be defined, or they can provide for different ordering possibilities, faster query processing, and quicker retrieval of data. An index is created from one or more keys in a table. If a table is created with no CLUSTERED indexes, then the data is not stored in any particular order. The storage structure in this type of table is suitably referred to as a "heap."

A few remaining topics that affect index usage, maintenance, and performance that have yet to be discussed are included in the sections that follow. A FILLFACTOR is a property of a SQL Server index that controls how densely the index is packed when it is initially created. The size of the FILLFACTOR used is determined by volatility. (FILLFACTORs are addressed more fully in the next section.) Indexes not only speed up the retrieval of rows for SELECT operations; they also usually increase the speed of UPDATEs and DELETEs because SQL Server must first find a row before it can update or delete the row. The increased efficiency of using the index to locate the row usually offsets the extra overhead needed to update the indexes, unless the table has plenty of indexes.

Deciding which particular set of indexes will optimize performance depends on the mix of queries in the system. A CLUSTERED index works well if most queries referencing a table have equality or range comparisons on the index key in their WHERE clauses. Consider using the most commonly referred to field as a CLUSTERED index. (This may mean that a name is used instead of a numeric ID.) Of course, there are many trade-offs—efficiency of storage over speed of access is one of the most common dilemmas.

FILLFACTOR

A FILLFACTOR specifies how full SQL Server should make each index page. A FILLFACTOR value can be anywhere between 1 and 100. If you don't specify a value, the default is 0. The lower the FILLFACTOR, the more space is made available for new index entries. If there is insufficient space for new entries, more space must be added dynamically. This allocation of space can affect performance.

If a table is volatile—there will be many updates and inserts after initial creation—you should create an index with a low FILLFACTOR, leaving room for future keys. If a table is nonvolatile, as in the case of a read-only table that does not change after initial creation, you should create an index with a high FILLFACTOR. A high FILLFACTOR reduces the physical size of the index, which lowers the number of disk reads that SQL Server uses to navigate through the index.

> **NOTE** The FILLFACTOR is only applied when an index is created.

The FILLFACTOR specifies how full SQL Server should make the leaf level of each index page. After that, time must be taken to divide the page to make room for more rows when an index page fills up. A properly chosen FILLFACTOR value yields better update performances in volatile tables. The value of the original FILLFACTOR is stored with the index in sysindexes, but it is not used after creation. As keys are inserted and deleted, the index eventually stabilizes at a certain density.

> **NOTE** The number of items on an interior index page is never fewer than two.

When FILLFACTOR is set to 0, only the leaf pages are filled. Space is left in non-leaf pages for at least two entries. You can change this default FILLFACTOR setting by executing sp_configure.

You will almost never use a FILLFACTOR of 100. The only situation where this would be relevant is when no INSERT or UPDATE statements are executed against the table. If the FILLFACTOR is 100, SQL Server creates indexes with leaf pages that are 100 percent full. A FILLFACTOR of 100 makes sense only for read-only tables. If subsequent INSERT or UPDATE operations are made to an index that is 100 percent full, page divisions have to be made on almost every change. Setting FILLFACTOR to 100 completely fills the leaf pages, leaving no space for additional entries. Setting FILLFACTOR to 100 fills the index node pages except for space for two entries.

Smaller FILLFACTOR values cause SQL Server to create new indexes with pages that are not full. Smaller FILLFACTOR values generally cause each index to take more storage space, which can be an issue in some implementations. It is a good practice to track the volatility of a table by using SQL Server Profiler, so that the correct size of FILLFACTOR is used when new indexes are created. (SQL Server Profiler is discussed in the section, "Index Maintenance.")

When FILLFACTOR is set to any value other than 0 or 100, space is left in non-leaf pages for one entry for most indexes. Space is left for two entries in non-unique CLUSTERED indexes. Space is left in leaf pages so that no leaf page is more full than the percentage specified by FILLFACTOR.

194 CHAPTER 4 Creating a Physical Database

> **NOTE** Creating a CLUSTERED index with a FILLFACTOR affects the amount of storage space that the data occupies because SQL Server redistributes the data when it creates the CLUSTERED index.

DROP_EXISTING

The DROP_EXISTING parameter specifies that the given table's CLUSTERED index should be dropped and rebuilt. Then, all existing NONCLUSTERED indexes are updated. If the same index name and columns as the original index are provided, SQL Server does not sort the rows. If a different index name and columns from the original index are provided, SQL Server sorts the rows. If the leaf level of the index is not sorted, the CREATE INDEX statement fails.

> **NOTE** When executing a CREATE INDEX statement with the DROP_EXISTING option, SQL Server assumes that the index is not corrupt. The rows in the specified index should be sorted by the specified key that is referenced in the CREATE INDEX statement.

PAD_INDEX

Using the PAD_INDEX parameter specifies the space to leave open on each interior node. Each page in an index is called an *index node*. By default, each index node accommodates at least two rows of the index as the maximum size. If the setting specified for PAD_INDEX falls below this two-row maximum size, SQL Server overrides the specified setting to allow a minimum of two rows. The PAD_INDEX setting is useful only when FILLFACTOR is also specified because PAD_INDEX uses the same percentage that is specified by FILLFACTOR.

Index Maintenance

Because many applications have a complex mix of queries, it can be difficult to estimate the usage of a particular table. SQL Server 7 provides two tools to assist with determining usage and fine-tuning indexes: The

SQL Server Profiler measures activity and the Index Tuning Wizard helps design indexes in a database. These two tools can be used together to produce appropriate indexes for any database schema.

The easiest way to design indexes for large schemas with complex access patterns is to use the Index Tuning Wizard. You provide the Index Tuning Wizard with a set of SQL statements that you build to reflect a typical mix of statements in the system. To build the statement list based on the actual activity, however, you usually use a SQL Server Profiler trace. The SQL Server Profiler produces a script that contains the actual SQL statements that are processed on the system during a period of time that reflects the typical load on the system. The Index Tuning Wizard runs the script and analyzes how effectively the existing indexes meet the processing load that is generated from the script. The wizard then produces a report, recommending exactly which indexes the query optimizer should use to maximize performance. You can also allow the wizard to implement the indexes.

Index Tuning Wizard

The Index Tuning Wizard is a new tool that allows you to create and implement indexes without an expert understanding of the structure of the database, how hardware platforms and components work, or how end-user applications interact with the relational engine. The Index Tuning Wizard analyzes your workload and recommends an optimal index configuration.

The Index Tuning Wizard provides the capability to compare, contrast, and select the best mix of indexes, allowing the system administrator to tune the database for a small set of problem queries without changing the index configuration.

The Index Tuning Wizard can analyze output from an SQL Server Profiler trace and make recommendations regarding the effectiveness of the current indexes. Recommendations can then be saved to an SQL script to be executed manually by the user at a later time, immediately implemented, or scheduled for another time.

SQL Server Profiler captures a continuous record of server activity in real-time and monitors events produced through SQL Server. SQL Server Profiler filters events, based on user-specified criteria; and then directs the trace output to the screen, a file, or a table. SQL Server

Profiler allows you to replay previously captured traces. Some common uses of the profiler are listed as follows:

- To determine the most resource-intensive queries
- To monitor locking, including blocked locks and deadlocks
- To debug and resolve server errors

Both the Index Tuning Wizard and SQL Server Profiler are discussed in detail in Chapter 5, "Maintaining a Database."

Database Population

After a database schema is created, there are several alternatives for getting the objects and data into a database. Depending on where the data is stored, you can restore information from database backups, transfer information directly from another SQL Server, or copy information from any other datasource, including ODBC databases and text files.

The creation of database backups allows you to copy data from one server to another. A database can be copied to another server to act as a standby server, to act as a warm backup server, or simply to create a redundant server to provide some load balancing. To provide a standby server, the database and the transaction logs are periodically copied to another server, which can be brought online if the primary server fails for some reason. It is possible to back up a database running on one computer and restore the backup to a separate computer, as long as some basic criteria are met. The following list provides the criteria for using the Backup/Restore mechanism to transfer data:

- The code page/character set and sort order used by SQL Server must be the same on both computers.
- The Unicode collation and locale used by SQL Server must be the same on both computers.
- The database backup cannot be from SQL Server version 6.5 or earlier.

Other methods for copying data from one server running SQL Server to another (and to and from other data sources) include the Data Transformation Services, the bcp utility, and the INSERT statement. Data Transformation Services are a series of import and export wizards that copy and modify data between any ODBC, OLE DB, or text data source and SQL Server. The bcp utility copies data between SQL Server and a data file by using native, character, or Unicode mode. The INSERT statement copies data into a table by using a distributed query as the select list to extract data from another data source. The next few sections focus on the bulk copy process and Data Transformation Service wizards, and the COM interfaces that facilitate data population.

Bulk Copy

A bulk copy transfers data to or from SQL Server by using another data source. A bcp operation can be performed as a logged (slow bcp) or non-logged (fast bcp) operation (each is discussed in separate sections that follow). The SQL Server bulk copy feature supports the transfer of large amounts of data into or out of a SQL Server table or view. The data is moved between SQL Server and an operating-system data file, such as an ASCII file. Thus, it is a two-stage operation: copying out and copying in. The data file can have different formats; the format is defined to bulk copy in a format file. Data can be loaded into program variables and transferred to SQL Server by using bulk copy functions, which are typically much faster than using INSERT statements.

The bulk copy utility (bcp) inserts large numbers of new rows into a table. To properly use the bcp utility, you must have an understanding of the table structure that is being copied into, and know the types of data that are valid for the rows in the table.

The bcp utility is a command line utility, not an SQL statement. Because of this, bcp is useful when combined within batch files that can perform a copy process using similar parameters, and also execute other NT or SQL processes within the same batch. The syntax description of the bcp utility is as follows:

```
bcp [[database name.][owner].]table name {in | out | format} data
↪file [options]
```

The available options and their descriptions for the bcp procedure are included in Table 4.3.

TABLE 4.3

bcp COMMAND LINE OPTIONS

Option	Description
-m *max errors*	Maximum number of errors before copy is abandoned; default is 10
-f *format file*	Full path to a format file
-e *err file*	Full path for the storage of errors
-F *first row*	Number of the first row; default is 1
-L *last row*	Number of the last row; default is 0 (last row in file)
-b *batch size*	Number of rows to be included in a transaction batch; all data in one batch by default
-n	Native database data types
-c	Character data type
-w	Unicode characters
-N	Native for non-character data types; Unicode for character data types
-6	Uses version 6.x data types
-q	Quoted identifiers are required
-C *code page*	Code page of the data
-t *field term*	Field terminator; default is \t (tab)
-r *row term*	Row terminator; default is \n (new line or hard return)
-i *input file*	Response file
-o *output file*	Output redirected from command prompt
-a *packet size*	Bytes per network packet
-S *server name*	SQL Server name
-U *login id*	Login ID
-P *password*	Password
-T	Use trusted connection
-v	bcp version and copyright
-k	Empty columns retain NULL, not DEFAULT
-E	Identity values not to be reinitialized
-h "*hint* [, ...*n*]"	SQL Server 7 bcp hints

In most cases, many of these options are not required. For a standard bulk copy operation to be performed, you are required to specify only the character format (usually -n, -c or -w).

Fast BCP

A fast bulk copy is a copy process in which the transaction log is not used to record the inserts that occur as a result of putting data into a table. SQL Server bulk copies that import data into SQL Server are run in fast mode if the following occur:

- The database option select into/bulkcopy is set to true.
- The target table has no indexes or triggers.
- The target table is not being replicated.

Slow BCP

A slow bulk copy is similar the fast bulk copy process. In fact, the state of the destination table determines whether or not a slow bulk copy or fast bulk copy is performed—it is not a bcp command option. All row-insert operations performed during a bulk copy operation are logged in the transaction log. Although minimal logging occurs when bulk copying data into a table that has indexes, the transaction log can become full. When bulk copying a large number of rows into a table with indexes, it can be faster to drop all the indexes, perform the bulk copy, and recreate the indexes. You can even have this operation performed via a batch file if the bulk copy process needs to be applied again in the future.

Data Transformation Services

Data Transformation Services (DTS) allow for the import, export, and transformation of data between multiple sources by using an OLE DB-based architecture. Using DTS, it is possible to build data warehouses and data marts in SQL Server by importing and transferring data from multiple sources interactively or automatically on a regularly scheduled basis. You can use DTS to create custom transformation objects that can be integrated into third-party products. With DTS, you can access applications by using third-party OLE DB providers. This allows applications, for which an OLE DB provider exists, to be used as sources and destinations of data.

Importing and exporting data is the process of exchanging data between applications by reading and writing data in a common format. DTS can import data from an ASCII text file into SQL Server. Alternatively, data can be exported from SQL Server to an OLE DB destination. A *transformation* is the set of operations that is applied to source data before it is stored at the destination. DTS allows for the calculation of new values from one or more source fields, or even breaking a single field into multiple values to be stored in separate destination columns.

DTS allows you to move and transform data to and from native OLE DB providers, ODBC data sources, ASCII fixed-field length text files, and ASCII-delimited text files. DTS components include the DTS Import Wizard, DTS Export Wizard, and DTS Package Designer, which are available through SQL Server Enterprise Manager. DTS also includes COM programming interfaces that you can use to create customized import, export, and transformation applications (discussed in the sections that follow).

DTS Import Wizard

To use the DTS Import/Export Wizards is a simple manner of following the wizard and providing the requested information on each screen. Follow these steps:

1. Determine the source of the data, including the type of provider (such as SQL Server, FoxPro, or Paradox); and any server name, file name, database name, and logon information that are required to access the provider.

2. Select the destination database for the transfer again, including the type of provider and any other information required for access.

3. Select the tables to be imported or provide a query as the basis for the import. During this stage, you can provide transformation information for the data.

4. Decide whether or not you want to run the package immediately, whether or not you want to create a replication publication, whether or not you want to save the package, and (if so) whether or not you want to schedule the package for later execution.

Maintaining Integrity 201

> **NOTE** If you select that you want to create a replication publication, the Create Publication Wizard executes after the data transfer.

Transformation information can be provided during Import or Export operations. When transforming the data, you may want to change the nullability of a column or other column characteristics such as size, precision, or scale. If desired, you can generate scripts or edit the SQL directly while generating a transformation.

DTS Package Design

Package components are implemented in the DTS Package Object Library. *Package objects* create a data-transformation package, which defines the source columns, destination columns, and information about how the data is manipulated during the transformation. The package object controls how the data is changed when it is moved and how the data pump moves the data.

The DTS package defines one or more tasks to be executed in a coordinated sequence. The DTS package can be created manually by using a language that supports OLE automation, such as Visual Basic, or interactively by using the Data Transformation Services wizards. The DTS package can be stored in a COM-structured storage file; in the Microsoft Repository, making package metadata available to other applications; or in the SQL Server msdb database. Each package creates and stores a series of steps that defines the order of tasks to be performed and all the details necessary to perform the tasks. Tasks may perform such operations as running a separate executable program, running an ActiveX script, or sending an e-mail message. Using COM-structured storage files makes it easy to schedule a package for execution or distribute DTS packages by using e-mail or network file servers, without the need to use the Repository. SQL Server provides the SQL-DTS object model that can be accessed from any COM-compliant environment.

After a DTS package is created and saved, it is completely self-contained, and can be retrieved and run by using SQL Server Enterprise Manager or the dtsrun utility. The syntax definition for the dtsrun utility is as follows:

```
dtsrun [{/? | {/[~]s server name {/[~]u user name [/~p password] |
```

202 CHAPTER 4 Creating a Physical Database

```
➥/e} ¦ /[~]f filename}
              {/[~]n package name [/[~]m package password] ¦ [/[~]g
➥package guid string]
              ¦ [/[~]v package version guid string]} [/!x] [/!d]
➥[/!y] [/!c]}]
```

The available arguments and their descriptions for the `dtsrun` utility are included in Table 4.4.

TABLE 4.4

dtsrun UTILITY ARGUMENTS

Argument	Description
/?	Displays the command-prompt option assistance.
~	Hexadecimal encrypted value of parameter.
/s server name	SQL Server name.
/u user name	Login ID.
/p password	Password used with a login ID.
/e	Use a trusted connection.
/n package name	DTS package name.
/m package password	DTS package password.
/g package guid string	DTS package ID; the package ID is a GUID.
/v package version	DTS package version ID; the guid string version ID is a GUID.
/f filename	UNC filename containing DTS packages.
/!x	Retrieves the DTS package from SQL Server.
/!d	Deletes the DTS package from SQL Server.
/!y	Displays the encrypted command used to execute the DTS package.
/!c	Copies the command used to execute the DTS package to the Clipboard.

The `dtsrun` utility allows a DTS package to be retrieved, executed, deleted, or overwritten. Also, the command used to execute the package may be displayed. To execute a DTS package saved as a COM file, use the following:

    dtsrun /FFileName /NPackageName /MPackagePassword

To execute a DTS package saved in the msdb database, use the following:

    dtsrun /SServerName /UUserName /Ppassword /NPackageName
    ➥/MPackagePassword

It is also possible to schedule a package for execution using SQL Server Enterprise Manager, by creating a SQL Server job that executes the DTS package utility. You can also schedule package execution when you create the package by using the Data Transformation Services Import and Export wizards.

Full-Text Implementation

SQL Server full-text indexing and query capabilities help solves the problem of retrieving data from a database by allowing users to issue full-text queries against plain character-based data in SQL Server tables (including words and phrases, or multiple forms of a word or phrase). This means that applications can be developed to give users the information they want without having to learn about the aspects of the database, server, and the rest of the environment. The implementation of full-text search includes the definition levels needed to achieve full-text search capabilities, and often requires a lot of forethought or guesswork about which English statements might be used for any given query.

One step is necessary prior to using full-text editing on a newly installed server. First, check that the full-text service is started. Starting the full-text service is part of the auto-startup of SQL Server. The service should be running if needed, but may have to be started manually the first time. If necessary, the service can be started and stopped in one of these ways:

- Right-click on the Full-Text Search object in SQL Server Enterprise Manager and select Start or Stop from the menu.
- Use the SQL Server through the Service Control Manager. In the Service Control Manager, this service is named Microsoft Search Service.
- Type **net start mssearch** or **net stop mssearch** from a command prompt.

A table that will use full-text processing features must have a unique single-column index, usually but not necessarily the PRIMARY KEY.

The Full-Text Indexing Wizard offers a step-by-step, screen-driven operation to simplify the implementation of full-text indexing. As you will see later in the chapter, the alternative stored procedures can be rather involved and have to be executed carefully to avoid problems. To use the wizard, run the following process:

1. Select the database, table, and unique key you want to use as a basis for the full-text index.
2. Select one or more character base columns that you want to be eligible for queries.
3. Select or create a full-text catalog.
4. Select or create the population schedule for the catalog.
5. Populate the catalog.

A similar process can be performed by using stored procedures. At any time, you can find out if a database has been enabled for full-text processing by executing a SELECT query against the database properties (like the use of the Pubs database in the following example). The statement returns 1 if the service is enabled and 0 if it is not:

```
SELECT DatabaseProperty ('Pubs', 'IsFulltextEnabled' )
```

If the database is not enabled, you can enable full-text processing by using the sp_fulltext_database stored procedure, as follows:

```
USE Pubs
sp_fulltext_database 'enable'
```

You can create a full-text catalog named by invoking the sp_fulltext_catalog stored procedure, as shown in the example that follows. This procedure creates metadata about a full-text catalog in system tables and builds an empty full-text catalog in the file system:

```
sp_fulltext_catalog 'PubsCatalog', 'create'
```

To register tables for full-text processing, invoke the sp_fulltext_table stored procedure once for each table, as shown in the following example. Notice that both tables use the PubsCatalog full-text catalog. The effect of these calls is to create the metadata for both full-text indexes:

```
sp_fulltext_table 'writers', 'create', 'PubsCatalog',
↪'writer_id_index'
sp_fulltext_table 'books', 'create', 'PubsCatalog', 'isbn_index'
```

Specify the names of the columns that are to support full-text queries by invoking the sp_fulltext_column stored procedure once for each column, as shown in the following example. The effect of these calls is to augment metadata for both the full-text indexes:

```
sp_fulltext_column 'writers', 'organization', 'add'
sp_fulltext_column 'writers', 'bio', 'add'
```

```
sp_fulltext_column 'books', 'titles', 'add'
sp_fulltext_column 'books', 'the words', 'add'
sp_fulltext_column 'books', 'abstract', 'add'
```

Create a full-text index for these tables by invoking the `sp_fulltext_table` stored procedure once for each table, as illustrated in the following example. Note that this does not actually create the full-text indexes; it simply registers the tables in the full-text catalog so that data from these tables will be included in the next population:

```
sp_fulltext_table 'writers', 'activate'
sp_fulltext_table 'books', 'activate'
```

Start a full population of the `PubsCatalog` full-text catalog by invoking the `sp_fulltext_catalog` stored procedure, as follows (you may have a short wait because the population of a full-text catalog is an asynchronous operation and it takes some time for the full-text indexes to be created):

```
sp_fulltext_catalog 'PubsCatalog', 'start_full'
```

`FullTextCatalogProperty` allows you to verify the progress of the population of the PubsCatalog full-text catalog, as shown in the following example query. This statement returns 0 if the service is idle, and 1 or more to indicate various stages of population:

```
SELECT FulltextCatalogProperty ( 'PubsCatalog', 'PopulateStatus' )
```

Advanced Text Searches

Searching can be performed by using any form of a specific word. You can search for all the different tenses of a verb, or for both the singular and plural forms of a noun—but not in the same query. Verbs and nouns must be approached by using two separate queries. Use the `FORMSOF()` function to allow for word variations, whereas `INFLECTIONAL` searches for both singular and plural words when looking for any form of a word within the `CONTAINS` option of the `WHERE` clause. A `CONTAINS` predicate can be used only with tables that have columns enabled for full-text querying. One or more table columns can be enabled for full-text querying. A given full-text predicate against that table can either access a single enabled column or all of the enabled columns in a table.

Some examples of the use of the `CONTAINS` predicate are in the following paragraphs. The following returns matches on `"spirit"`, `"spirits"` and `"spirited"`:

```
SELECT Description, CategoryName
FROM Categories
```

```
WHERE CONTAINS (Description, 'FORMSOF(INFLECTIONAL, "spirit")')
```

Searching for multiple forms of words or phrases is permitted through the use of wildcards. You can search a word or phrase in which the word or words begin with specified text. In the case of a phrase, each word within the phrase is considered to be a prefix term. The following returns any phrase beginning with the word `"blue"`:

```
SELECT Description, CategoryName
FROM Categories
WHERE CONTAINS (Description, ' "blue*" ' )
```

All text that matches the text specified before the wildcard is returned. The following example returns various forms of the word set `"light batter"`, `"lightly battered"`, `"lighter batter"`, or `"lighter battered"`:

```
SELECT Description, CategoryName
FROM Categories
WHERE CONTAINS (Description, ' "light batter*" ' )
```

When searching for specific words or phrases in any single-byte languages, a word that is framed by spaces and/or punctuation can easily be accommodated. In the following example, the word `"computers"` is found if it is framed in such a manner:

```
SELECT title_id, title, notes
FROM titles
WHERE CONTAINS(notes, 'computers')
```

A wildcard used in place of a column name indicates all full-text enabled columns for the table. In the following example, the '*' represents the words `"Canadian Developer"`, which should be sought out in each column of the select list:

```
SELECT title_id, title, description, price
FROM titles
WHERE CONTAINS( *, ' "Canadian Developer" ' )
```

Searching for words or phrases close to another word or phrase by proximity can be performed by using NEAR() or a ~ (tilde), if you prefer. In addition, you can specify two words or phrases in any order and get the same result. For instance, this example searches for the word "socks" close to the word "mending":

```
SELECT title, notes
FROM titles
WHERE CONTAINS (notes, 'socks NEAR() mending')
```

However, you can also reverse the words in the WHERE clause to get the same result:

```
WHERE CONTAINS (notes, 'mending NEAR() socks')
```

You can specify the tilde (~) in place of the NEAR() keyword in the previous queries and get the same results:

```
WHERE CONTAINS (notes, 'mending ~ socks')
```

Searching for words or phrases using weighted values is done by establishing the weight for each word to be applied in the search. A *weight value*, any value between 0.0 and 1.0, indicates the degree of importance for each word and phrase within a set of words and phrases. A weight value of 0.0 is the lowest value, and a weight value of 1.0 is the highest. In the example that follows, the words following "Washburn" in the address are given different priorities. The end result gives a greater value to "Washburn Central" than to "Washburn Road", and gives the greatest value to "Washburn Central Road":

```
SELECT CompanyName, ContactName, Address
FROM Customers
WHERE CONTAINS(Address, 'ISABOUT ("Washburn*",
Road WEIGHT(0.5),
Central WEIGHT(0.9))' )
```

By combining the options of the CONTAINS parameter, you can essentially use any search criteria desired or develop an application that allows for the user to have complete freedom over the criteria being selected. Many of the principles discussed here are the basis for the most powerful search engines.

What Is Important to Know

The following bullets summarize the chapter and accentuate the key concepts to memorize for the exam:

- Storage structure has moved away from .DAT files and now uses .MDF, .NDF, and .LDF files.

- Files can be placed and maintained in filegroups, files cannot belong to more than one filegroup, and a filegroup can only be used in a single database.

- Use ALTER DATABASE to change database and files settings or increase space; use DBCC SHRINKFILE and DBCC SHRINKDATABASE to decrease space.

- Use sp_helpdb to obtain information about a database; use sp_dboption to set database options.

- CLUSTERED indexes, one per table, physically reorder the table and are usually used for the PRIMARY KEY.

- NONCLUSTERED indexes, up to 249 per table, do not reorder the data in the table, used for alternative index keys.

- A Fill Factor, used only at the time of index creation, provides a percentage of how full to fill the pages while leaving room for inserted keys.

- Constraints are used to maintain referential and data integrity by enacting on events to prevent invalid alterations to table data.

- Unique constraints create unique indexes, ensuring that each row of data maintained by the index is unique from all others.

- The CONTAINS option of the WHERE clause is used against FULL-TEXT indexes within queries to locate desired text.

OBJECTIVES

- Evaluate and optimize the performance of an execution plan by using
  - DBCC SHOWCONTIG
  - SET SHOWPLAN_TEXT
  - SET SHOWPLAN_ALL
  - UPDATE STATISTICS
- Evaluate and optimize the performance of query execution plans.
- Diagnose and resolve locking problems.
- Identify SQL Server events and performance problems by using SQL Server Profiler.

CHAPTER 5

Maintaining a Database

Optimizing and Tuning SQL Server Implementations

This chapter, the final chapter covering the exam topics, discusses the optimizing and tuning techniques used within SQL Server. To achieve optimum performance with any implementation, the logical and physical design is only the beginning. A fully efficient implementation requires ongoing maintenance, monitoring, and tweaking of the entire system.

When fine-tuning an implementation, several SQL statements and SQL Server utilities are available to assist you and make this process as painless as possible. This chapter discusses DBCC statement usage, tools to assist with query execution plans, diagnosis and resolution of locking problems, and the use of SQL Server Profiler to look at server activity. By looking into each of these topics carefully, you will be able to fine tune any installation and correctly answer questions on the exam that relate to tuning and optimization.

This chapter begins with a look behind the scenes, under the hood, and into the engine. You'll see how SQL Server 7 gets the optimum performance out of statement execution stored procedures and the production of resultsets from the execution of queries. Known as an execution plan, SQL Server determines the optimum techniques to execute statements in a dynamic fashion, making adjustments to the plan as warranted by changes in the data. When performing a query operation, you can select to view the execution plan and the resultset. Positioning the cursor over each component of the plan displays information about that element of the plan (see Figure 5.1). Note that the toolbar specifies that the execution plan is to be shown as an available tab along with the output (see Figure 5.2).

A more complex operation will have a more complex execution plan, which produces a full, graphic illustration of how SQL Server solves a given query (see Figure 5.3). By studying the execution plan and the resulting statistics, you might be able to determine a more efficient means of executing a process.

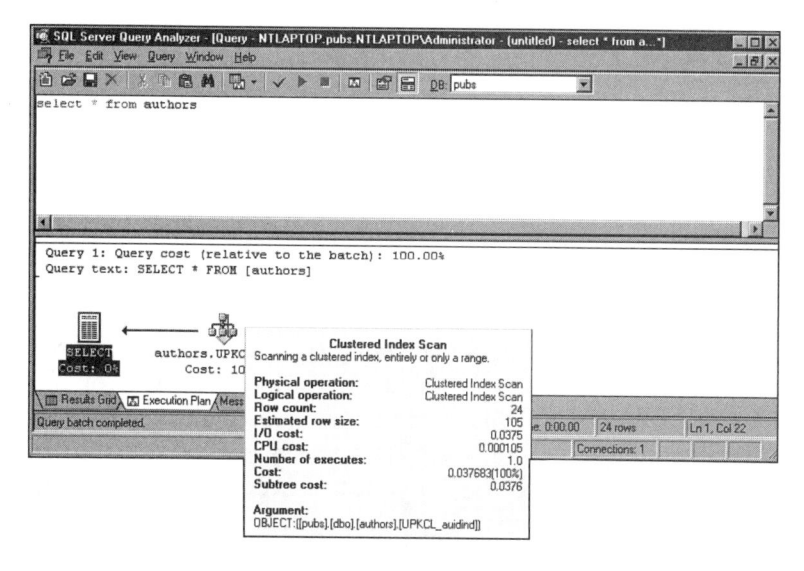

Optimizing and Tuning SQL Server Implementations 211

FIGURE 5.1
Plan and additional information for a simple query.

FIGURE 5.2
Toolbar icon identifying the execution plan to be shown.

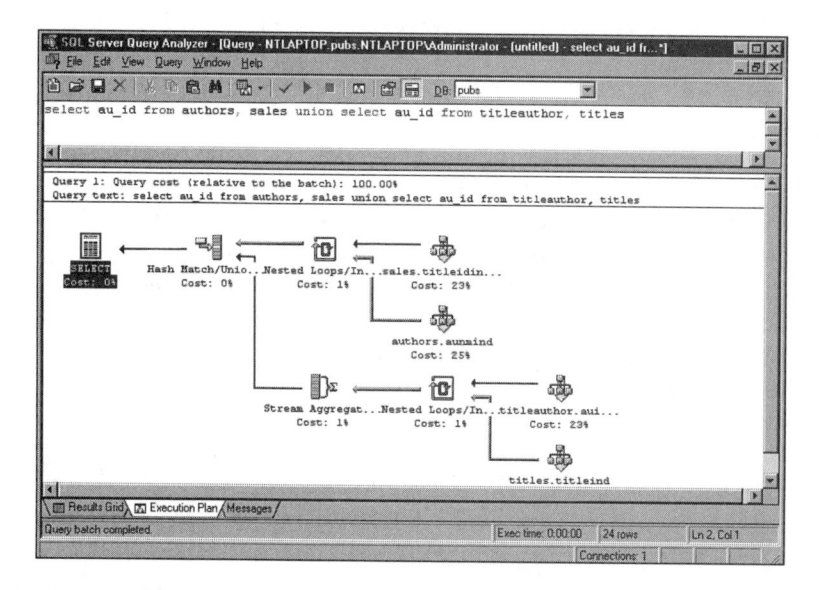

FIGURE 5.3
Complex query plan.

Execution Plans

An execution plan is what SQL Server uses to determine the best possible techniques to execute a given query. The SQL Server engine creates an execution plan as part of the preparation process prior to the actual execution of a SQL query.

SQL Server 7 brings about some huge performance improvements over previous versions, mostly due to the architecture behind the query-processing capabilities and compilation techniques. The improved support for large systems with enhanced handling of large databases and complex queries provide for some of this performance improvement. The handling of data warehouses, decision support systems, and OLAP (OnLine Analytical Processing) applications, and query processing in general offer enhancements that greatly improves performance in most scenarios.

SQL Server 7 uses hash join, merge join, and parallel query execution. A *hash join* is the process that bases query resolution on mapping summary values from a query operation to a hash table. A *merge join* operation simultaneously passes over two sorted inputs to perform a join. Complex queries with subquery operations can be run as a *parallel query* to improve the use of resources in a multiple processor environment and provide better performance. The use of these techniques can allow a system to scale to much larger database structures than those previously performed through a nested-loop join technique. New OLAP tools enable the implementation of star and snowflake schemas for very large data warehouse systems.

The star schema is a relational database structure in which data is maintained in a single fact table at the center of the schema. This central table is related to a dimensional table with additional stored data. The snowflake schema is an extension of the star schema in which one or more levels of dimensional data is stored in other related tables with only the primary levels directly associated to the fact table and other levels associated to a table in the primary level.

> **NOTE** This book concentrates on the implementations other than those used in data warehouses. Data warehousing is now a separate exam provided by Microsoft and, thus, is not the focus of this book.

SQL Server 7 uses index intersection and union techniques on multiple indexes to filter data before it retrieves rows from the database. All indexes on a table are maintained concurrently and constraint evaluations are part of the query's execution plan. This simplifies and speeds up the updating of multiple rows of a table.

Evaluation of Execution Plans

Several statements can be used to obtain information from SQL Server about which execution plans the server is utilizing. The following paragraphs give you a quick outline of these statements and the information that each provides. In later sections of this chapter, the statements are closely examined to see how they can be utilized as information gathering tools.

SET SHOWPLAN_ALL can be used to look at detailed information about how the statements are executed and estimates of the resource requirements for the statements. SET SHOWPLAN_TEXT contrasts this by providing detailed information about how the statements are executed. A couple of DBCC parameters can be used to provide information about execution plans and update system tables so that more appropriate information can be retrieved. DBCC SHOWCONTIG can be used to display fragmentation information for the data and indexes of the specified table. UPDATE STATISTICS is a statement used update information about the distribution of key values for one or more indexes in the specified table. UPDATE STATISTICS is run automatically. Alternatively, the table owner can execute UPDATE STATISTICS at will.

DBCC MEMUSAGE helps you find the system hogs. When specifying the PROCEDURE option, DBCC MEMUSAGE returns a resultset that explains the amount of memory in use by the 12 largest objects in the procedure cache. DBCC MEMUSAGE shows the sizes of the trees and plans and the total trees and plans used to evaluate the largest objects.

Optimizing Performance

The SQL Server Query Optimizer manages statistics gathering in an attempt to guarantee the most efficient evaluation plan possible. New algorithms implemented with SQL Server 7 provide a basis for sampling statistics to produce the most efficient means of performing a query. The query processor automatically recognizes common join types and provides the optimum response times. SQL Server 7 even applies OLE DB to the query processor to optimize this operation.

New to SQL Server 7 are the optimization hints *merge* and *hash*. If joined fields are indexed and the columns represented in the index cover a given query, then a merge join is preferable to a standard join mechanism. A merge join can take advantage of the binary tree storage structure of indexes. Merge and hash joins are useful in performing inner, outer, semi-joins, and unions. If you were working with a large heap or other nonindexed table, hashing would provide performance benefits. These instructions (referred to as hints) can give the Query Optimizer a basis for deciding which execution plan to use in a given scenario.

Merge and Hash Optimization

A merge join is used as an optimization technique in queries dealing with indexed data. A merge join simultaneously passes over two sorted inputs. For a merge join to be accommodated, both inputs must be sorted on the columns to be used in the merge. When a query contains ordering of multiple input sets (see Figure 5.4), a merge join is used.

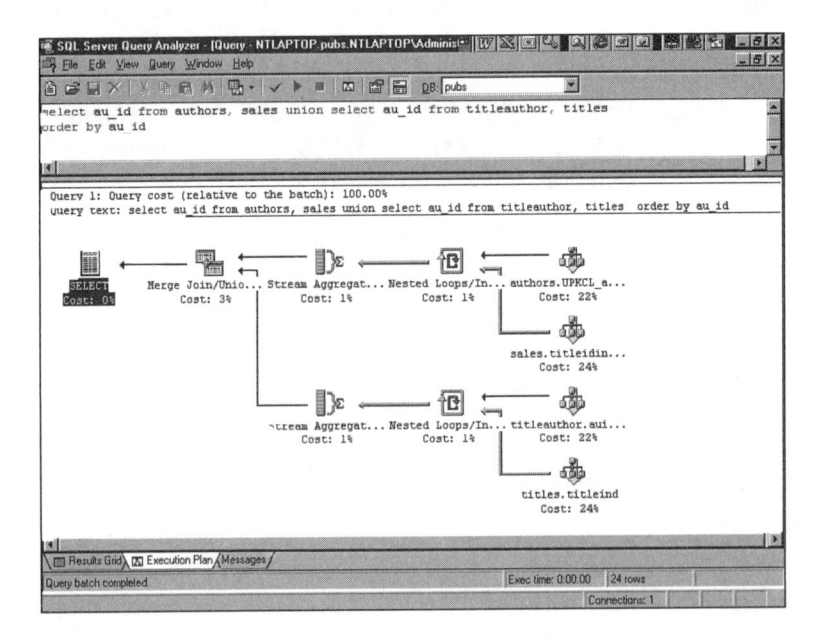

FIGURE 5.4
Merge join plan.

The Query Optimizer scans an index, (if one exists on the proper set of columns) or places a sort operator below the merge join. In some cases, there might be multiple equality clauses, but the merge columns are taken from only some of the available clauses. Because each input is sorted, the Merge Join operator gets a row from each input and compares them. A merge join is relatively fast, but it can be expensive if sorting needs to be accomplished over large recordsets.

Hashing is used as an optimization technique on heap, nonindexed data. Two styles of hashing optimization exist: hash joins and hash teams. A hash join uses two inputs. The first input is referred to as the build input and the second, the probe input. The Query Optimizer assigns these roles. It assigns the roll of the build input to the smaller of the two inputs. Hash joins are used in set-matching operations. The hash join is similar to the merge join in that there is at least one equality in the join. The set of columns in the equality is referred to as the hash key that will be used to evaluate the joining of the inputs.

The Query Optimizer uses three forms of hash joins. An *in-memory hash join*, first scans or computes the entire build input and then builds a hash table in memory. It then scans the remaining input one row at a time producing matches. A *grace hash join* is used if the build input does not fit in memory. It accommodates a hash join in several steps. Each of these steps has its own build and probe operations. A *recursive hash join* is performed when the build input is so large that inputs for a standard external merge sort would require multiple merge levels. It is possible to perform a hybrid of these joins in those cases where the build input is larger—but not much larger—than the available memory.

It is not always possible during optimization for the Query Optimizer to determine which hash join to use. In some cases, the engine starts by using an in-memory hash join and gradually moves to a grace hash join and a recursive hash join depending on the size of the build input. If the Query Optimizer incorrectly judges which of the two inputs is smaller and should have been the build input, the build and probe roles are reversed dynamically by the Optimizer.

In most cases, SQL Server chooses the best form of optimizations. You can supply specific hints with a variety of SQL statements, but a hint is provided only in rare instances when the default behavior of the SQL Server Optimizer is not wanted. The HASH:() predicate with a list of columns used to create a hash value can appear in the argument column.

If a `RESIDUAL:()` predicate is present, that predicate must also be satisfied for rows to be considered a match. The merge join operator contains a `MERGE:()` predicate if the operation is performing a one-to-many join or a `MANY-TO-MANY MERGE:()` predicate if the operation is performing a many-to-many join.

Semi-joins are often performed as part of an execution plan, especially when a star schema is utilized. A *left anti semi-join* outputs each row satisfying the join predicate from the left input for which no rows exist in the right input. A *left semi-join* outputs each row satisfying the join predicate from the left input for which there exists a row in the right input. A *right anti semi-join* outputs each row satisfying the join predicate from the right input for which no rows exist in the left input. A *right semi-join* outputs each row satisfying the join predicate from the right input for which a row exists in the left input.

Database Consistency Checker (DBCC)

The `DBCC` statement has undergone a complete overhaul from previous versions. Although previously it was used for little more than information gathering, it can now actually repair some problems rather than just report on them. `DBCC` statements check the logical and physical consistency of the database, but improved engine-checking procedures require the `DBCC` operations to be performed less frequently than in previous server versions. `DBCC`, when it is executed, now performs faster than in previous releases.

Because `DBCC` now (in some cases) repairs the errors that it finds, it need not be used as often as in past versions. Transact-SQL provides `DBCC` to check the physical and logical consistency of a database. Many `DBCC` statements can fix the problems that are detected. The `DBCC` option `SHOWCONTIG` can display fragmentation information for the data and indexes of the specified table, as defined in the following paragraphs.

The `SHOWCONTIG` statement passes across the page chain at the leaf level. `DBCC SHOWCONTIG` scans the data pages of the specified table and determines whether the table is heavily fragmented. Table fragmentation can occur when modifications are made against the table data. If a table is found to be heavily fragmented, you can reduce fragmentation to improve performance by dropping and re-creating a clustered index. Recreating a clustered index without the SORTED_DATA option allows the data to be reorganized. The index will not be altered by the DBCC command directly and will have to be done as a subsidiary process.

DBCC SHOWCONTIG returns information about the level of fragmentation and other related data. The resultset includes the number of pages in the table or index. It also includes the number of extents in the table or index, the number of times the DBCC statement moved from one extent to another while it passed across the pages of the table or index, and the number of pages per extent in the page chain. Density information is provided so that you can easily determine the ideal number of extent changes if everything is contiguously linked. The amount of fragmentation given as a percentage of out-of-order pages is returned from scanning the leaf pages of an index.

Graphical SHOWPLAN

The SQL Query Analyzer provides the graphical SHOWPLAN mechanism to illustrate the techniques that the Optimizer uses to execute a query in a graphically representational format. As shown earlier in this chapter, this tool provides a lot of information about how a query will be optimized to produce the resultset. It can be enlightening to see what goes on behind the scenes for the execution of a given statement. The information provided permits you to see how a resultset is formulated and can provide some indication of how a query could be restructured to provide faster execution.

If either of the SHOWPLAN options—SET SHOWPLAN_TEXT and SET SHOWPLAN_ALL—are used, the graphical plan is replaced by a textual information tab; in which case, the query is not actually executed and the graphical plan is not shown. To see a complete listing of the graphical showplan icons and their respective definitions see "Graphical Showplan—Execution Plan—Graphically Displaying the Execution Plan Using SQL Server Query Analyzer," in SQL Server books online.

Graphical SHOWPLAN uses logical and physical operators to illustrate how a query or update was executed. The physical operators describe each step of the actual implementation algorithm that was used to process a given query or update. The logical operators describe the relational algebraic operations that were used to process a given query or update. The SHOWPLAN statement that was available in previous version of SQL Server has been replaced in SQL Server 7 by two switches. SHOWPLAN_TEXT and SHOWPLAN_ALL can be turned on or off within a SET operation to alter the appearance and handling of the query by the Query Analyzer.

SET SHOWPLAN_TEXT

The query is never really executed when you use SHOWPLAN_TEXT; instead SQL Server returns summary, text information about how the statements are to be executed. When you use the SET SHOWPLAN_TEXT ON statement, the execution plan for any subsequent Transact-SQL statement is returned in text format until you use the SET SHOWPLAN_TEXT OFF statement (see Figure 5.5).

When SET SHOWPLAN_TEXT is turned off, SQL Server executes all statements normally. SET SHOWPLAN_TEXT and SET SHOWPLAN_ALL cannot be specified in a stored procedure; they must be the only statements in a batch, as shown in the previous example. Remember that a batch ends in a GO. Statements following the GO represent a new batch. Each statement reflected in the output contains a single row with the text of the statement, followed by several rows with the details of the execution steps.

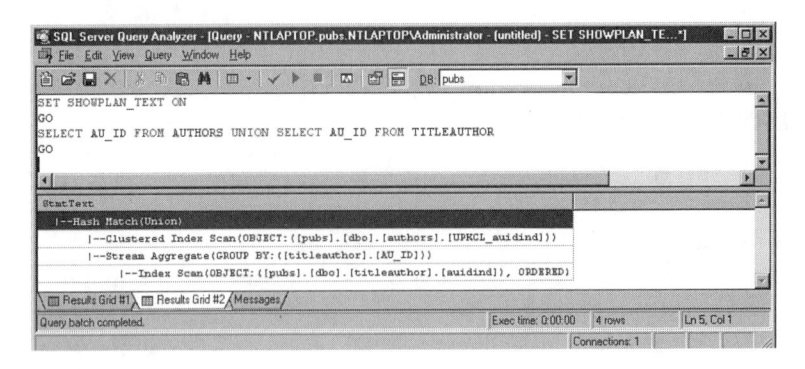

FIGURE 5.5
SHOWPLAN_TEXT when set on.

SET SHOWPLAN_ALL

SET SHOWPLAN_ALL returns more detailed output than SET SHOWPLAN_TEXT (see Figure 5.6.) and should be used with programs designed to handle its output. Again, the statements following SHOWPLAN_ALL ON are not executed; instead, SQL Server returns detailed information about how the statements are to be executed and estimates of the resource requirements needed for their execution. SET SHOWPLAN_ALL is intended to be used by applications written to handle its output. Use SET SHOWPLAN_TEXT to return readable output for command line applications, such as the OSQL utility.

The SHOWPLAN_ALL option provides more detail than SHOWPLAN_TEXT. The information is given in a set of columns providing one row for each step of the execution. Table 5.1 represents the column information provided.

TABLE 5.1

SHOWPLAN_ALL RESULTS

Column	Description
StmtText	This column contains the text of the Transact-SQL statement or a description of the operation.
StmtId	Number of the statement within the current batch.
NodeId	ID of the node within the current query.
Parent	Node ID of the parent step.
PhysicalOp	Physical implementation algorithm for the node.
LogicalOp	Relational algebraic operator this node represents.
Argument	Provides additional information about the operation.
DefinedValues	Contains a comma-separated list of values introduced by the operator.
EstimateRows	Estimated number of rows output by this operator.
EstimateIO	Estimated I/O cost for the operator.
EstimateCPU	Estimated CPU cost for the operator.
AvgRowSize	Estimated average row byte size of the row being passed through the operator.

continues

TABLE 5.1 continued

Column	Description
TotalSubtreeCost	Estimated cumulative cost of the operation and all child operations.
OutputList	Contains a comma-separated list of columns being projected by the current operation.
Warnings	Contains a comma-separated list of warning messages relating to the current operation.
Type	Node type.
Parallel	0 = Operator is not running in parallel. 1 = Operator is running in parallel.
EstimateExecutions	Estimated number of times this operator will be executed while running the current query.

In Figure 5.6, not all columns are shown due to the limited width of the screen. Not all columns will contain data for every statement plan. It is recommended that you run several statements and view the results of the columns to get used to the format of the nongraphic plans.

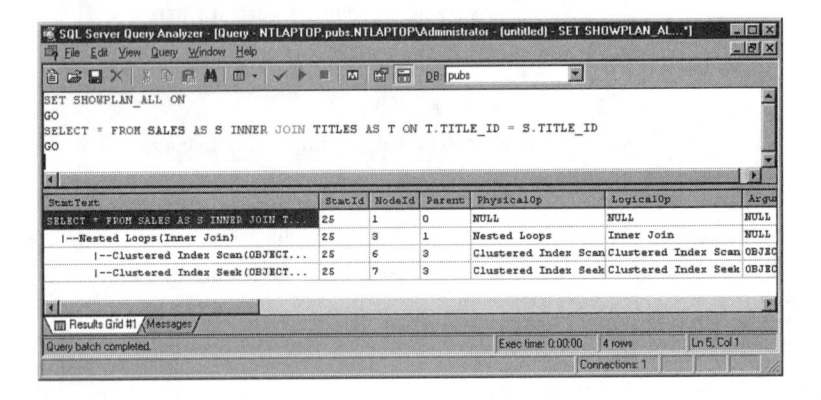

FIGURE 5.6
SHOWPLAN_ALL when set on.

UPDATE STATISTICS

UPDATE STATISTICS updates information about the distribution of key values for one or more statistics groups (collections) in the specified table. UPDATE STATISTICS runs automatically when an index is created on a table that already contains data. The syntax of the UPDATE STATISTICS command is as follows:

```
UPDATE STATISTICS table
    [index ¦ (statistics name[,...n])]
    [ WITH [ [FULLSCAN] ¦ SAMPLE number {PERCENT ¦ ROWS}]]
    [[,] [ALL ¦ COLUMNS ¦ INDEX]
    [[,] NORECOMPUTE]
```

The table name must be specified because index names are not unique within each database. However, specifying the database or table owner is optional. If no index is specified, the statistics for all indexes within the table will be updated. The index statistics are updated based on the information about the statistics group/collection in the system histogram. The histogram records statistical information reflecting index page usage. The creation of statistics groups is accommodated through the use of the CREATE STATISTICS statement. The SQL syntax structure of the CREATE STATISTICS statement follows this paragraph. When using UPDATE STATISTICS, you can specify whether the statement is to affect column statistics, index statistics, or all existing statistics. If no option is specified, the UPDATE STATISTICS statement affects all statistics. Only one type (ALL, COLUMNS, or INDEX) can be specified in an UPDATE STATISTICS statement.

```
CREATE STATISTICS statistics name ON table (column [,...n])
    [ WITH [ [ FULLSCAN ¦ SAMPLE number PERCENT ] [,] ] [
    ↪NORECOMPUTE] ]
```

The CREATE STATISTICS statement creates the histogram and associated density groups over the supplied column(s). UPDATE STATISTICS can then work with the associated information when called upon to keep the statistics up to date. Only the table owner can create statistics on that table. The owner of a table can create a statistics group at any time even if there is no data in the table. Users can create statistics on nonindexed columns by using the CREATE STATISTICS statement.

You can specify FULLSCAN when creating or updating statistics. When you do, all rows will be read to gather statistics. This behavior is identical to SAMPLE 100 PERCENT; thus, FULLSCAN cannot be used with SAMPLE. When sampling for the creation or updating of statistics, you supply the percentage of the data to be read. SQL Server uses a random sampling algorithm to gather statistics. If you do not supply the SAMPLE or FULLSCAN option, a sample fraction is computed by SQL Server to use as a basis for the statistics. When updating statistics, you can specify the number of rows to sample; this is advantageous when collecting statistics for larger tables. SQL Server ensures that a minimum number of values are sampled to provide useful statistics. If you set the sample value of the sample too low, SQL Server will make an adjustment and correct the sampling based on the number of existing rows in the table. When statistics are created or updated, the SQL Server default behavior is to perform a sample scan on the target table. SQL Server automatically computes the required sample size. A table smaller than eight megabytes will always be scanned completely.

You can choose to disable the automatic tabulation of out-of-date statistics by specifying the NORECOMPUTE option. If this option is specified, SQL Server continues to use previously created statistics. These statistics can become outdated as the data changes. If the statistics are not automatically updated and maintained by SQL Server, the execution plans might result in less than optimal performance. Whether statistics become outdated depends upon the number of INSERT, UPDATE, and DELETE operations performed on indexed columns. It is strongly recommended that you allow SQL Server to update the statistics so that this option is used only in rare circumstances.

If you want to set NORECOMPUTE and then at a later date revert back to the automatic recalculation of statistics, simply reissue the UPDATE STATISTICS statement without the NORECOMPUTE option or execute sp_autostats. The sp_autostats stored procedure displays or changes the automatic setting for an index and statistics. It is also possible to tell SQL Server not to maintain statistics for a given column or index by using the STATISTICS_NORECOMPUTE clause of the CREATE INDEX statement. The SQL syntax for the sp_autostats stored procedure is as follows:

```
sp_autostats [@tblname =] 'table name' [, [@flagc =] 'ON | OFF']
➥[, [@indname =] 'index name']
```

Execution Plans 223

The `sp_autostats` stored procedure returns a resultset if no ON or OFF setting is provided. If ON or OFF is declared, the stored procedure simply reports the action that was taken. The resultset provides the name of the index, the current ON or OFF setting for UPDATE STATISTICS, and the date that the statistics were last updated.

SQL Server maintains statistics about the distribution of the key values in each index and uses these statistics to determine which index(es) it uses to process any given statement. Query optimization depends on the accuracy of the distribution steps. If there is a significant change in the key values in the index, rerun UPDATE STATISTICS on that index. You would also use UPDATE STATISTICS in a case where a large amount of data has been added, changed, or removed, or if the table has been truncated using the TRUNCATE TABLE statement and then repopulated. You can determine the last date that statistics were updated by using `sp_autostats` or by using the STATS_DATE function.

SQL Server enables you to create statistical information regarding the distribution of values in a column. The Query Processor can then use this statistical information and attempt to determine the optimal strategy for evaluating a query. SQL Server stores statistical information regarding the distribution of values in the indexed column(s) when you create an index. The Query Optimizer in SQL Server uses these statistics to estimate the cost of using the index for a query. You can see these cost figures by using Graphical Showplan or the SHOWPLAN_ALL/SHOWPLAN_TEXT as illustrated earlier in this chapter.

> **NOTE** The presence of outdated or missing statistics is indicated by warning errors when the execution plan of a query is graphically displayed using SQL Server Query Analyzer.

SQL Server updates statistical information as the data in the tables changes. By performing random sampling across data pages, SQL Server reads data to gather statistics. After a data page has been read from disk, all the rows on the data page are used within the sampling to update the statistical information. Sampling the data minimizes the cost of the automatic update. If desired, you can set the Auto Create Statistics and Auto Update Statistics database properties to false using the `sp_dboption` system stored procedure, but this requires more administration than using a manual update and/or manual creation of statistics.

If you choose not to maintain statistics automatically, you should perform manual updates on a regular basis. If desired, you can create statistics on all columns in all user tables using the `sp_createstats` system stored procedure. Columns not eligible for statistics include computed columns, or columns of image, text, and *n*text data types. You can delete statistics generated for a column if you no longer want to retain and maintain them. Statistics created on columns by SQL Server are automatically deleted when no longer used.

The manual creation of statistics does have some advantages, but these statistics could be created in addition to the automatically generated statistics provided by SQL Server. Statistics can be created to allow for multiple columns. Creating statistics on two or more columns together permits SQL Server to make a better estimate for a query that uses these columns.

QUERY EXECUTION PLANS

The SQL Server 7.0 Query Processor extracts information from the statistics and regathers statistics automatically, using fast sampling. This ensures that the Query Processor uses the most current statistics and reduces maintenance requirements. SQL Server implements what is known as a cost-base query analyzer as opposed to a syntax-based optimizer. The benefit of using this style of optimization is that with the cost-based solution, a choice between a variety of executions is made on the current statistics of a database, unlike a syntax-based system, which always execute the same plan regardless of the changing statistics of a database. During the life of a database, the index utilization changes as more applications that use the data are derived. The data also expands and possibly undergoes schema changes that make other indexes more relevant than those originally used. A dynamic plan takes into account any changes in database activity and always selects a plan based on the current situation.

SQL Server easily recognizes common query formats and develops execution plans that are suitable for the query type. Schemas, such as star or snowflake schemas, and queries that execute inner, outer, and self-joins, as well as standard unions can all have optimum plans developed based on the needs of the individual query. SQL Server selects an execution plan based on a careful cost analysis.

SQL Server 7.0 is less sensitive to index-selection issues than previous releases. It is now far easier to maintain an implementation with less concern for administrative configuration and developer fine tuning. The cost-based Query Optimizer can be rapidly adapted for new or refined execution strategies. SQL Server constantly redefines the execution plan to suit the changing needs of a database.

Some query limitations that were present in past releases have been loosened or completely removed. A single query can now reference 32 tables. The number of internal worktables used by a query is no longer limited. OLE DB provides the SQL Server Query Processor with distributed and heterogeneous query capabilities. SQL Server 7.0 supports parallel execution of a single query across multiple processors. A CPU-bound query that must examine a large number of rows often benefits if portions of its execution plan run in parallel on other available processors. SQL Server 7.0 makes the determination as to which queries benefit from parallelism and generates a parallel execution plan.

As defined previously, SQL Server supports new query hints. Knowing the available hints and when each is normally used will benefit you when you are determining what is actually being performed during the preparation of SQL statements and their subsequent execution. Knowing the important role that statistics play in execution plan development will also greatly benefit you. The next two sections examine the evaluation and optimization of query plans.

Evaluation of Query Plans

To evaluate a query plan when considering alterations or overriding SQL Server, you first use the Graphical Showplan to get an idea of what the server is actually doing. As seen earlier in the chapter, you can gain further knowledge of the plan by using the text tools SHOWPLAN_ALL and SHOWPLAN_TEXT. Other tools you can use to diagnose the server activity include the SQL Server Profiler and NT/SQL Server Performance Monitor, both discussed later in this chapter.

Other techniques that you need to fully evaluate a query include the DBCC SHOW_STATISTICS statement and the ability to run a SELECT query against any of the system tables. DBCC SHOW_STATISTICS displays the current distribution statistics for the specified target on the specified table. System Tables provide the information used by SQL Server and its components.

DBCC SHOW_STATISTICS returns a resultset that indicates the selectivity of an index. The lower the density returned by the statement, the higher the selectivity. The statistics provide the basis for determining whether an index is useful to the Optimizer. The results returned by SQL Server are based on distribution steps of the index.

System Tables

System tables provide the essential information needed for SQL Server to perform its operations. Some of the tables reside only in the master database, others in the MSDB SQL Server Agent database, and still others in user databases. Additionally, there is a whole category of system tables responsible for the distribution/replication process. System tables should not be altered directly by any user but can be queried at any time by using a standard SELECT operation.

Although it's possible to query the system tables directly, you should not write applications to do so; instead, you should use information schema views, system stored procedures database API calls, or SQL-DMO. If you are working directly with the server, however, you may want simply to access the system tables through the use of Transact-SQL. This is desirable when you are after the true information or want to query a series of tables. The format of the system tables is dependent upon the internal architecture of SQL Server and can change from release to release. Therefore, you might have to change applications that directly access the system tables before they can access a later version of SQL Server.

Table 5.2 summarizes the complete set of system tables available in SQL Server. We will discuss a few of these tables in more detail but it is recommended that you get more information from SQL Server books online with regard to the others. The types of tables available are as follows:

- **System Tables in the Master Database Only.** These tables store server-level system information.
- **System Tables in Every Database.** These tables store database-level system information for each database.
- **SQL Server Agent Tables in the MSDB Database.** These tables store information used by SQL Server Agent.
- **Tables in the MSDB Database.** These tables store information used by database backup and restore operations.
- **Tables Used to Store Replication Information.** These tables are used by replication and stored in the master database.
- **Tables Used by Replication and Stored in the Distribution Database.**
- **Tables Used by Replication and Stored in the User's Database.**

TABLE 5.2

System Tables in the Master Database Only

sysaltfiles	sysdevices	sysoledbusers
syscacheobjects	syslanguages	sysperfinfo
syscharsets	syslockinfo	sysprocesses
sysconfigures	syslogins	sysremotelogins
syscurconfigs	sysmessages	sysservers
sysdatabases		

System Tables in Every Database

sysallocations	sysfiles	sysobjects
syscolumns	sysforeignkeys	syspermissions
syscomments	sysfulltextcatalogs	sysprotects

continues

TABLE 5.2 continued

System Tables in Every Database

sysconstraints	sysindexes	sysreferences
sysdepends	sysindexkeys	systypes
sysfilegroups	sysmembers	sysusers

SQL Server Agent Tables in the MSDB Database

sysalerts	sysjobschedules	systargetservergroupmembers
syscategories	sysjobservers	systargetservergroups
sysdownloadlist	sysjobsteps	systargetservers
sysjobhistory	sysnotifications	systaskids
sysjobs	sysoperators	

Tables in the MSDB Database

backupfile	backupset	restorefilegroup
backupmediafamily	restorefile	restorehistory
backupmediaset		

Tables Used to Store Replication Information

sysarticles	syspublications	sysservers
sysdatabases	sysreplicationalerts	syssubscriptions
sysobjects		

Tables Used by Replication and Stored in the Distribution Database

MSagent_parameters	MSmerge_agents	Msrepl_originators
MSagent_profiles	MSmerge_history	MSrepl_transactions
MSarticles	MSmerge_subscriptions	MSrepl_version
MSdistpublishers	MSpublication_access	MSsnapshot_agents
MSdistributiondbs	Mspublications	MSsnapshot_history
MSdistribution_agents	Mspublisher_databases	MSsubscriber_info
MSdistribution_history	MSreplication_objects	MSsubscriber_schedule
MSdistributor	MSreplication subscriptions	MSsubscriptions
MSlogreader_agents	MSrepl_commands	MSsubscription_properties
MSlogreader_history	MSrepl_errors	

Tables Used by Replication and Stored in the User's Database

MSmerge_contents	MSmerge_tombstone	sysmergeschemachange
MSmerge_delete_conflicts	sysarticleupdates	sysmergesubscriptions
MSmerge_genhistory	sysmergearticles	sysmergesubsetfilters
MSmerge_replinfo	sysmergepublications	

The following list describes the new system tables available in SQL Server 7. A short description of the table purpose has been provided for quick reference. For more detailed information, check SQL Server books online with regard to each table. You will note that many of the topics covered in this book are included within the new system tables listing. It is helpful to understand the new tables and how they are implemented within any new version of a Microsoft product, not only from the exam perspective but also to be able to implement the new information into custom procedures and processes of a database environment.

- backupfile. This table contains one row per data or log file that was backed up. Each time a backup process is performed, the information is added to this system table.
- backupmediafamily. This table is used to describe each medium involved in the backup family backup set to allow for reference to each media family.
- backupmediaset. This table is used to describe the backup media set to allow for reference to each media set.
- backupset. This table is used to describe the backup set to allow for reference to each backup set.
- MSagent_parameters. This table contains parameters associated with an agent profile. Each parameter name reflects the same name as the associated property supported by the agent.
- MSagent_profiles. This table contains one row for each defined replication agent profile.
- MSarticles. This table contains one row for each article assigned to be replicated by a publisher.

- `MSdistpublishers`. This table contains one row for each remote publisher supported by the local distributor.
- `MSdistributiondbs`. This table contains one row for each distribution database defined on the local distributor.
- `MSdistribution_agents`. This table contains one row for each distribution agent running at the local distributor.
- `MSdistribution_history`. This table contains history rows for the distribution agents associated with the local distributor.
- `MSdistributor`. This table contains the distributor properties.
- `MSlogreader_agents`. This table contains one row for each log reader agent running at the local distributor.
- `MSlogreader_history`. This table contains history rows for the log reader agents associated with the local distributor.
- `MSmerge_agents`. This table contains one row for each merge agent running at the subscriber.
- `MSmerge_contents`. This table contains one row for each row modified in the current database since it was published. The merge replication process utilizes this table to determine which rows have changed.
- `MSmerge_delete_conflicts`. This table contains tombstone information for rows that were deleted and subsequently had the delete undone because it conflicted with an update performed at another replica. A row could be deleted if it lost the conflict or the delete was undone to achieve data convergence. This table is stored in the database used for conflict logging, which is usually the publishing database but can be the subscribing database if there is decentralized conflict logging.
- `MSmerge_genhistory`. This table contains one row for each generation that a subscriber knows about within the retention period. This table is used to avoid sending common generations during exchanges and to resynchronize subscribers that are restored from backups.
- `MSmerge_history`. This table contains history rows for previous updates to the subscriber.

- `MSmerge_replinfo`. This table contains one row for each replica made from the local server. This table tracks internal information about the sent and received generation.

- `MSmerge_subscriptions`. This table contains one row for each subscription serviced by the merge agent at the subscriber.

- `MSmerge_tombstone`. This table contains information on deleted rows and allows deletes to be propagated to other subscribers.

- `MSpublication_access`. This table contains a row for each SQL Server login that has access to the specific publication or publisher.

- `MSpublications`. This table contains one row for each publication that is replicated by a publisher.

- `MSpublisher_databases`. This table contains one row for each publisher/publisher database pair serviced by the local distributor.

- `MSreplication_objects`. This table contains one row for each object that is associated with replication in the subscriber database.

- `MSreplication_subscriptions`. This table contains one row or replication information for each distribution agent servicing the local subscriber database.

- `MSrepl_commands`. This table contains rows of replicated commands.

- `MSrepl_errors`. This table contains rows with extended replication agent failure information.

- `MSrepl_originators`. This table contains one row for each updateable subscriber from which the transaction originated.

- `MSrepl_transactions`. This table contains one row for each replicated transaction.

- `MSrepl_version`. This table contains one row with the current version of replication installed.

- `MSsnapshot_agents`. This table contains one row for each snapshot agent associated with the local distributor.

- `MSsnapshot_history`. This table contains history rows for the snapshot agents associated with the local distributor.

- `MSsubscriber_info`. This table contains one row for each publisher/subscriber pair that is being pushed subscriptions from the local distributor.
- `MSsubscriber_schedule`. This table contains default merge and transactional synchronization schedules for each publisher/subscriber pair.
- `MSsubscriptions`. This table contains one row for each subscription serviced by the local distributor.
- `MSsubscription_properties`. This table contains rows for the parameter information for pull distribution agents.
- `restorefile`. This table contains one row per file restore.
- `restorefilegroup`. This table contains one row per restored filegroup.
- `restorehistory`. This table contains one row per restore operation.
- `sysallocations`. This table contains one row for each allocation unit.
- `sysaltfiles`. This table contains one row for each file in a database.
- `sysarticleupdates`. This table contains information on the articles that are updated.
- `syscacheobjects`. This table contains information on how the cache is being used. The table will show the cache lookup keys.
- `syscategories`. This table contains the categories used by SQL Server Enterprise Manager to organize jobs, alerts, and operators.
- `sysdownloadlist`. This table holds the queue of download instructions for all target servers.
- `sysfiles`. This table contains information that describes each database file. This table is a virtual table that cannot be modified directly.
- `sysfilegroups`. This table contains information that describes each database filegroup. There is always at least one entry for the primary filegroup.
- `sysfulltextcatalogs`. This table provides a list of the set of full-text catalogs.

- `sysjobhistory`. This table contains information about the execution of scheduled jobs by SQL Server Enterprise Manager.
- `sysjobschedules`. This table contains schedule information for jobs to be executed by SQL Server Enterprise Manager.
- `sysjobs`. This table stores the information for each scheduled job to be executed by SQL Server Enterprise Manager.
- `sysjobservers`. This table stores the association or relationship of a particular job with one or more target servers.
- `sysjobsteps`. This table contains the information for each step in a job to be executed by SQL Server Enterprise Manager.
- `syslockinfo`. This table contains information on all granted, converting, and waiting lock requests. This table provides a denormalized tabular view of all of the internal data structures related to the Lock Manager.
- `sysmembers`. This table contains a row for each member of a database role.
- `sysmergearticles`. This table contains one row for each merge article defined in the local database.
- `sysmergepublications`. This table contains one row for each merge publication defined in the database.
- `sysmergeschemachange`. This table contains information about the last schema change.
- `sysmergesubscriptions`. This table contains one row for each known subscriber and is a local table at the publisher.
- `sysmergesubsetfilters`. This table contains join filter information for partitioned articles.
- `sysperfinfo`. This table contains a SQL Server representation of the internal performance counters that can be displayed through the Windows NT Performance Monitor. This table has no information in it when using the Windows 95/98 desktop version of SQL Server.
- `syspermissions`. This table contains information about permissions that have been granted and denied to users, groups, and roles in the database.

- `sysoledbusers`. This table contains one row for each user and password mapping for the specified linked server.

- `sysprocesses`. This table includes the addition of the open_tran column, which indicates how many transactions a process has. These processes can be client or server processes.

- `sysreplicationalerts`. This table contains information about the conditions that cause a replication alert to fire.

- `systargetservergroupmembers`. This table is used to record the target servers that are currently enlisted into this multiserver group.

- `systargetservergroups`. This table is used to record the target server groups that are currently enlisted into this multiserver environment.

- `systargetservers`. This table is used to record the target servers that are currently enlisted into this multiserver operation domain.

- `systaskids`. This table contains a mapping of tasks created in earlier versions of SQL Server to SQL Server Enterprise Manager jobs in the current version.

System tables store configuration information and definitions for all objects, users, and permissions in SQL Server. Server-level configuration information is stored in system tables in the master database. Every database contains system tables defining the users, objects, and permissions contained by the database. The master database and its system tables are created during SQL Server Setup. System tables in a user database are created automatically when the database is created. SQL Server contains system, stored procedures to report and manage the information in system tables.

Optimizing Performance

Optimizing the performance of an installation involves plenty of configuration and constant fine tuning. There are several categories in which SQL Server allows for the fine tuning of resource usage, response time, and data availability. Each of these categories is discussed briefly within this section. There is a substantial amount of information available on server fine tuning within SQL Server books online. Because the fine tuning of an implementation drastically depends upon the implementation itself, an overview of some frequently used procedures are discussed within. It is important to realize that system tuning needs to be constantly monitored and adjusted throughout the lifetime of any implementation.

Optimization falls into several different categories which are discussed in the following individual sections.

Backup/Restore Optimization

To optimize the performance of backup and restore operations, you can use several methods offered by SQL Server.

Using multiple backup devices is a sure technique that was initially implemented because of the slow performance of tape systems. Although tape performance has improved drastically, using multiple backup devices is still a cost-effective method for improving performance. It is important to note that if you use multiple drives for the backup, it is not necessary to have the same number of drives available for the restore. This allows the restore to be performed on a separate server with a different configuration, or in the event of a failure, to one of the drives.

You should implement a combination of backup strategies including full database, differential database, and transaction log backups to minimize the time necessary to recover from a failure and to maximize the server usage while a dynamic backup is being performed. Although substantial improvements have been made to the techniques the SQL Server uses to perform a dynamic backup, you might still notice a reduction in performance while a backup is taking place. As in previous versions, there is no need to take the data offline to perform a backup.

Differential database backups reduce the size of the transaction log that must be applied to recover the database and they perform operations in less time than the time it would take to create a full database backup. The creation of a differential-database backup copies only the data that has changed since the last full backup.

Spreading the database files among several logical drives can increase parallel read operations. The performance of parallel writes can be improved by using more backup devices.

Generally, the bottleneck will be either the database files or the backup devices. If the total read throughput is greater than the total backup device throughput, the bottleneck is on the backup device side. Adding more backup devices and better hard-drive controllers can improve performance. If the total backup throughput is greater than the total read throughput, you can increase the read throughput by adding more database files on devices or by using more disks in the RAID device.

Optimizing tempdb Performance

There are a couple of methods for improving the performance of temporary operations through the fine tuning of tempdb. Remember that tempdb is utilized anytime SQL Server needs a temporary storage location for recordsets. The common recommendations for the physical placement and database options for the tempdb database are set so that tempdb can automatically expand as needed. Set the original size of the tempdb database files to a reasonable size to avoid the files from automatically expanding as more space is needed. If the tempdb database expands too frequently, performance can be affected. The definition of reasonable varies from system to system and must be periodically tested to ensure optimum performance.

Set the file growth increment percentage to a reasonable size to avoid the tempdb database files from growing by too small a value. If the file growth is too small compared to amount of data being written to the tempdb database, tempdb might need to expand constantly, which affects performance. Again, reasonable varies from system to system.

Place the tempdb database on a fast I/O subsystem to ensure good perfomance. Stripe the tempdb database across multiple disks for better performance. Use filegroups to place the tempdb database on disks different than those used by user databases.

Optimizing Bulk Copy Performance

To bulk copy data as quickly as possible, several options are available to specify how data should be bulk copied into SQL Server using the bcp utility or the BULK INSERT statement. In some cases, it is faster to drop indexes and perform a fast bulk copy than to recreate the indexes. In cases where there are a considerable number of complex indexes, it is probably faster to perform a slow bulk copy. Using the BULK INSERT statement almost always produces faster results than using the bcp command-line utility.

There are essentially two contributing factors that help to determine the performance in which a bulk operation performs its activity. The first of these factors is the amount of existing data in the table compared to the amount of data to be copied into the table. The second factor, as previously discussed, is the number, types, and sizes of indexes. Additionally, you can expect variations on the performance levels when data is bulk copied into a table from a single client or in parallel from multiple clients.

If nonclustered indexes are also present on the table, drop these before you copy data into the table. It is generally faster to bulk copy data into a table without nonclustered indexes and then recreate the nonclustered indexes, than to bulk copy data into a table with the nonclustered indexes in place.

When you load data in parallel from multiple clients, you achieve higher performance if you run SQL Server on a computer with more than one processor. Because SQL Server automatically multithreads this operation, you achieve faster results where the data to be bulk copied into the table can be partitioned into separate data files. You must drop all indexes from the table. Consider recreating the secondary indexes in parallel by creating each secondary index from a separate client at the same time.

With all forms of bulk copy operations use a TABLOCK hint. The TABLOCK hint causes a table-level lock to be taken for the duration of the bulk-copy operation. Use a single batch with the ROWS_PER_BATCH hint set to the size of the entire recordset. When you are copying data between computers perform all bulk-copy operations using either native or unicode native format.

Optimizing Database and Transaction Log Performance

Create the transaction log on a separate, physical disk. The transaction log file is written sequentially, and using a separate, dedicated disk allows the disk heads to stay in place for the next write operation. Ensure that the original size of the transaction log is sufficient to prevent the file from automatically expanding as more transaction log space is needed. Monitor the size of the log and attempt to have sufficient space available at all times. Set the file growth increment percentage to a reasonable size to prevent the file from growing by too small a value. If the file growth is too small compared to the number of log records being written to the transaction log, the transaction log might need to expand constantly, affecting performance. This is true for most database and log files.

You gain some performance by manually shrinking files rather than allowing SQL Server to shrink the files automatically. Shrinking the transaction log can affect performance on a busy system due to the movement and locking of data pages. Shrinking other files can affect system performance especially where the number of records in a file fluctuates frequently.

Optimizing Server Performance

You can improve server memory and I/O performance through adjustments to the server configuration options for the memory manager and the I/O system. Because the memory in SQL Server 7 is configured dynamically, the server can be seriously effected if options are not optimized. I/O is needed in every level of SQL Server operations; fine-tuning the operations from the outset for high performance should be the mandate of any database implementor or administrator.

You can use the `Min Server Memory` configuration option to ensure that SQL Server starts with the minimum amount of allocated memory. Use the `Max Server Memory` configuration option to specify the maximum amount of memory SQL Server can allocate when it starts and while it runs. An overview of all operations performed by the server will be necessary in fine tuning these options.

> **NOTE** Server configuration is a must for database administrators. If you are taking the administering certification exam, you should spend a lot of time on the configuration options available for SQL Server 7.

You can use the `Max Worker Threads` configuration option on a server running on NT to specify the number of threads used to support the users connected to SQL Server. The default setting of 255 might be too high for some configurations, depending on the number of concurrent users.

Set the configuration value to the number of concurrent connections, but it cannot exceed 1,024. A Windows 95/98 SQL Server installation doesn't support this option.

The Index Create Memory configuration option controls the amount of memory used by sort operations during index creation. Index creation should be performed as seldom as possible on a production server, and it should be left to off-peak times. Increasing this value can improve the performance of index creation. Keep the Min Memory Per Query configuration option at a lower number.

The Min Memory Per Query configuration option can specify the minimum amount of memory that will be allocated for the execution of a query. When there are many queries executing concurrently in a system, increase this value to improve the performance of memory-intensive queries, such as substantial sort and hash operations. You should not set the value too high on busy systems. The query will have to wait until it can secure the minimum memory requested or until the value specified in the query wait server configuration option is exceeded.

You can use the Max Async IO configuration option to configure the maximum number of outstanding asynchronous disk I/O requests that the computer can issue against a file. For very sophisticated I/O subsystems with many disks and controllers, you can increase the value from the default of 32 to 64 or higher. Monitor disk write activity using Windows NT Performance Monitor, and watch for spikes caused by the lazy writer. If spikes occur that cause the LogicalDisk: %Disk Time counter to peak, lower the value of this configuration option.

The Recovery Interval configuration option controls when SQL Server issues a checkpoint. By default, SQL Server determines the best time to perform checkpoint operations. To determine whether the value is appropriate for this setting, monitor disk write activity on the database files using Windows NT Performance Monitor. Spikes of activity that cause disk utilization to reach 100 percent can affect performance.

Much of the performance within SQL Server depends on the usage of the server. The number of concurrent users, the types of operations they perform, and the tables in which the activity is performed against all affect server performance. In cases where users all access the same data for different activities, the loss in performance is related to the loss of access to data due to locking. The next section examines locking behavior in more detail and looks at how to resolve problems relating to locking.

Locking Problems

As multiple users require access to the same data, it becomes a challenge for the implementor to provide access to those requiring and maintain the integrity of the data. Several problems relate to the locking of data. The blocking of user-requested data by another user or process is the most common problem. The deadlocking of data, where two processes request data in which the other has locked, provides a particularly interesting problem; data is needed by both processes but can't be obtained by either without the release of the other's lock.

SQL Server 7 implements locking in a far more granular style than previous versions. This granularity helps to resolve some of the possible locking problems. By allowing for locking of individual rows, less data is kept from other users who need to perform their own operations free from the restrictions of locks. With row-level locking comes a substantial amount of overhead as the number of locks increase. SQL Server dynamically adjusts locking to the page or table level if it deems it necessary because of the amount of data needing to be locked.

Although locking strategies from an application development process have not changed considerably, there are some new developments and some traditional techniques useful for avoiding excessive locking. One of the main developmental rules to remember as you develop applications is to maintain the scope of activity within the application. That is, if an application does not need to update data, make sure to use a cursor that has applicable limitations. Not only does this improve the performance of the application itself, but it also allows others to access the data without unnecessary locking levels.

The next two sections investigate the techniques you can use to diagnose possible locking problems and the methods to solve some of these problems. Keep in mind that the strategies used for locking and solving locking problems have to be adjusted to suit each application and the system in which the application runs.

Locking Diagnosis

Several tools, utilities, and procedures are available to help you find information about the levels, types, and numbers of locks that are in effect. You can obtain general information about the number and types of locks currently in place by using the Enterprise Manager and the following procedure:

1. Select the desired server and unfold the listing of objects by selecting the plus sign (+).

2. Open the management folder to display the management tools and statistics objects.

3. Select and open the Current Activity object.

In the Current Activity object, you can find out information about the server processes, database users, and current locking activity. Process Info provides a listing of all processes active on the server and identifies the spid (server process identifier) and current user and database information (see Figure 5.7).

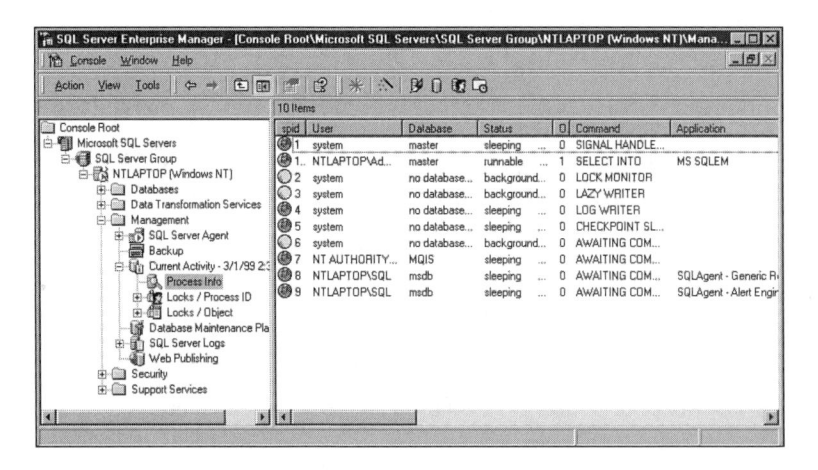

FIGURE 5.7
Process Info.

242 CHAPTER 5 Maintaining a Database

The remainder of the information found under the Current Activity option relates to the current process and object locks in effect within the server. The lock information is organized in two folders. The first folder identifies the locks by processor ID, and the second organizes locks by object. Using these folders, you can view the databases that are currently holding locks and the number and types of locks being held.

Alternatively, you can use the `sp_lock` stored procedure to obtain information about the current locks being held by the server. The active lock information is displayed in report format (see Figure 5.8).

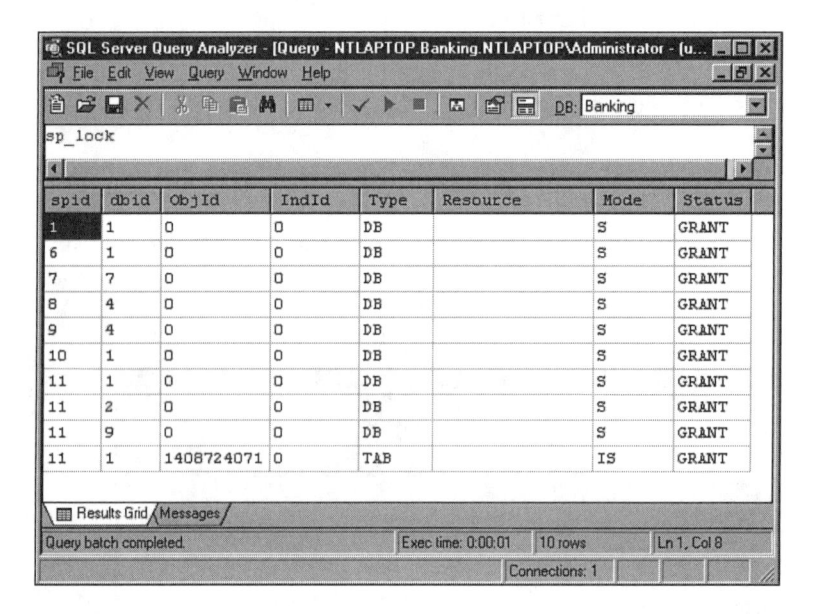

spid	dbid	ObjId	IndId	Type	Resource	Mode	Status
1	1	0	0	DB		S	GRANT
6	1	0	0	DB		S	GRANT
7	7	0	0	DB		S	GRANT
8	4	0	0	DB		S	GRANT
9	4	0	0	DB		S	GRANT
10	1	0	0	DB		S	GRANT
11	1	0	0	DB		S	GRANT
11	2	0	0	DB		S	GRANT
11	9	0	0	DB		S	GRANT
11	1	1408724071	0	TAB		IS	GRANT

FIGURE 5.8
Output from `sp_lock`.

The Type column shows the type of the resource currently locked by the server, as shown in the Table 5.3.

TABLE 5.3
Resource Lock Types

Resource Type	Description
RID	Row identifier, used to individually apply row-level locking on a single row within a table.
KEY	Rowlock within an index that protects index key ranges in serializable transactions.
PAG	Identifies either a data or index page.
EXT	Indicates an extent lock of a contiguous group of eight data or index pages.
TAB	Entire table, including all data and indexes.
DB	Database.

The Resource column provides information about the resource being locked by the server, as shown in Table 5.4.

TABLE 5.4
Resources Locked

Resource Type	Description
RID	Row identifier of the locked row within the table. The row is identified by a file ID : page : rid combination, where rid is the row identifier on the page.
KEY	Hexadecimal number used internally by SQL Server.
PAG	Page number. The page is identified by a file ID : page combination, where file id is the file ID in the sysfiles table, and page is the logical page number within that file.
EXT	First page number in the extent being locked. The page is identified by a file ID : page combination.
TAB	No information is provided because the ObjId column already contains the object ID of the table.
DB	No information is provided because the dbid column already contains the database ID of the database.

The mode column describes the type of lock being applied to the resource. The types of locks include any multigranular lock. The multigranular locks are identified by the following characteristics:

- Shared (S). Used for operations that do not change or update data and require only read-only types of locks.
- Update (U). Used on resources that can be updated. Prevents a common form of deadlock that occurs when multiple sessions are reading, locking, and then potentially updating resources later.
- Exclusive (X). Used for data-modification operations to ensure that multiple updates cannot be made to the same resource at the same time.
- Intent(I). Used to establish a lock hierarchy.
- Schema(Sch-M, Sch-S). Used when an operation dependent on the schema of a table is executing. There are two types of schema locks: schema stability (Sch-S) and schema modification (Sch-M).
- Bulk update (BU). Used when bulk copying data into a table and the TABLOCK hint is specified.

The Status column shows whether the lock has been obtained (GRANT), is blocking on another process (WAIT), or is being converted to another lock (CNVT). A lock being converted to another lock is held in one mode but waits to acquire a stronger lock mode. When diagnosing blocking issues, a CNVT can be considered similar to a WAIT.

There are many other SQL Server tools for monitoring locking activity; using sp_lock or the Enterprise Manager to display locking information may not always be feasible when many locks are held and released faster than they can be displayed. In this case, SQL Server Profiler can be used to monitor and record locking information. SQL Server Profiler is discussed later in this chapter. Windows NT Performance Monitor can be used to monitor lock activity using the SQL Server Locks Object counter. Many counters are available for observance of SQL Server behavior, including those involving locking.

SQL Server Profiler tracks engine process events, such as the start of a batch or a transaction. Windows NT Performance Monitor gives you the ability to monitor server performance and activity using predefined objects and counters or user-defined counters to monitor events.

Windows NT Performance Monitor collects counts of the events rather than data about the events. Thresholds can be set on specific counters to generate alerts that notify operators. Windows NT Performance Monitor mainly tracks resource usage, such as the number of buffer manager page requests that are in use.

Windows NT Performance Monitor works only on Microsoft Windows NT and can monitor SQL Server running only on Windows NT. At times, Performance Monitor can be used to monitor server behavior. For more information about using Windows NT Performance Monitor, see Windows NT Performance Monitor Help or your Windows NT documentation. SQL Server Profiler provides you with the ability to monitor server and database activity. You can capture SQL Server Profiler data to a SQL Server table or a file for later analysis and replay the events captured on SQL Server.

After locking information has been gathered, you have to determine which (if any) configuration alterations or application modifications can resolve locking problems. Some information to be considered is presented in the following section. Not all methods will be utilized in all cases. Continued monitoring helps to determine whether the proposed solutions had the desired effect on the system.

Resolving Locking Problems

There is no one bona fide solution that resolves all locking situations. You can selectively set priorities for locking resolutions and hope to minimize the impact of locking. There are some common practices that you can use to design applications to implement different locking mechanisms. There are also statements you can use to fine tune locking behavior.

One configuration option that you can use is the selection of a deadlock victim. Normally, SQL Server selects the process that can most easily be reversed as the victim of a deadlock situation and rolls back anything the process has already done. You can control the way the session reacts when in deadlock situation occurs by setting the DEADLOCK_PRIORITY to LOW or a specific value to within a character variable. Deadlock situations arise when two or more processes have data locked and each individual process cannot release its lock until other processes have released their locks.

Setting the priority to LOW specifies that the current session is the preferred deadlock victim. The deadlock victim's transaction is automatically rolled back by the server, and the deadlock error message 1204 is returned to the client application. Alternatively, a character variable specifying the deadlock-handling method can be set where a content of 3 identifies LOW, and a 6 is NORMAL.

You can specify the number of milliseconds a statement waits for a lock to be released. LOCK_TIMEOUT can be used to set a time in milliseconds that will pass before SQL Server returns a locking error. A value of -1 (default) indicates no time-out period (wait forever). A value of 0 means not to wait at all and return a message as soon as a lock is encountered.

Locking hints can be used within SQL Server to allow for a specific level of locking behavior overriding level selected by the server lock manager. You can select from four different behaviors READ_ONLY, OPTIMISTIC WITH VALUES, OPTIMISTIC WITH ROW VERSIONING, and SCROLL LOCKS. Behavior changes based on the hints given with the SQL statement.

With READ_ONLY behavior, positioned updates through the cursor are not allowed and no locks are held on the rows that make up the resultset. When using OPTIMISTIC WITH VALUES, no locks are held on the underlying rows, which helps maximize throughput. The OPTIMISTIC WITH ROW VERSIONING behavior acts each time a row with a timestamp column is modified in any way; the server stores the current database timestamp value in the column. SCROLL LOCKS behavior implements pessimistic data control and locks the data as soon as the fetch of data is performed.

These cursor concurrency options might generate scroll locks, depending on the hints specified in the SELECT statement in a cursor definition. Scroll locks acquired on each row are held until the next fetch or the close of the cursor. Scroll locks are independent of transaction locks and can persist past a commit or rollback operation. If the option to close cursors on commit is off, a COMMIT does not close any open cursors and scroll locks are preserved past the commit to maintain the isolation of the fetched data.

The types of scroll locks acquired depend on the cursor concurrency option and the locking hints in the cursor SELECT statement. Table 5.5 summarizes the locking activity in various combinations.

TABLE 5.5

LOCKING COMPARISON: CONCURRENCY USING SEPARATE HINTS

Locking Hints	Read Only	Optimistic with Values	Optimistic with Row Versioning	Locking
No Hints	No locking	No locking	No locking	Update
NOLOCK*	No locking	No locking	No locking	No locking
HOLDLOCK	Share	Share	Share	Update
UPDLOCK	Error	Update	Update	Update
TABLOCKX	Error	No locking	No locking	Update
All Others	No locking	No locking	No locking	Update

*Makes a cursor read-only.

In Transact-SQL cursors, the READ_ONLY, SCROLL_LOCK, and OPTIMISTIC keywords are indicated on the DECLARE CURSOR statement. The OPTIMISTIC keyword specifies optimistic with row versioning; Transact-SQL cursors do not support the optimistic with values concurrency option. In ADO applications, you indicate adLockReadOnly, adLockPessimistic, adLockOptimistic, or adLockBatchOptimistic in the LockType property of a Recordset object. In ODBC applications, you can set the statement attribute SQL_ATTR_CONCURRENCY to SQL_CONCUR_READ_ONLY, SQL_CONCUR_ROWVER, SQL_CONCUR_VALUES, or SQL_CONCUR_LOCK. In DB-Library applications, you can set the dbcursoropen parameter *concuropt* to CUR_READONLY, CUR_OPTCC (for optimistic using row versioning), CUR_OPTCCVAL, or CUR_LOCKCC. For additional information, see Locking Hints in SQL Server books online.

To fully diagnose locking behavior, you can use the SQL Server Profiler to monitor the locking behavior over time. The next section describes the considerations and usage of this tool.

SQL SERVER PROFILER

The SQL Server Profiler is a graphic tool that captures a continuous record of server activity in real time (see Figure 5.9). SQL Server Profiler can monitor many different server events and event categories, filter

248 CHAPTER 5 Maintaining a Database

these events with user-specified criteria, and output a trace to the screen, a file, or another server. SQL Server Profiler is the ideal tool to use for observing system activities. You can use the Profiler to step through problematic queries, find and diagnose slow-running queries, capture the series of SQL statements that lead to a problem, and monitor the performance of the server.

> **NOTE**
> This is the new toy in SQL Server and you can count on it being covered on the exam. In fact, it will be covered on all three SQL-related exams.

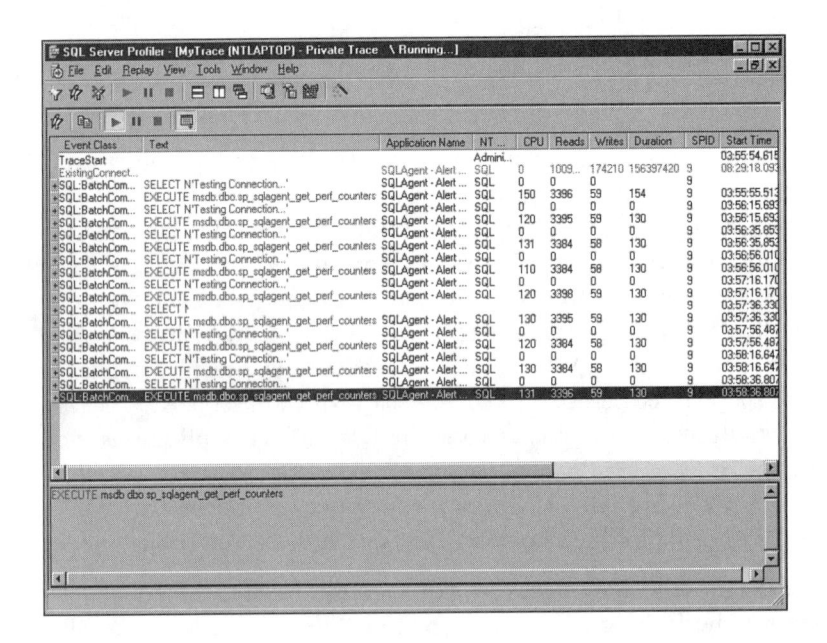

FIGURE 5.9
SQL Server Profiler.

SQL Server Profiler is essentially used to monitor engine events. You can use the Profiler to see security-related events by monitoring login connects, fails, and disconnects. SQL Server Profiler is an excellent tool fog diagnosing system usage, particularly the use of Transact-SQL SELECT, INSERT, UPDATE, and DELETE statements. You can also use Profiler to monitor the batch status of a remote procedure call. It is useful for monitoring stored procedures to find a long-running procedure or to identify the start or end of statements. The Profiler also serves as a debugging tool in that it can identify errors written to the SQL Server error log. You can also use Profiler to monitor locking for the purpose of locating deadlock situations.

Data about each monitored event can be captured and saved to a file or SQL Server table for later analysis. Creating traces collects data about the engine events. The data captured can be in the form of the type/class of event, the name of the computer on which the client is running, the text of the Transact-SQL statement or stored procedure being executed, and other information identifying the time and place of the event.

The captured event data can be filtered so that only a subset of the event data is actually collected. This can enable you to collect only the event data in which you are interested. SQL Server Profiler allows captured event data to be replayed against SQL Server, thereby effectively re-executing the saved events as they originally occurred. SQL Server Profiler provides a graphical user interface to a set of extended stored procedures. You can also use these extended stored procedures directly.

The next section looks at SQL Server Profiler's ability to monitor performance, select events, and filter events to obtain the desired captured data.

Identifying Events Using Profiler

When you create a new trace using SQL Server Profiler, the trace is defined with a set of default event classes. You can remove any of these event classes and/or add others (see Figure 5.10). Each time a new trace is created, the default event classes will be present unless explicitly removed. The default event classes are Connect, Disconnect, Existing Connection, RPC:Completed and SQL:Batch Completed. Each of these defaults are defined as follows:

250 CHAPTER 5 Maintaining a Database

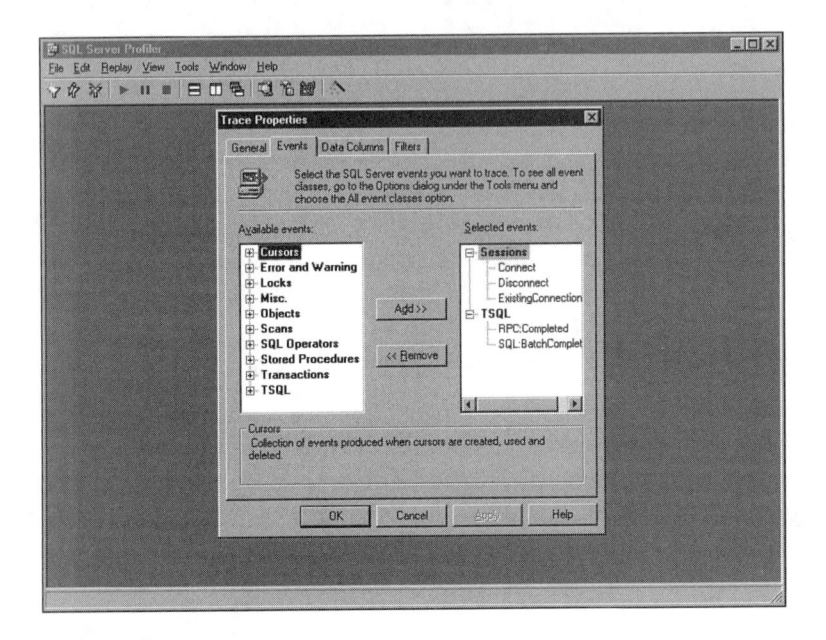

FIGURE 5.10
Trace Properties dialog box.

- Connect. The connection event has occurred, such as a client requesting a connection to a server running SQL Server. These events are grouped within the Session event category.

- Disconnect. The disconnect event has occurred, such as a client issuing a disconnect command. These events are grouped within the Session event category.

- Existing Connection. The activity by all users that were logged on before the trace started has been detected. These events are grouped within the Session event category.

- RPC:Completed. RPC has completed. This event is grouped within the TSQL event category.

- SQL:Batch Completed. Transact-SQL batch has completed. This event is grouped within the TSQL event category.

Other events that you can select enable you to monitor locking, transactions, cursor, errors and warnings, and essentially all SQL Server engine activity.

You can use the Cursors event classes to monitor all cursor operations including opening, closing, executing, and a wide array of other classes and subclasses. By monitoring the cursor classes, you can determine when a cursor is executed and what type of cursor is used. These event classes are useful for determining the actual cursor type used for an operation by SQL Server rather than the cursor type specified by the application. For more information on cursor classes and subclasses, and their use with SQL Server, see SQL Server Books Online, Cursor Events.

You can use the errors and warnings event classes to monitor many of the errors and warnings that are raised by SQL Server and other components, such as OLE DB. By monitoring these errors, you can determine whether there are errors occurring within the server engine, in a particular database, or through the use of user executed operations. The Execution Warnings event class can be monitored to determine if and how long queries had to wait for resources before proceeding. Use the Sort Warnings event class to monitor query performance. The Hash Warning event class can monitor when a hash recursion or hash bail has occurred during a hashing operation. For more information on errors and warnings classes and subclasses, and their use with SQL Server, see SQL Server Books Online, Error and Warning Events.

You use the locks event classes to monitor SQL Server lock activity. By monitoring the locks event classes, you can investigate contention issues caused by concurrent users and applications. Use the Lock:Acquired and Lock:Released event classes to monitor when objects are being locked. Use the Lock:Deadlock, Lock:Deadlock Chain, and Lock:Timeout event classes to monitor when deadlocks and time-out conditions occur. Because lock events are so constantly occurring, capturing the lock event classes can incur significant overhead on the server being traced and result in very large trace files or trace tables. For more information on locks classes and subclasses, and their use with SQL Server, see SQL Server Books Online, Locks Events.

You use the miscellaneous event classes to monitor a variety of event classes not found in the other event categories, such as failed logins and query plans. By monitoring the Attention event class, you can determine whether attention events are occurring. The generation of a high number of attention events could indicate a network communication problem between the clients and SQL Server that needs further investigation. Monitoring the LoginFailed event class is useful for monitoring security and performing logon auditing. By monitoring the Event Subclass, and the SQL User Name or NT User Name default data columns, you can determine which users are failing to connect to SQL Server and why. For more information on miscellaneous classes and subclasses and their use with SQL Server, see SQL Server Books Online, Miscellaneous Events.

Use the objects event classes to monitor when an object, such as a database, table, index, view, or stored procedure is opened, created, deleted, or used. By monitoring the Object:Opened event class, you can determine which objects are most commonly used. The Object:Created and Object:Deleted event classes determine if many ad hoc objects are being created or deleted. By monitoring the SQL User Name and NT User Name default data columns in addition to the objects event classes, you can determine the name of the user who is creating, deleting, or accessing objects. Because practically everything in SQL Server is an object, capturing the objects event classes can incur significant overhead on the server being traced and result in large trace files or trace tables. For more information on objects classes and subclasses, and their use with SQL Server, see SQL Server Books Online, Objects Events.

You use the scans event classes to monitor when a table or index is being scanned during the execution of a query. By using the Scan:Started and Scan:Stopped event classes, it is possible to monitor the type of scans being performed by a query on a specific object. By monitoring the Index ID default data column, you can determine the identification number of the index being used by a specific query. For more information on scans classes and subclasses, and their usage with SQL Server, see SQL Server Books Online, Scans Events.

Use the SQL operators event classes to monitor when a DELETE, INSERT, SELECT, or UPDATE query occurs. You can use the Event Subclass data column for each operator that can be used for monitoring whether the Query Optimizer generates a parallel query execution plan for the specific SQL operator. For more information on SQL Operators classes and subclasses, and their use with SQL Server, see SQL Server Books Online, SQL Operators Events.

Use the stored procedures event classes to monitor the execution of stored procedures. By monitoring the SP:CacheHit and SP:CacheMiss event classes, you can determine how often stored procedures are found in the cache. By monitoring the Object ID of the SP:CacheHit event class, you can determine which stored procedures reside in the cache.you can use the `SP:CacheInsert`, `SP:CacheRemove`, and `SP:Recompile` event classes to determine which stored procedures are brought into cache, first executed, and then later removed from the cache. Monitoring the `SP:Starting`, `SP:StmtStarting`, `SP:StmtCompleted`, and `SP:Completed` event classes and all the TSQL event classes monitors the execution of a stored procedure. Use the `SP:ExecContextHit` event class to monitor execution contexts. If the `SP:ExecContextHit` event class is not generated for a stored procedure, the stored procedure has no execution-time, cachable queries. For more information on stored procedure classes and subclasses, and their use with SQL Server, see SQL Server Books Online, Stored Procedure Events.

You use the transactions event classes to monitor the status of transactions. Use the `DTCTransaction` event class to monitor the state of MS DTC transactions. You should monitor the `SQLTransaction` event class when testing your application stored procedures or triggers. Use the `TransactionLog` event class when you want to monitor activity in the SQL Server transaction log. For more information on Transaction classes and subclasses, and their use with SQL Server, see SQL Server Books Online, Transaction Events.

The TSQL event classes can be used to monitor the execution and completion of a remote procedure call, a batch, and a Transact-SQL statement. By monitoring the TSQL event classes and the events using single stepping, you can monitor your application queries. The `SQL:BatchStarting` event class shows the Transact-SQL submitted in a batch; whereas the `SQL:StmtStarting` event class shows the individual statement within a batch. By replaying the `SQL:BatchCompleted` and `RPC:Completed` event classes, any results returned by the batch or RPC are displayed and you can check them to ensure that they match the results you are expecting. Monitoring the Start Time, End Time, and Duration default data columns shows when the events start and complete, and how long each RPC, batch, or statement takes to complete. By grouping events based on the Duration default data column, you can easily determine the longest running queries. You can also monitor the NT User Name and SQL User Name default data columns to identify users who submit these queries.

PUTTING IT ALL TOGETHER

By using the entire set of SQL tools, system tables, and configuration capabilities, you can provide for an environment that is best suited to the needs of the user. The following example provides a basic illustration of the application of design basics through to the diagramming actual resulting code.

Although you will not see this identical topic on the exam, it does bring together elements of four or five questions that I saw on the exam. I have placed the material here as a conclusion to this portion of the book, providing an overview of several exam topics. The example I have chosen represents a self-join where a table is joined to that same table for the purpose of combining elements in a hierarchical fashion.

In this case, a listing of employees and their managers is desired from a singular employee table. Each employee record contains the employee code of their manager under the `mgr_id` column. The first step in this exercise would be to design a foreign key constraint tying the `mgr_id` column to the `emp_id` column of the employee table. Figure 5.11 shows the physical design diagram of just such a relationship. It is important to note that this type of relationship is the only way to get a connected listing of this sort.

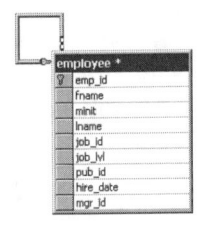

FIGURE 5.11
Foreign Key constraint `mgr_id` to `emp_id`.

After the appropriate constraint has been placed, the next step is to design a select query that will produce the desired results. This query would need to be a joining of two resultsets from the same table using aliases. A sample of the code to get a listing of all employees with their manager's ID number would be as follows:

```
Select E.Emp_ID, E.FName, E.LName, E.Mgr_ID From Employee AS E
```

Next, the basic query would need to be modified so that information about the manager could be listed with the employee. This would be done through a join using aliases to allow for the same table to be used twice in the join. The query would use syntax similar to the following:

```
Select E.Emp_ID, E.FName, E.LName, M.LName From Employee AS E Inner
↪Join Employee As M On E.Mgr_ID = M.Emp_ID
```

The estimated execution plan for this query is shown in Figure 5.12.

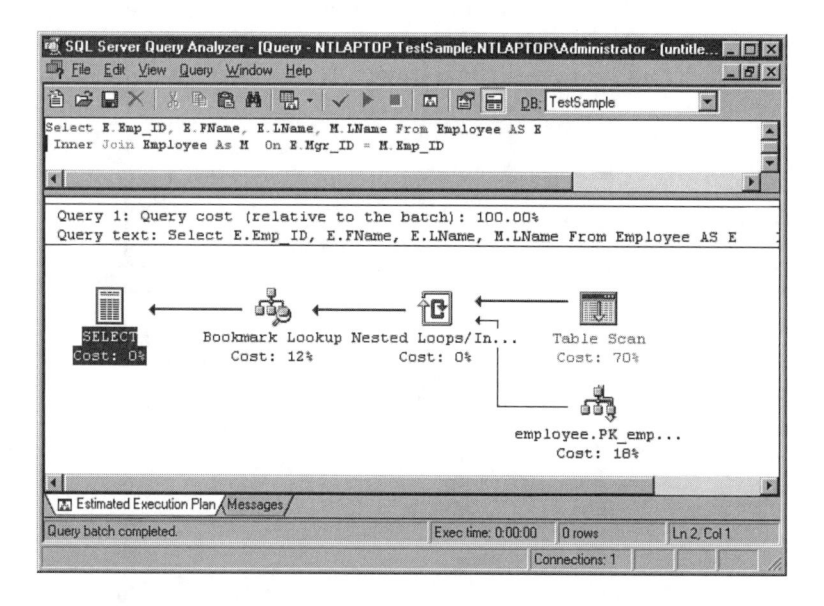

FIGURE 5.12
Query plan for an inner-join.

256 CHAPTER 5 Maintaining a Database

An inner-join would not show the entire list of employees. Any employees that did not have a manager would not show up in the list. To show a listing of all employees including those who would have a <NULL> entry for the manger, you would need an outer-join; the syntax of which could be similar to the following:

```
Select E.Emp_ID, E.FName, E.LName, M.LName From Employee AS E Left
↪Outer Join Employee As M On E.Mgr_ID = M.Emp_ID
```

A left outer-join is used because the first or left table represents the employees; the second or right table represents the managers. The estimated query plan would be similar to that of the inner-join. Now, to make the resultset easier to read, we will make it a little more attractive with the use of column headings. The end results are illustrated in Figure 5.13.

After the desired results have been achieved, note what happens to the execution plan as conditions are added to the statement; first, add a simple WHERE condition based on the manager's rows as illustrated in Figure 5.14. A similar condition on the employee's rows would not affect the execution plan.

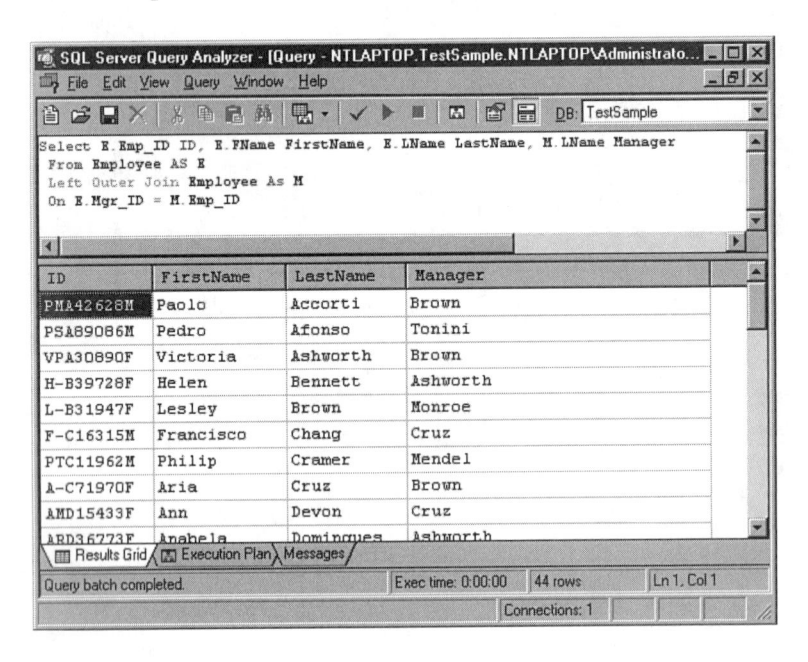

FIGURE 5.13
Resulting output of employees and their managers.

Putting It All Together   257

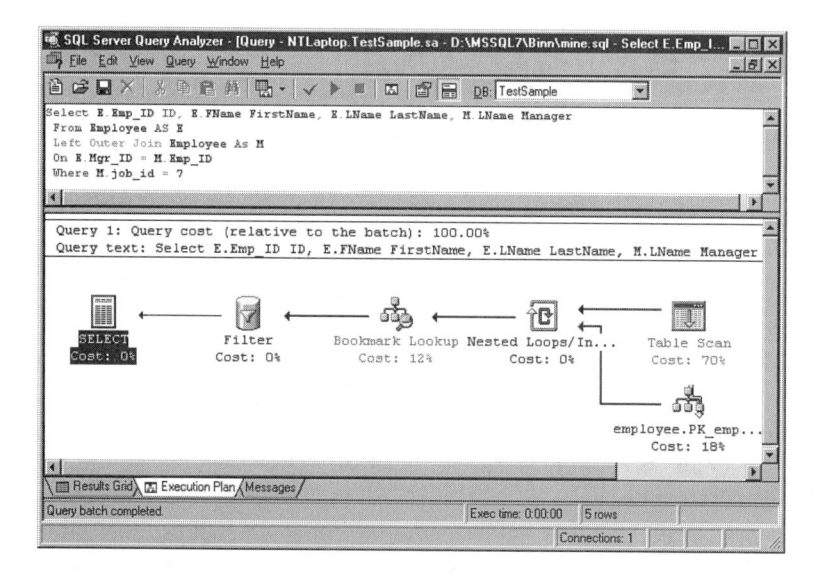

FIGURE 5.14
Resulting output of employees and their managers.

You can play out are numerous options and see their effect on the execution plan. In preparing for the exam, you should try to become comfortable with looking at plans to see what is actually being done within the engine to solve a query. Look at the effects of subqueries and complex joins involving three or more tables. Try ORDER, COMPUTE, GROUP and WHERE in different combinations to see the resulting plans.

What Is Important to Know

The following list summarizes the chapter and accentuates the key concepts to memorize for the exam:

- SQL Server uses dynamic execution plans that monitor statistics to determine the most efficient techniques for executing a query.
- The Graphical Showplan option of the SQL Server Query Analyzer will graphically illustrate a plan so you can determine the efficiency of any query.
- The server automatically maintains statistics unless configured otherwise, but you could give additional statistics to the server to enhance queries that are often used but don't rely on the default makeup of the database.
- The optimization of SQL Server performance is a combination of hardware, configuration, and database design coupled with the appropriate knowledge to utilize the resources available to achieve the optimum results.
- Locking is a foregone conclusion in multiuser environments, but the effects of locking can be greatly reduced by applying appropriate levels for the task at hand.
- The SQL Profiler is a powerful tool that enables you to investigate and monitor all facets of the server and the data maintained therein to make informed decisions about system improvements.

OBJECTIVES

Think of this as your personal study diary—your documentation of how you'll pass the exam.

The Objective Review Notes section is provided so that you can personalize this book to maximum effect. This is your workbook, study sheet, notes section—whatever you want to call it. You will ultimately decide exactly what information you'll need, and this section has been provided for your personal notes. As I have learned from my teaching experiences, there's absolutely no substitute for taking copious notes and using them throughout the study process.

Each subobjective covered in this book has its own section (there are two on a page). Each subobjective section falls under the main exam objective category, where you would expect to find it. I strongly suggest that you review each subobjective, make note of your knowledge level, and then return to the Objective Review Notes section repeatedly and document your progress. Your ultimate goal should be to review this section by itself and know if you are ready for the exam.

OBJECTIVE REVIEW NOTES

Here is how I suggest you use the Objective Review Notes:

1. Read the objective. Refer to the part of the book where it's covered.
2. If you already know this material, check "Got it" and make a note of the date.
3. If you need to brush up on the objective area, check "Review it" and make a note of the date. While you're at it, write down the page numbers you check, since you'll need to return to that section soon enough.
4. If this material is something you're largely unfamiliar with, check the "Help!" box and write down the date. Now you can get to work.
5. You get the idea. Keep working through the material in this book and in any other study materials you have. The more you understand the material, the quicker you can update and upgrade each Objective Review Notes section from "Help!" to "Review it" to "Got it."
6. Cross-reference using all your exam preparation materials. Most people who take certification exams use more than one resource. Write down where this material is covered in other books, software programs, and videotapes you're using.

OBJECTIVE REVIEW NOTES 261

Developing a Logical Data Model

► Objective: Group data into entities by applying normalization rules.

☐ Got it	☐ Review it	☐ Help!
Date:	Date:	Date:

Notes:

Fast Track cross reference, see pages:

Other resources cross reference, see pages:

► Objective: Identify primary keys.

☐ Got it	☐ Review it	☐ Help!
Date:	Date:	Date:

Notes:

Fast Track cross reference, see pages:

Other resources cross reference, see pages:

OBJECTIVE REVIEW NOTES

OBJECTIVE REVIEW NOTES

▶ Objective: Choose the foreign key that will enforce a relationship between entities and ensure referential integrity.

- ☐ Got it Date:_____
- ☐ Review it Date:_____
- ☐ Help! Date:_____

Notes:

Fast Track cross reference, see pages:

Other resources cross reference, see pages:

▶ Objective: Identify the business rules that relate to data integrity.

- ☐ Got it Date:_____
- ☐ Review it Date:_____
- ☐ Help! Date:_____

Notes:

Fast Track cross reference, see pages:

Other resources cross reference, see pages:

OBJECTIVE REVIEW NOTES

▶ **Objective:** Incorporate business rules and constraints into the data model.

☐ Got it ☐ Review it ☐ Help!
Date:_____ Date:_____ Date:_____

Notes:
_____
_____
_____
_____
_____

Fast Track cross reference, see pages:
_____
_____

Other resources cross reference, see pages:
_____
_____
_____

▶ **Objective:** In a given situation, decide whether denormalization is appropriate.

☐ Got it ☐ Review it ☐ Help!
Date:_____ Date:_____ Date:_____

Notes:
_____
_____
_____
_____
_____

Fast Track cross reference, see pages:
_____
_____

Other resources cross reference, see pages:
_____
_____
_____

Deriving the Physical Design

Objective: Assess the potential impact of the logical design on performance, maintainability, extensibility, scalability, availability, and security.

☐ Got it ☐ Review it ☐ Help!
Date:____ Date:____ Date:____

Notes:

Fast Track cross reference, see pages:

Other resources cross reference, see pages:

Creating Data Services

▶ Objective: Access data by using the dynamic SQL model.

☐ Got it ☐ Review it ☐ Help!
Date:_____ Date:_____ Date:_____

Notes:
_____
_____
_____
_____
_____

Fast Track cross reference, see pages:
_____
_____
_____

Other resources cross reference, see pages:
_____
_____
_____

▶ Objective: Access data by using the stored procedures model.

☐ Got it ☐ Review it ☐ Help!
Date:_____ Date:_____ Date:_____

Notes:
_____
_____
_____
_____
_____

Fast Track cross reference, see pages:
_____
_____
_____

Other resources cross reference, see pages:
_____
_____
_____

OBJECTIVE REVIEW NOTES

Objective: Manipulate data by using Transact-SQL cursors.

☐ Got it ☐ Review it ☐ Help!
Date:_____ Date:_____ Date:_____

Notes:

Fast Track cross reference, see pages:

Other resources cross reference, see pages:

Objective: Create and manage explicit, implicit, and distributed transactions to ensure data consistency and recoverability.

☐ Got it ☐ Review it ☐ Help!
Date:_____ Date:_____ Date:_____

Notes:

Fast Track cross reference, see pages:

Other resources cross reference, see pages:

OBJECTIVE REVIEW NOTES

▶ **Objective:** Write **INSERT, DELETE, UPDATE**, and **SELECT** statements that retrieve and modify data.

- ☐ **Got it**
  Date:_____
- ☐ **Review it**
  Date:_____
- ☐ **Help!**
  Date:_____

Notes:
_____
_____
_____
_____
_____

Fast Track cross reference, see pages:
_____
_____

Other resources cross reference, see pages:
_____
_____

▶ **Objective:** Write Transact-SQL statements that use joins or subqueries to combine data from multiple tables.

- ☐ **Got it**
  Date:_____
- ☐ **Review it**
  Date:_____
- ☐ **Help!**
  Date:_____

Notes:
_____
_____
_____
_____
_____

Fast Track cross reference, see pages:
_____
_____

Other resources cross reference, see pages:
_____
_____

OBJECTIVE REVIEW NOTES

▶ Objective: Create scripts using Transact-SQL. Programming elements include control-of-flow methods, local and global variables, functions, and error-handling methods.

☐ Got it
*Date:*____

☐ Review it
*Date:*____

☐ Help!
*Date:*____

Notes:
_____
_____
_____
_____
_____
_____

Fast Track cross reference, see pages:
_____
_____
_____

Other resources cross reference, see pages:
_____
_____
_____

▶ Objective: Design, create, use, and alter views.

☐ Got it
*Date:*____

☐ Review it
*Date:*____

☐ Help!
*Date:*____

Notes:
_____
_____
_____
_____
_____
_____

Fast Track cross reference, see pages:
_____
_____
_____

Other resources cross reference, see pages:
_____
_____
_____

OBJECTIVE REVIEW NOTES

▶ **Objective:** Create and execute stored procedures to enforce business rules, to modify data in multiple tables, to perform calculations, and to use input and output parameters.

☐ **Got it**
Date:_____

☐ **Review it**
Date:_____

☐ **Help!**
Date:_____

Notes:
_____
_____
_____
_____
_____

Fast Track cross reference, see pages:
_____
_____

Other resources cross reference, see pages:
_____
_____

▶ **Objective:** Create triggers that implement rules, enforce data integrity, and perform cascading updates and deletes.

☐ **Got it**
Date:_____

☐ **Review it**
Date:_____

☐ **Help!**
Date:_____

Notes:
_____
_____
_____
_____
_____

Fast Track cross reference, see pages:
_____
_____

Other resources cross reference, see pages:
_____
_____

OBJECTIVE REVIEW NOTES

▶ Objective: Create result sets that provide summary data. Query types include **TOP *n* PERCENT** and **GROUP BY**—specifically, **HAVING**, **CUBE**, and **ROLLUP**.

☐ Got it ☐ Review it ☐ Help!
*Date:*____ *Date:*____ *Date:*____

Notes:
_____
_____
_____
_____
_____

Fast Track cross reference, see pages:
_____
_____

Other resources cross reference, see pages:
_____
_____

▶ Objective: Configure session-level options.

☐ Got it ☐ Review it ☐ Help!
*Date:*____ *Date:*____ *Date:*____

Notes:
_____
_____
_____
_____
_____

Fast Track cross reference, see pages:
_____
_____

Other resources cross reference, see pages:
_____
_____

OBJECTIVE REVIEW NOTES

▶ Objective: Access data from static or dynamic sources by using remote stored procedures, linked servers, and openrowset.

☐ **Got it**
  *Date:*_____

☐ **Review it**
  *Date:*_____

☐ **Help!**
  *Date:*_____

Notes:

Fast Track cross reference, see pages:

Other resources cross reference, see pages:

Creating a Physical Database

▶ Objective: Create and manage files, file groups, and transaction logs that define a database.

☐ Got it ☐ Review it ☐ Help!
Date:_____ Date:_____ Date:_____

Notes:
_____
_____
_____
_____
_____
_____

Fast Track cross reference, see pages:
_____
_____
_____

Other resources cross reference, see pages:
_____
_____
_____

▶ Objective: Create tables that enforce data integrity and referential integrity.

☐ Got it ☐ Review it ☐ Help!
Date:_____ Date:_____ Date:_____

Notes:
_____
_____
_____
_____
_____
_____

Fast Track cross reference, see pages:
_____
_____
_____

Other resources cross reference, see pages:
_____
_____
_____

OBJECTIVE REVIEW NOTES

▶ Objective: Create and maintain indexes.

☐ Got it ☐ Review it ☐ Help!
Date:_____ Date:_____ Date:_____

Notes:

Fast Track cross reference, see pages:

Other resources cross reference, see pages:

▶ Objective: Populate the database with data from an external data source. Methods include bulk copy program and Data Transformation Services (DTS).

☐ Got it ☐ Review it ☐ Help!
Date:_____ Date:_____ Date:_____

Notes:

Fast Track cross reference, see pages:

Other resources cross reference, see pages:

▶ Objective: Implement full-text search.

☐ Got it   ☐ Review it   ☐ Help!
*Date:*_____   *Date:*_____   *Date:*_____

Notes:

Fast Track cross reference, see pages:

Other resources cross reference, see pages:

Maintaining a Database

▶ Objective: Evaluate and optimize the performance of an execution plan by using **DBCC SHOW CONTIG**, **SHOWPLAN_text**, **SHOWPLAN_ALL**, and **UPDATE STATISTICS**.

☐ Got it ☐ Review it ☐ Help!
Date:____ Date:____ Date:____

Notes:

Fast Track cross reference, see pages:

Other resources cross reference, see pages:

▶ Objective: Evaluate and optimize the performance of query execution plans.

☐ Got it ☐ Review it ☐ Help!
Date:____ Date:____ Date:____

Notes:

Fast Track cross reference, see pages:

Other resources cross reference, see pages:

OBJECTIVE REVIEW NOTES

Objective: Diagnose and resolve locking problems.

- ☐ Got it Date:_____
- ☐ Review it Date:_____
- ☐ Help! Date:_____

Notes:

_____
_____
_____
_____
_____

Fast Track cross reference, see pages:

_____
_____

Other resources cross reference, see pages:

_____
_____
_____

Objective: Identify SQL Server events and performance problems by using SQL Server Profiler.

- ☐ Got it Date:_____
- ☐ Review it Date:_____
- ☐ Help! Date:_____

Notes:

_____
_____
_____
_____
_____

Fast Track cross reference, see pages:

_____
_____

Other resources cross reference, see pages:

_____
_____
_____

PART II

INSIDE EXAM 70-029

Part II is designed to round out your exam preparation by providing you with chapters that do the following:

- "Fast Facts Review" is a digest of all "What Is Important to Know" sections from all Part I chapters. Use this chapter to review just before you take the exam: It's all here, in an easily-reviewable format.
- "Insider's Spin on Exam 70-029" grounds you in the particulars for mentally preparing for this examination and for Microsoft testing in general.
- "Hotlist of Exam-Critical Concepts" is your resource for cross-checking your technical terms. Although you're probably up to speed on most of this material already, double-check yourself anytime you run across an item you're not 100 percent certain about; it could make a difference at exam time.
- "Sample Test Questions" provides a full length practice exam that tests you on the actual material covered in Part I. If you mastered the material there, you should be able to pass with flying colors here.
- "Did You Know?" is the "last day of class" bonus chapter: A brief touching-up of peripheral information designed to be helpful and of interest to anyone using this technology to the point that they wish to be certified in its mastery.

6   **Fast Facts Review**

7   **Insider's Spin on Exam 70-029**

8   **Hotlist of Exam-Critical Concepts**

9   **Sample Test Questions**

10 **Did You Know?**

OBJECTIVES

The exam is divided into five objective categories:

▶ **Developing a Logical Data Model**

▶ **Deriving the Physical Design**

▶ **Creating Data Services**

▶ **Creating a Physical Database**

▶ **Maintaining a Database**

CHAPTER 6

Fast Facts Review

What to Study

A review of the key topics discussed in the first five chapters follows. After you are certain that you understand the principles given in those chapters and you have practiced creating, writing, testing, and optimizing your own databases and stored procedures, study these key points on the day of the exam.

Because much of the exam will center on the proper use of statements and their syntax, it is strongly recommended that you spend some time developing some statements of your own. As an aid in the study process, you can copy from the help facility and alter existing code to make better use of your time. The other significant exam activities focus on recognizing different database situations with no other resource but the database diagram. You will see many different diagrams within the exhibits on the live exam.

Developing a Logical Data Model

An *entity* is a table. An *attribute* is a column. A *dependency* is a relationship. Entity integrity is maintained through the use of primary keys. Relationships tie the foreign key of one table to the primary key of another table (or the same table in the case of a self-join).

Business rules are used to help maintain data integrity. Business rules can be implemented through the use of constraints, rules, triggers, and defaults.

Normalization rules are applied to a database in an attempt to remove data redundancy. Denormalization is then applied to increase efficiency and provide better response times within user procedures. Normalization rules for database design are based on these definable goals for table content:

- There should be no decomposable columns.
- Data must directly relate to the entire primary key.
- There should be no repeating columns.
- Columns should never supply redundant information.

Denormalization purposefully adds redundant information at the column, table, and database or server level to provide for a faster system where data is more readily available.

Deriving the Physical Design

The performance of a physical database can be improved using several different methods. The most successful methods will involve an appropriate hardware configuration that tries to keep index, data, transaction logs, and system files on separate physical devices. File groups are used to help divide files among separate physical units and assign specific tasks to each unit.

Database diagrams can make the physical design and table interrelationships easier to work with. Also, through the diagram tool, you can enforce changes against the actual data and make foreign key ties within the database structure easier to implement.

When preparing the physical model, use foreign key ties from a table to the primary key of the same table to allow for the implementation of self-joins, providing hierarchical data display within a singular table. It is with this technique that you could print managers and their staff (similar to Figure 6.1), products and their components, and other data organizations where the records have a parent/child relationship.

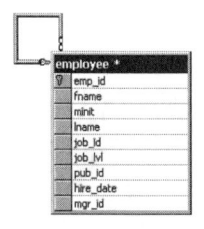

FIGURE 6.1
A self-join relationship.

Physical relationships are one-to-one, one-to-many, or many-to-many. A many-to-many relationship mandates the use of at least three tables in the database design. A central table is used to tie the main table relationships together, as shown in Figure 6.2.

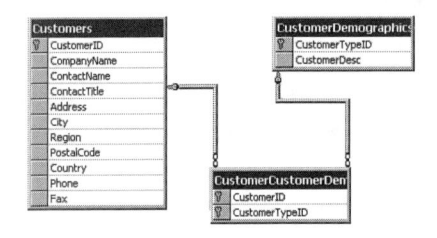

FIGURE 6.2
A many-to-many relationship.

Creating Data Services

INSERT operations make use of the "inserted" temporary table. This table can be referred to from within an INSERT TRIGGER to determine the content of the new record(s) being brought into a table.

DELETE operations make use of the "deleted" temporary table. It is referred to from within a DELETE TRIGGER to allow for manipulation or transfer of the deleted information to a backup location or other form of historical storage area.

UPDATE operations use both the "inserted" and "deleted" temporary tables. The entire operation occurs at the row level, even if only a couple of columns are being changed. One record will be deleted and then replaced with another record that could possibly contain some of the old field values accompanied by the new values being entered into the table. An UPDATE TRIGGER normally interacts with both temporary tables.

A trigger is a transaction in itself. When changes are made through the used of INSERT, UPDATE, or DELETE, the information is held within the transaction log as an uncommitted transaction until the trigger completes. If you want to cancel operations that caused the trigger to occur, you can use a "rollback transaction" within the trigger. Including explicit transactions within a trigger creates a nested transaction. You must be careful with the syntax and control of each portion of these nested situations.

@@Error can be used to see if there has been an error on the previous SQL statement. There is no facility to "trap" errors. You must use inline code to identify possible error situations. If used, @@Error must follow every statement that could possibly cause an error. Therefore, it's usually combined with variables and test conditions to determine the actual cause of an error and the corrective action to be taken when one occurs.

Explicit transactions are initiated with BEGIN TRANSACTION or BEGIN DISTRIBUTED TRANSACTION. A transaction is concluded with a COMMIT TRANSACTION statement. There is no end transaction statement (as found in other languages).

Creating a Physical Database

Use SELECT DISTINCT to eliminate duplicate IDs when you want only singular rows for a particular ID. This can be used as a technique within subqueries or joins to provide increased efficiency for the server's execution plans.

Use FILLFACTOR to indicate what percentages of leaf pages are to remain unoccupied during the index-creation process. If you have a high degree of volatility, with numerous records being added frequently, use a low setting. The reverse is also true. Use a high setting in cases where the table has few records added. A static table that never changes can have indexes created with a FILLFACTOR of 100.

IDENTITY columns help maintain entity integrity by providing a method of uniquely identifying a row within a table while, at the same time, having these values internally generated by the server. If records have been deleted and you want to reinsert them into the now-unused identities, you must use SET IDENTITY_INSERT ON to allow for values to be specified for the identity column within the insert operation.

Maintaining a Database

Use Performance Monitor only when activity for the entire server is to be monitored. It is a preference to use SQL Server Profiler when diagnosing problems related to a specific application, database, or other related activity.

The graphical SHOWPLAN option of the SQL Server Query Analyzer allows you to see a graphic representation of the plan that the server will use to execute any given operation.

Several DBCC commands can be used to help diagnose and repair database and index errors within the server. Use DBCC CHECKALLOC to check the allocation and use of all pages in the specified database. Use DBCC CHECKDB to check the allocation and structural integrity of all the objects in the specified database. Use DBCC DBREINDEX to rebuild one or more indexes for a table in the specified database. Use DBCC NEWALLOC to check the allocation of data and index pages for each table within the extent structures of the database. Use DBCC SHOW_STATISTICS to display the current distribution statistics for the specified target on the specified table. Use DBCC SHOWCONTIG to display fragmentation information for the data and indexes of the specified table. Use DBCC SHRINKDATABASE and DBCC SHRINKFILE to reduce the size of databases or specific files.

Use TABLOCK to specify that a table lock is to be used. Use HOLDLOCK to keep a lock in place until the end of a transaction. Use PAGELOCK to indicate that a page of data is to be locked instead of table locks or row locks. Use READCOMMITED to only view committed transactions. Use ROWLOCK to specify locking at the row level.

The Insider's Spin gives you the author's word on exam details specific to 70-029, as well as information you possibly didn't know—but could definitely benefit from—about what's behind Microsoft's exam preparation methodology. This chapter is designed to deepen your understanding of the entire Microsoft exam process. Use it as an extra edge—inside info brought to you by someone who teaches this material for a living.

CHAPTER 7

Insider's Spin on Exam 70-029

At A Glance: Exam Information

Exam Number	70-029
Minutes	90
Questions	*
Passing Score	*
Single-Answer Questions	Yes
Multiple-Answer With Correct Number Given	Yes
Multiple-Answer Without Correct Number Given	Yes
Ranking Order	No
Choices of A through D	Yes
Choices of A through E	Yes
Objective Categories	5

*At the time of publication, this information was unavailable.

The Designing and Implementing Databases with Microsoft SQL Server 7.0 exam is computer-administered and is intended to measure your ability to design a database system and implement that system in an efficient and optimized manner. It is as much a database design theory exam that could relate to any software environment as it is one that is specific to SQL Server 7. Although a number of questions (about one-quarter of them) relate specifically to the capabilities of SQL Server, there is a much more concerted effort to test general database design concepts and the implementation of procedures using SQL syntax. A person taking this exam could draw on database implementation experience from a variety of platform backgrounds. To be thoroughly prepared, you would need to supplement this knowledge with "What's New in SQL Server 7," as defined in this book and in SQL Server Books Online, and "What is the Microsoft SQL Syntax Slant," comparing Transact SQL to ANSI SQL.

The questions on this exam have a significant number of exhibits. In fact, you will probably see an exhibit for almost every question. Be prepared to see numerous database diagrams illustrating table interrelationships, as well as samples from Graphical SHOWPLAN.

A second focus of the exam is the usage of appropriate SQL syntax within stored procedures. This is not just a simple pick-the-correct-statement-to-solve-the-problem kind of problem, but complete illustrations of entire procedures in which you are expected to determine whether the procedure does what it is intended to do.

The third area you will be tested on is the application of database theories such as normalization/denormalization, table relationships (one-to-one, one-to-many), three-tier implementations, and data locking.

Finally, a portion of the exam relates specifically to SQL Server 7 implementation. Use of utilities (SQL Server Profiler, Index Maintenance Wizard) will be queried from the perspective of which utility you would use under certain circumstances.

The exam definitely will be a challenge for the database user who hasn't had much exposure to the design of database systems from the ground up to completion. It is clear that Microsoft wants to eliminate the possibility of anyone passing the exam through anything other than the application of database implementation knowledge to specific related problems. It is my opinion that you won't see much in the way of "braindumps" or other questionable study notes available for use in preparing for the exam.

The exam has three types of multiple-choice questions: single-answer (always readily identified by a radio button), multiple-answer with the correct number given, and multiple-answer with no correct number given. Overall, the questions are verbose and include a large number of exhibits.

This book has a number of notes on particular areas to watch out for, but I had the most difficulty with the long sections of code in the questions (about two or three questions out of 30). This was partially because the code was supposed to accomplish five or six different things that had to be diagnosed quickly and also because every programmer has his or her own coding style that doesn't necessarily mesh with that of the person creating the exam. These two points made it quite a challenge to review the code and choose the correct answer in a time-limited exam format.

Although Microsoft no longer releases specific exam information, at one time they said that 85 percent of those who take a certification exam fail it. Common logic then indicates that only 15 out of every 100 people who think they know a product know it well enough to pass—a remarkably low number.

Quite often, developers who do know a product very well and use it daily fail certification exams. Is it because they don't know the product as well as they think they do? Sometimes, but more often than not, it is because of other factors:

- They know the product from a real-world perspective, not Microsoft's perspective.
- They are basing their answers on the product's previous release(s), which might be significantly different from the new version.
- They are unaccustomed to so many questions in such a short time or they are unaccustomed to the electronic test engine.
- They don't use all the testing tools or pretest time available to them.

The purpose of this chapter is to try to prepare you for the exam and help you overcome these four items. If you've been taking exams daily and you don't think you need this information, skim this chapter and go on. Odds are that you will still uncover some helpful tips. On the other hand, if you haven't taken many electronic exams or you've been having difficulty passing them by as wide a margin as you should, read this chapter carefully.

Get into Microsoft's Mind-Set

When taking the exam, remember that Microsoft was responsible for writing the exam. Microsoft employees don't write the exams themselves. Instead, experts in the field are hired on a contract basis to write the questions. However, all questions must adhere to certain standards and be approved by Microsoft before they make it into the actual exam. What this translates into is that Microsoft will never put anything in an exam that reflects negatively on them. It will also use the exam for promotional marketing as much as possible.

Therefore, to successfully answer questions and pass the exam, you must put yourself into the Microsoft mind-set and see questions from their standpoint. Consider the following question, for example:

1. Which database development environment would offer a company the easiest implementation of a large enterprise corporate environment?

- **A.** Sybase SQL Anywhere
- **B.** Oracle
- **C.** SQL Server
- **D.** CA Unicenter

Although you could make a sincere argument for at least three of the answers, only one answer will be correct on the exam. Don't try to read too much between the lines and don't think you can put a comment at the end of the exam, arguing why another choice would be better. If you answer anything other than C, you might as well write this one off as a missed question.

Also, related to this, Microsoft will always promote the new technologies within its software. In cases where choices are given reflecting older versions of Microsoft products and newer capabilities, always choose the newer technologies over older equivalents. Consider the following question:

2. You are developing a client application that will access a database either across a local network or, in some cases, spanning a WAN link. Which technology would you implement in order to facilitate the application?

- **A.** DAO
- **B.** RDO
- **C.** ADO
- **D.** DDE

Again, arguments could be made for at least three of the choices, but since the ADO architecture represents the "new" solution to this situation, it is the correct choice.

Understand the Exam's Time Frame

When you take an exam, find out when it was written. In almost all cases, an exam goes live within three months of the final release of the product it is based on. Before the exam is released, it goes through a beta process in which all the questions that can be on the exam are written. This exam version is then available for a short time (typically a week), during which scores on each question can be gathered. Questions that exam-takers get right every time are weeded out as being too easy and those that are too hard are also weeded out.

When you take something like a major BackOffice system (which will remain nameless in this example) and create an exam for it, you end up with a time frame similar to the following:

1. The product goes into early beta.
2. A survey is done (mostly of beta testers) to find out which components of the product they spend most time with and consider the most important. The findings are used to generate the objectives and the weighting for each.
3. The product goes to final beta.
4. Contract writers are hired to write questions about the product using the findings from the survey.
5. The product goes live.
6. The exam is beta-tested for one to two weeks. After that, the results of each question are evaluated and the final question pool is chosen.
7. The service pack for the product is released.
8. The exam goes live.
9. Another service pack is released. It fixes problems from the first service pack and adds additional functionality.
10. Yet another service pack comes out.
11. An option pack that incorporates service packs is released.
12. You take the exam.

Now suppose that the product happens to be Windows NT Server 4 and you see a question such as this:

3. What is the maximum number of processors that Windows NT Server 4 can handle?

A. 2
B. 4
C. 8
D. 16

In the real world, the answer would be C or D, depending on how you look at it: The end-user license agreement states that 8 is the limit, but NCR and other vendors make SMP servers that can run NT on 16. When NT 4 first came out, however, the answer was B. Since the original exam questions were written to the final beta, the answer then was B, so the answer now is B. Microsoft has maintained that it will test only on core products, not add-ons. Service packs, option packs, and the like are considered something other than core product.

With this in mind, you must always answer the questions as if you were addressing the product as it exists when you pull it from the box, and before you do anything else with it—because that is exactly what the exam is written to. You must get into this mind-set and understand the time frame in which the exam was written or you will fail the exam consistently.

GET USED TO ANSWERING QUESTIONS QUICKLY

Every exam has a different number of questions and most stick with the 90-minute time frame. If you run out of time, every question you haven't answered is graded as a wrong answer. Therefore, keep the following in mind:

- Always answer every question; never leave any unanswered. If you start running out of time, answer all the remaining questions with the same letter and then go back and start reading them. Using the law of averages, if you do run out of time, you should get 25 percent of the remaining questions correct.

- Time yourself carefully. A clock runs in the upper-right corner of each screen. Mark all questions that require lots of reading or that have exhibits and come back to them after you've answered all the shorter questions.

- Practice, practice, practice. Get accustomed to electronic questioning and answering questions in a short period. With so many exam simulators available, there is no reason for anyone not to run through one or two before plunking down $100 for the real test. Some simulators aren't worth the code they're written in, and others are so close in style to the actual exam that they prepare you very well. If money is an issue, and it should be, look for demos and freebies on Web sites. http://www.MeasureUp.com is an excellent example of a site where you can try some sample exams online.

If you do run out of time, spend as much time as you want to on the last question. You will never time out with a question in front of you. You will time out only when you click Next to go from that question to the next one.

Taking the Test

An enormous amount of common sense is important here, and much of that common sense comes only as you get more used to the testing procedure. Here's a typical sequence of events:

1. You study for an exam for a considerable period of time.
2. You call Sylvan Prometric (1-800-755-EXAM) and register for the exam, or you register online at www.sylvanprometric.com.
3. You drive to the testing site, sit in your car, and cram on last-minute details.
4. You walk into the center, sign your name, show two forms of ID, and walk to a computer.
5. Someone enters your ID into the computer and leaves. You're left with the computer, two pieces of plain paper, and two No. 2 pencils.
6. You click the button on the screen to begin the exam and the 90 minutes begins.

When you call Sylvan, be sure to ask how many questions are on the exam so that you know before you go in. Sylvan is allowed to release very little information (for example, they can't tell you what constitutes a passing score). This is one of the few pieces of information they can pass along.

The exam begins the minute you click the button to start it. Before that, the 90-minute time frame hasn't started. After you walk into the testing center and sit down, you're free (within reason) to do whatever you want to. Why not dump everything from your brain (including those last-minute facts you studied in the parking lot) onto those two sheets of paper before you start the exam? The two sheets provide you with four sides—more than enough to scribble down everything you remember. You can refer to this information during the test.

When you click Start, the first question appears. Various types of questions are asked, including the type shown in Figure 7.1. Because Microsoft doesn't readily make available the capability to take screen shots of the exams (for obvious reasons), all the figures in this chapter are from a third-party emulator that closely resembles the real thing.

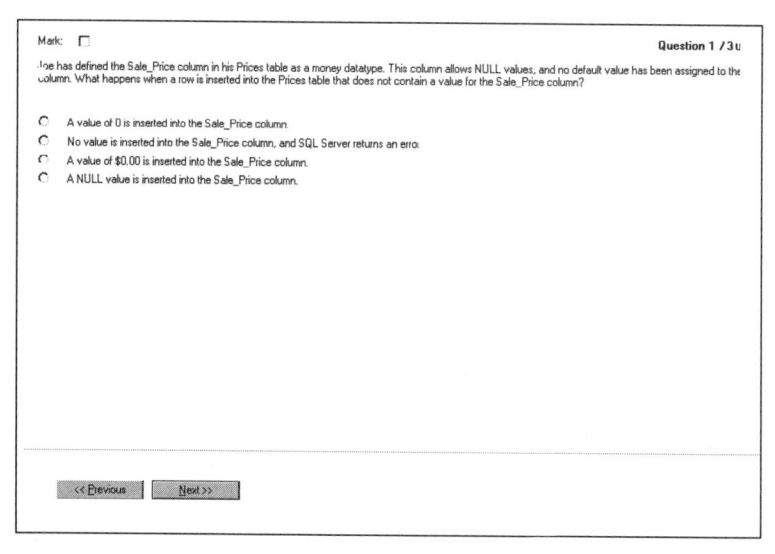

FIGURE 7.1
A sample test question.

Look at the sample question briefly, but more important, look at the information on the screen. First, you can mark this question. By doing so, you can see at the end of the exam any questions you thought were difficult and jump back to them. (However, if you're taking an adaptive exam, you can't go back and review a question once you move to the next one.) Never mark a question and then go to the next one without choosing an answer. Even if you don't read the question at all because you're saving it for later, mark it and answer C. That way, if you run out of time, you have a chance of getting the question right.

In the upper-right corner, you see the number of the question you are on. In the real exam, you also see the time remaining. Under the question are the possible answers. The radio buttons to the left of the answers indicate that there is only one correct answer.

Although this isn't always true, many times when there are four possibilities, one is so far off the mark as to not even be plausible, and another is too much of a gimme to be true, so you are left with two possibilities. For example:

4. In SQL Server 7, to view current locking information for the server, what option must you choose?

   A. From the View menu, choose Locks.

   B. From the Management folder, choose Current Activity.

   C. From the Support Services folder, choose Locking.

   D. From NT's Start menu, choose SQL Server 7 - Switch.

In this case, choice A is the gimme of a nonexistent option that fits the question too perfectly. Choice D is the blow-off answer—so far away from what's possible as to not be a possibility. That leaves choices B and C.

Even if you know nothing about SQL Server, a clue that B and C are legitimate possibilities is the similarity of their wording. Anytime you see two answers worded so closely, assume that they are the ones to focus on.

The buttons at the bottom of the screen allow you to move to the next question or to a previous question. The latter option is important, because if you come across a question whose wording provides the answer to a question you saw before, always use the Previous button to go back and change or check your answer. Never walk away from a sure thing.

When an exhibit is associated with the question, the command button for it is displayed as well. The problem with exhibits is that they appear on top of the question, or they can be tiled in such a way that you can't see either. Whenever you have an exhibit, read the question carefully, open the exhibit, memorize what is there (or scribble information about it on your two sheets of paper), close the exhibit, and answer the question.

Figure 7.2 shows an example of a question that has more than one correct answer, as evidenced by the check boxes next to the answers instead of radio buttons.

There are two types of these questions—one where you are told how many answers are correct (choose two, choose three, and so on), and another where you are not. In Figure 7.2, you are told to choose two correct answers. In Figure 7.3, you must select all the correct answers, and you don't know whether that is one, two, three, or four. In some cases, the questions are presented in a fashion to trip you up. Sometimes there is really only one correct answer, or all of the selections are correct and, thus, must all be chosen.

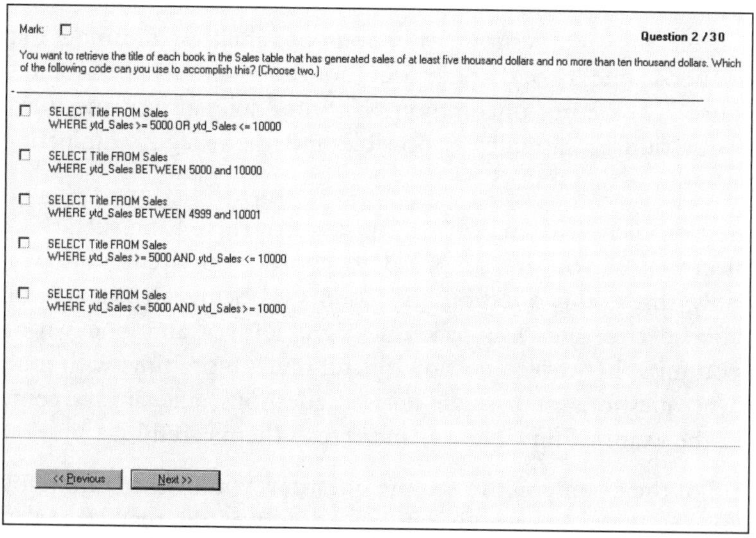

FIGURE 7.2
Another sample test question.

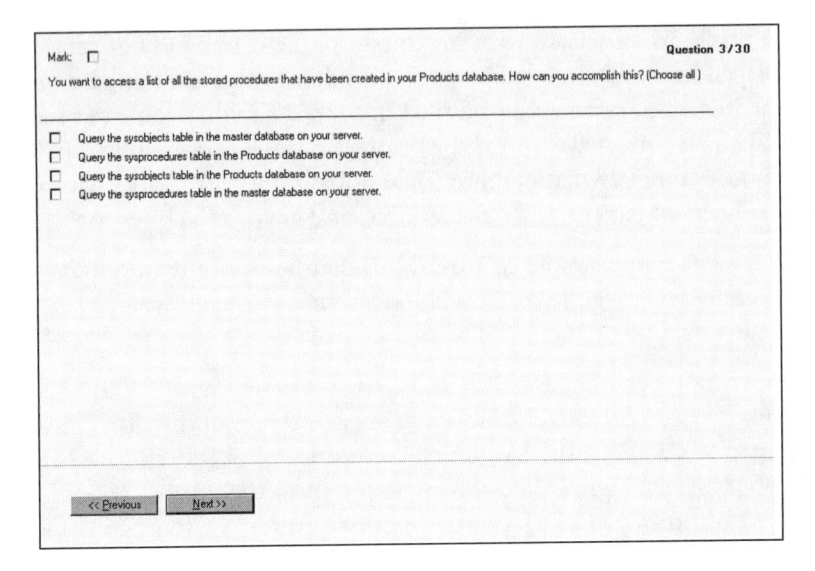

FIGURE 7.3
Another sample test question.

Most multiple-answer questions offer four possibilities, meaning that you must choose one, two, three or four, but those with five possibilities (as in Figure 7.2) are not uncommon. With multiple-answer questions, read the question as carefully as possible and then begin eliminating choices.

The biggest problem with multiple answers is that there is no such thing as partial credit. If you are supposed to choose four items, but you choose only three, the question still counts as being wrong. If you should choose two and you pick one right answer and one wrong answer, you miss the whole question. Spend much more time with multiple-answer questions than single-answer questions, and always come back after the exam (if time allows) and reread them carefully.

At the end of the exam you can see the questions you marked and jump back to them. If you've already chosen an answer on that screen, it remains chosen until you choose something else (the question also remains marked until you unmark it). The command buttons at the bottom of the question will now include an Item Review choice to let you jump back to the Item Review screen without going through additional questions.

Use the capability to mark and jump as much as you possibly can. All lengthy questions should be marked and returned to in this manner. Also note all answers that are incomplete. You can ill afford to not answer any question, so be certain to go back and answer them all before choosing to finish the exam (or before you run out of time).

After you click Finish, the grading is done, and the Examination Score Report appears. The one shown in Figure 7.4 is a bit misleading. Typically, you're shown only the bar graphs and a message as to your passing or failing. A section analysis doesn't appear on the screen—only on the printed documentation you walk out of the testing center with. The pass/fail score is based on the beta of the exam and on statistics gathered from the performance of those who took it.

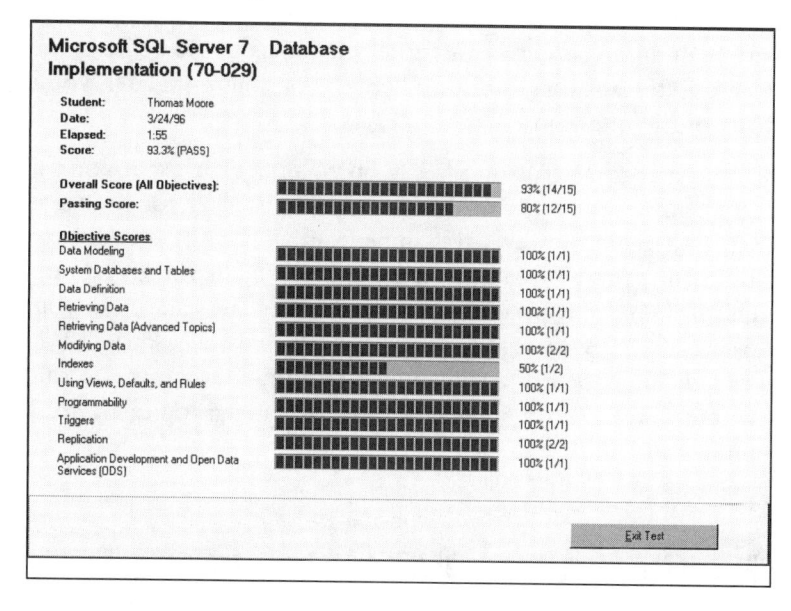

FIGURE 7.4
The Examination Score Report.

If you fail an exam—and everyone will, occasionally—never be lulled into a false sense of confidence by the Section Analysis. If it says you scored 100% in a particular section, you should still study that section before retaking the exam. Too many test-takers study only the sections they did poorly on. That 100% in Monitoring and Optimization could be the result of the first question pool containing only one question on that topic, and you had a 25 percent chance of guessing correctly. Also note that on the real exam, you are not given the number of questions in each section. What happens the next time, when there are three questions in the random pool from that objective category, and you don't know the answers? You're handicapping yourself right off the bat.

A good rule of thumb if you do fail an exam is to rush back to your car and write down all the questions you can remember (that is, perform your own "braindump"). Have your study materials in the vehicle with you and look up the answers then and there. If you wait until later, you'll forget many of the questions.

The new policy from Microsoft allows you to retake an exam you fail once without any waiting period (other than registering for it and so on). If you fail it again, however, you must wait 14 days before you can take it a third time (and 14 days from that point for the fourth try, and so on). This is to prevent people from memorizing the exam. Do your best to never fall into this category. If you fail an exam once, start all over again and study anew before trying it a second time. Make the second attempt within a week of the first, however, so that the topics are fresh in your mind.

WHERE THE QUESTIONS COME FROM

Knowing where the questions come from can be as instrumental as knowing how to prepare for the exam. The more you know about it, the better your odds of passing. Earlier, I discussed the time frame used to create the exam, and I mentioned that contract writers are hired for the exam. The contract writers are given a sizable document detailing how questions must be written. If you really want to pursue the topic with fervor, contact Microsoft and inquire about a contract writing position. Here are a few tidbits that can be gleaned from multiple-choice authoring:

- No question should have an All of the Above answer. When such a choice is available, it is almost always the correct answer, so it isn't a fair representation of a valid multiple-choice question.

- For the same reason, there should never be a None of the Above answer.

- Scenarios should be used when they increase the value of the question.

- Subjective words (such as best and most) should be avoided.

- Although there can be only one correct answer for the question, all other possibilities should appear plausible and should avoid all rationale or explanations.

- Single answers must be mutually exclusive (no A+C, B+C, and so on).

- Negative words (such as not and cannot) should be avoided.

Different Flavors of Questions

At one time, all questions were either single-answer or multiple-answer. There is a push today to go more toward ranking and performance-based questions, as well as simulations, case studies, and adaptive questions. Older exams still have only the first two types of questions, whereas newer ones offer the latter types.

Ranking questions give you a scenario, a list of required objectives, a list of optional objectives, and a proposed solution. You have to rank how well the solution meets the objectives. This used to be a commonplace question type on recent Microsoft exams. Although similar questions will be on the exam, they will have a slightly different flavor.

A simulation imitates a portion of the functionality of the product being tested. The person taking the exam is given a scenario and one or more activities to complete. Although this exam has no simulation questions, many of the Microsoft exams do have questions of this type.

Case study questioning provides smaller tests ("testlets") within the exam. Each testlet provides a case study and several questions to accompany the testlet. At this point, this question type is being used only in the MCSD core 70-100 exam.

After trying adaptive testing styles, Microsoft recently revisited its traditional format. However, Microsoft makes no promises as to the type of exam you will get when you actually sit down to take it. The current format (at the time this book was written) used by Microsoft in the majority of its newer tests is a 30-question, 90-minute exam with a very high passing score. For example, at last look, the Networking Essentials exam had a passing score of 833. This new standard certainly raises the bar for those attempting Microsoft certification exams.

The breadth and depth of your technical vocabulary is a significant measure of your knowledge as applied to the exam you're about to be tested on. You should refer to the hotlist of exam-critical concepts every time you run across a term or word you're unsure about. Double-check your knowledge by occasionally reviewing this section. Do you have a slightly different definition for a term? Why? The answer can deepen your understanding of the technology.

Do you need to add your own definitions or new terms? It's more than likely, because no two exam candidates will find the same list of terms equally useful. That's why there's room to add your own terms and concepts at the end of this section.

CHAPTER 8

Hotlist of Exam-Critical Concepts

Term	Definition
10Base2	A type of coaxial cabling similar to that of television cable wire used to connect two or more computers over short distances.
ACID	Atomicity, Consistency, Isolation, Durability.
Aggregate	A function that is used to summarize data, such as SUM, AVG, and so on.
Alphanumeric	Data containing any combination of numbers, letters, and/or special characters.
ANSI	American National Standards Institute.
ASCII	American Standard Code for Information Interchange: A standard coding for character data, pertaining to a standard "txt" format.
Associative entity	An entity used to tie or associate kernel entities to each other.
Atomicity	An all-or-nothing state for transactions.
Attribute	A field in a table.
Autoclose	A setting that causes a database to automatically close when the last user disconnects.
Automatic recovery	Recovery that occurs every time SQL Server is restarted. Automatic recovery protects your database in the event of system failure.
Autoshrink	A setting for database files that lets them use background processing to shrink in size if there is an excessive number of empty pages.
Availability	Making data (including data updates) available in a timely fashion with a quick response time and data redundancy.

Term	Definition
Bitwise	Breaking data down into individual bits.
Boolean	Resulting in true or false, 1 or 0.
Bound connection	A connection between objects that requires overhead for maintenance.
Bulkcopy	A two-stage process of moving information from one data store to another.
Business rule	A rule applied against the data to prevent bad information from entering a database. Coincides with a business goal.
Business services	Procedures that enforce business rules, taking some of the processing load of determining invalid data and the user interface away from the database engine.
Cache	Computer memory used to hold frequently used data and procedures, permitting faster access.
Cascading delete	A delete that erases all related database rows or columns.
Cascading update	An update that updates all related database rows or columns.
Characteristic entity	An entity that provides additional information or further defines a kernel or associative entity.
Check constraint	Enforces domain integrity by limiting the values that can be placed in a column.
Checkpoint	The point at which all changed data pages are written to disk.
Client configuration utility	Used to manage the client configuration for DB-Library, Net-Libraries, and custom-defined network connections.

Term	Definition
Client-side cursor	A cursor implemented on the client. The entire result set is first transferred to the client, and then the client API software implements the cursor functionality from this cached result set. Client cursors typically don't support all types of cursors—only static and forward-only cursors.
Clustered index	A singular table index that defines the order of the data stored.
Coaxial	*See* 10Base2.
Column	A field in a database that corresponds to a set of data for all records in a database, such as First Name and Street Address.
Commit	The process of completing a transaction and updating the physical table.
Committal phase	In a two-phase commit, the process of all servers committing a transaction.
Comparison operator	An operator such as greater than, equal to, or less than performed against two expressions.
Compound key	A key that references data in more than one field.
Concatenate	The uniting of character strings and/or string variables to form a sentence out of phrases or a message from the combination of variable information and character strings.
Consistency	Having transactions always perform in the same predictable manner.
Constant	Any constant or literal string, built-in function, or mathematical expression. This value can't include the names of any columns or other database objects.
Constraint	Defines rules regarding the values allowed in columns.

Hotlist of Exam-Critical Concepts

Term	Definition
Contention	A situation where locking prevents a process from obtaining data needed to complete its operation.
Control-of-flow	Transact-SQL keywords that control the flow of execution of SQL statements, statement blocks, and stored procedures.
Convergence	Comparing two databases and the changes made against each to try to have equivalent content.
Cross-join	*See* equi-join.
Cube	A function used to produce super-aggregate data.
Cursor	A tracking mechanism that allows movement through a set of records. Also, the basis in which a set of records is created.
Data integrity	The correctness of the data and the ability to maintain the accuracy of the information presented from the data.
Data services	Procedures responsible for performing alterations directly against the data.
Data Transformation Services (DTS)	A SQL Server component used to import, export, and transform data from different data sources.
Data warehouse	A method used to control extremely large databases.
Database	A complete set of related tables and other objects for a given implementation.
Database Consistency Checker (DBCC)	A statement used to check the logical and physical consistency of a database, check memory usage, decrease the size of a database, check performance statistics, and so on. DBCC helps ensure the physical and logical consistency of a database, but it isn't corrective.
Database Object Owner (DBOO)	Anyone who creates a SQL Server object and thus becomes the owner of the object.

Term	Definition
Database Owner (DBO)	A single person or group of people assigned to be the owner of the database for the purpose of evaluating permissions.
DB-Library	The interactive driver that performs client-to-server communications and translations.
dbo Use Only	A setting of the database that permits only database owner access. All other user connections are refused.
Deadlock	A situation in which two users, each having a lock on one piece of data, attempt to acquire a lock on the other's piece. Each user waits for the other to release the lock. SQL Server detects deadlocks and kills one user's process.
Default	A value automatically inserted into a column if the user doesn't explicitly enter one. In a relational database management system, every data element (a particular column in a particular row) must contain a value, even if that value is NULL. Because some columns don't accept NULL values, another value must be entered, either by the user or by SQL Server. Also, the behavior exhibited by a statement or component unless overridden by the user.
DELETE	The statement used to remove a row or rows from a table.
Denormalization	The process of disobeying normalization rules for the purpose of improving performance and usability.
Dependency	In a logical design, a relationship between two or more tables. In a stored procedure usage, the resources needed by the stored procedure to complete its tasks.
Device file	In SQL Server 6.x, a method used to reserve space on the hard drive for use as data and log storage. In SQL Server 7, it is used only to store backups.

Hotlist of Exam-Critical Concepts

Term	Definition
Differential backup	The process of backing up only the information that has changed since the last backup.
Dirty read	A read that contains uncommitted data. For example, suppose transaction1 changes a row. Transaction2 reads the changed row before transaction1 commits the change. If transaction1 rolls back the change, transaction2 reads a row that is considered to have never existed.
Dirty write	Taking updates that remain in RAM and writing them to disk.
Disaster recovery plan	A documented procedure that dictates the steps to be taken in the event of a catastrophe to fully recover and get back up and running as normal.
Disk striping	Laying out data across multiple hard drives so that the reading and writing of data can be performed across these drives, at the same time increasing performance.
Disk striping with parity	Similar to disk striping with the added feature of providing a recovery mechanism for the data upon failure. Uses an algorithm to produce a data check mechanism.
Distinct	Different from all others in a result set.
Distributed query	A query that can reference multiple linked servers and can perform either update or read operations against each individual linked server.
Distributed transaction	A transaction that can span two or more servers, known as resource managers.
Drop	To permanently delete.
DSN	Data Source Name: A friendly name used by a client computer to point to a database's network location and driver type.

Chapter 8 Hotlist of Exam-Critical Concepts

Term	Definition
DTS package	A job that defines the tasks for the data transformation system.
Durability	A system's ability to survive service, hardware, or software failure.
Dynamic cursor	A cursor that can reflect data modifications made to the underlying data while the cursor is open. Updates, deletes, and inserts made by users are reflected in the dynamic cursor.
Dynamic row-level locking	The lock manager dynamically adjusts the locking and chooses between page locking (preferable for table scans) and row-level locking (preferable for inserting, updating, and deleting data).
Dynamic SQL	In Embedded SQL for C or Transact-SQL, a SQL statement built and executed at runtime.
Entity	A table within a logical database model.
Equi-join	A join in which the values in the columns being joined are compared for equality, and all columns are included in the results.
Exclusive lock	A lock that prevents any other access to the data and/or schema.
Explicit transactions	A group of SQL statements enclosed in the transaction delimiters BEGIN TRANSACTION and COMMIT TRANSACTION.
Extended stored procedure	A SQL Server-provided procedure that dynamically loads and executes a function within a dynamic link library (DLL) in a manner similar to a stored procedure. Extended stored procedures seamlessly extend SQL Server functionality. Actions outside of SQL Server can be easily triggered and external information returned to SQL Server. Return status codes and output parameters (identical to their counterparts in regular stored procedures) are also supported.

Hotlist of Exam-Critical Concepts 311

Term	Definition
Extensibility	The ability to add additional objects to a system after its initial implementation.
Fact table	Contains detail-level data representing the underlying business transactions.
Fast bulkcopy	If a destination database has no triggers or indexes, SQL Server permits a bcp process to occur without logging separate inserts to the transaction log.
Fault tolerance	The ability to recovery quickly from a hardware or other type of failure.
Fetch cursor	Forward-only cursors support only a FETCH NEXT statement. Scrollable cursors support FETCH NEXT as well as FETCH FIRST, FETCH LAST, FETCH PRIOR, FETCH RELATIVE(n), and FETCH ABSOLUTE(n). FETCH RELATIVE(n) fetches the row that is *n* rows from the current position in the cursor. FETCH ABSOLUTE(n) fetches the *n*th row in the cursor. Transact-SQL batches, stored procedures, and triggers use the FETCH statement to fetch from Transact-SQL cursors. Applications use API functions, such as the ODBC SQLFetch and SQLFetchScroll functions.
Field	*See* column.
File group	A named collection of one or more files that forms a single unit of allocation and administration.
Fill factor	A setting that specifies the amount of free space to leave for future expansion of indexes.
First normal form (1NF)	An attribute of an entity shouldn't have more than one definable piece of data or repeating groups. Normalization rule #1.

312 CHAPTER 8 Hotlist of Exam-Critical Concepts

Term	Definition
Foreign key	The column or combination of columns whose values match the primary key (PK) or unique key in the same table or another table. A foreign key doesn't have to be unique. A foreign key is often in a many-to-one relationship with a primary key. Foreign key values should be copies of the primary key values. No value in the foreign key except NULL should ever exist unless the same value exists in the primary key. A foreign key may be NULL. If any part of a composite foreign key is NULL, the entire foreign key must be NULL.
Forward-only cursor	A cursor that can't be scrolled. Rows can only be read in sequence from the first row to the last row.
FULLSCAN	The process used by SQL Server to scan all the data in the table to prepare statistics for optimization.
Full-text catalog	A logical connection of one or more tables to provide for full-text processing.
Full-text index	The portion of a full-text catalog that stores all the full-text words and their locations for a given table.
Full-text query	The ability to type an English question or phrase and have a data result set returned.
Function	A set of instructions that operates as a single logical unit, can be called by name, accepts input parameters, and returns information. In programming languages such as C, a function is a named subroutine of a program that encapsulates some logic. The function can be called by name, using parameters to pass data to the function and retrieve data produced by the function. In Transact-SQL, a function is a unit of syntax consisting of a keyword and, usually, a set of parameters. There are several categories of Transact-SQL functions: string, math, system, niladic, text and image, date, aggregate, and conversion.
Global	An object that can be referenced by any user or stored procedure. @@ for variables, ## for procedures.
Granularity	The level to which an object is broken down into smaller objects.

Term	Definition
Graphical showplan	An option of SQL Server Query Analyzer and SQL Server Enterprise Manager that shows the execution plan for a query.
Grouping	Putting data into logical groups to present more meaningful information.
GUID	Globally Unique Identifier: A unique system identifier given to all objects.
Hash	A computed check value for each row.
Heap	A table with no defined clustered index.
Hold lock	Extends the locking period to the duration of the lifetime of a process.
Hub	A connection point on a twisted-pair network where all cables extend to the workstations.
Identifier	A column or set of columns that can be used to identify any single record exclusively from the other records in the table.
Identity	A column in a table that uses the identity property for a system-generated, monotonically increasing number.
Immediate guaranteed consistency	A level of transaction consistency in which all participating sites are guaranteed to have the same data values at the same time, and the data is in a state that could have been achieved if all the work had been done at one site.
Implicit transaction	A transaction in which each single SQL statement is considered an atomic unit.
Index	An organizational technique used to permit faster location of data by referencing it in a sequence other than the one in which it was stored (such as alphabetical order).

314 CHAPTER 8 Hotlist of Exam-Critical Concepts

Term	Definition
Inner-join	A join in which records from two tables are combined and added to a query's results only if the values of the joined fields meet certain specified criteria.
Input parameter	A parameter that will receive information from another procedure or calling function.
Insensitive	A cursor that doesn't reflect data modifications made to the underlying data by other users while the cursor is open. Insensitive cursors are typically used in Transact-SQL batches, stored procedures, and triggers using the INSENSITIVE keyword on the DECLARE CURSOR statement.
INSERT	The statement used to add a record or records to a table.
Intent lock	Indicates that SQL Server wants to acquire a shared or exclusive lock on a more specific resource. An intent lock prevents another transaction from acquiring an exclusive lock on the resource containing that page or row.
Isolation	Keeping one operation from being disturbed by the actions of another.
Isolation level	An option that allows you to customize locking for an entire SQL Server session. When you set the isolation level, you specify the default locking behavior for all SELECT statements in your SQL Server session.
Join	The process of connecting data from one or more tables to produce a result set that contains data from each table but appears to the user to be a singular unit.
Kernel entity	A table that exists on its own; it doesn't define or provide descriptive information for other entities.
Keyset cursor	A cursor that shows the effects of updates made to its member rows by other users while the cursor is open, but doesn't show the effects of inserts or deletes.

Hotlist of Exam-Critical Concepts

Term	Definition
Latent guaranteed consistency	A level of transaction consistency in which all participating sites are guaranteed to have the same data values at the same time, and the data is in a state that could have been achieved if all the work had been done at one site.
Leaf level page	The bottom level of a clustered or nonclustered index. In a clustered index, the leaf level contains the actual data pages of the table. In a nonclustered index, the leaf level points to either the data pages or the clustered index (if one exists), rather than containing the data itself.
Linked server	An abstraction of an OLE DB data source that looks like another server to the local SQL Server. A linked server has an associated OLE DB provider that manages the data source.
Load	The process of restoring a table with backup data or initializing a table with content from another file.
Local	Referenced only by the procedure that initialized it and only for the life of the procedure.
Locking	The protection of data while it is being updated so that no other process can make changes to the data that might compromise the accuracy and handling of the data.
Log	A file or set of files containing a record of a database's transactions.
Log file (LDF)	A file or set of files containing a record of a database's transactions.
Logical model	A graphic representation of a database schema.
Logical operator	The operators AND, OR, and NOT. Used to connect search conditions in WHERE clauses.
Maintainability	The ability to easily upgrade and change a system.

316 CHAPTER 8 Hotlist of Exam-Critical Concepts

Term	Definition
Many-to-many	A table relationship where multiple records in one table coincide with multiple records in another.
Master database	A system database used to keep track of all objects stored on a server. Holds all system configuration settings and is essential for the operation of the server.
Mathematical operators	Any of a set of operators used to perform arithmetic.
Mbps	Megabits per second: A network speed rating.
Metadata	Provides information about the database and its objects.
Model database	A system database that is used as a template for each newly created database.
MSDB database	A system database used for the storage of user-defined alerts, jobs, and operators.
Named pipe	A network communications technique that facilitates the exchange of data.
Nested	A statement that contains a similar statement or a procedure that executes other procedures.
Nonclustered index	An index in which the logical order of the index doesn't match the physical, stored order of the rows on disk.
Nonlogged	Any operation performed against the database that doesn't reflect the action of the operation to the transaction log. *See also* fast bulkcopy.
Normal form	A rule applied to normalize a database. *See also* normalization.
Normalization	A set of five rules to implement a database plan that utilizes storage as efficiently as possible.
Null	Having no value. Not the same as empty or space.

Hotlist of Exam-Critical Concepts

Term	Definition
ODBC	Open Database Connectivity: A process used to allow clients to connect to databases across the network regardless of database type or manufacturer.
Offline	A state set for a database to indicate that it is not available for use.
OLE	An application programming interface (API) for sharing objects among applications.
OLE DB	A data storage material CLI for COM environments. OLE DB supports accessing any format of data storage (databases, spreadsheets, text files, and so on) for which an OLE DB provider is available.
One-to-many	One record in a table coincides with many records in another table tied together by a foreign key.
One-to-one	One record in a table coincides with one record in another table tied together by a foreign key.
Outer-join	A join that includes all rows from the joined tables, regardless of whether there is a matching row between the joined tables.
Output parameter	A parameter used by a stored procedure for output to another stored procedure or calling function.
Ownership chain	The ownership of dependent objects.
Parallel query execution	Executing portions of a query against all available processors.
Parameter	A placeholder in a query or stored procedure that can be filled in when the query or stored procedure is executed. Parameters allow you to use the same query or stored procedure many times, each time with different values. Parameters can be used for any literal value, and in some databases, for column references as well.
Parsing	The process of the engine breaking down a SQL statement for the purposes of compilation.

Term	Definition
Performance	The speed in which queries are processed, calculations are performed, and results are sent back to the client.
Performance Monitor	An NT utility that allows for the monitoring of performance using object counters.
Pessimistic locking	Locking data from the point at which it is read, not just the time it takes to update.
Physical design	The process of converting a logical model into the actual database with all its objects.
Physical model	The layout and interrelationships of all tables in the actual database.
Preparation phase	In a two-phase commit, the process of having each of the participating servers see if a particular transaction can be executed.
Prepared execution	Sending a SQL operation to the server ahead of time before the execution is actually performed.
Prepared procedure	A procedure that is compiled and held in memory, awaiting execution.
Primary data file (MDF)	The initial file created for the storage of data within a database.
Primary key	The column or combination of columns that uniquely identifies one row from any other row in a table. A primary key must be nonnull and must have a unique index. A primary key is commonly used for joins with foreign keys (matching nonprimary keys) in other tables.
Profiler	A utility that allows the inspection of SQL Server processes as they relate to a specific database and its users.
Property	A variable that holds a value that may change in appearance, or the handling of an object.
Query	A procedure performed against a table or tables to return a set of records.

Term	Definition
Query execution plan	Used by SQL Server to determine the fastest method to execute a SQL statement.
Query optimization	The process of compiling and preparing a query in memory so that it executes as quickly and efficiently as possible.
RAID	Redundant Array of Inexpensive Drives: Using multiple hard drive volumes to provide fault tolerance and increase performance.
RAM	Random Access Memory.
Read ahead	The server reads data before it is actually requested.
Read committed	Identifying that only data that has been committed should be read.
Read uncommitted	Allows for the reading of data that has not yet been committed.
Record	One complete set of columns for one data element.
Recursive trigger	A trigger that causes another trigger to fire, which in turn causes the original trigger to fire a second time.
Referential integrity	Maintaining the validity of records stored in related tables.
Relationship	The tying of two tables using foreign and primary keys to develop a dependency between the two.
Remote server	A SQL server on the network that can be accessed through a user's local server. The Setup program can install, upgrade, and configure remote servers.
Remote stored procedure	A collection of SQL statements and optional control-of-flow statements stored under a name on a remote server. Remote stored procedures can be called by clients or SQL Server.
Removable media	Any form of media that isn't permanently attached to the system, such as a CD or diskette.

Term	Definition
Repeatable read	Allowing data to be read repeatedly within the cursor's lifetime.
Replication	(1) Duplication of table schema and data or stored procedure definitions and calls from a source database to a destination database, usually on separate servers. (2) The copying of data from one server to another to provide redundancy and increase availability.
Result set	The set of rows returned from a SELECT statement. The format of the rows in the result set is defined by the column-list of the SELECT statement.
Return code	A value returned by a procedure to indicate success or failure or to provide an answer for the task that a process performed
Role	An administrative unit within SQL Server that contains SQL Server logins, Windows NT logins, groups, or other roles. *See also* grouping.
Rollback	The ability to remove partially completed transactions after a database or other system failure.
Rollup	An operator to produce super-aggregates.
Row	*See* record.
Rowset	The OLE DB object used to contain a result set. It also exhibits cursor behavior, depending on the rowset properties set by an application.
Rule	A set of code that controls the content of data prior to entering the database.
Save point	A marker that the user includes in a user-defined transaction. When transactions are rolled back, they are rolled back only to the save point.
Scalability	The ability of a database to support an increasing number of users over time.

Term	Definition
Scalar	A function applied to all the rows in a table (producing a single value per function). An aggregate function in the SELECT list with no GROUP BY clause applies to the whole table and is an example of a scalar.
Schema lock	A lock put in place to allow for the alteration of a table's structure.
Script	A collection of Transact-SQL statements used to perform an operation. Transact-SQL scripts are stored as files, usually with an .sql extension.
Scrollable	The ability to move a cursor around in directions other than forward-only. Users can move the cursor up and down at will.
SCSI	The manufacturer of a controller card for hard drives. A standard for communication between compatible drives and the card.
Second normal form (2NF)	A nonkey attribute of an entity must depend on the entire primary key, not just a portion of the key. Normalization rule #2.
Secondary data file (NDF)	Any file created for the data storage of a database after the initial file has been created.
Security	Roles, permissions, and ownership regulations established to prevent data tampering.
SELECT	A SQL statement used to return a set of rows.
Self-join	A join that compares rows within the same table. In database diagrams, a self-join is called a reflexive relationship.
Sensitive	A cursor that can reflect data modifications made to underlying data by other users while the cursor is open. Updates, deletes, and inserts made by other users are reflected in the sensitive cursor. Sensitive cursors are typically used in Transact-SQL batches, stored procedures, and triggers by omitting the INSENSITIVE keyword on the DECLARE CURSOR statement.

Term	Definition
Serializable	A transaction isolation level. Ensures that a database changes from one predictable state to another. If multiple concurrent transactions can be executed serially, and the results are the same, the transactions are considered serializable.
Server cluster	A group of servers set up to share the processing load and to have one take over if another fails.
Server-side cursor	A cursor implemented on the server. The cursor itself is built at the server, and only the rows fetched by an application are sent to the client.
Session	The amount of time for which a current user is logged on or a stored procedure is executing.
Shared lock	A lock created by nonupdate (read) operations. Other users can read the data concurrently, but no transaction can acquire an exclusive lock on the data until all the shared locks have been released.
Showplan	A report showing the execution plan for a SQL statement. SET SHOWPLAN_TEXT and SET SHOWPLAN_ALL produce textual showplan output. SQL Server Query Analyzer and SQL Server Enterprise Manager can display showplan information as a graphical tree.
Slow bulkcopy	In a database where triggers and/or indexes exist, each insert to the destination database is logged in the transaction log.
Snowflake schema	A variation of the star schema in which dimension tables are stored in a more normalized form. This can help improve performance for queries by reducing the number of disk reads. *See also* star schema.
SQL Server Agent	Used to create and manage local or multiserver jobs, alerts, and operators. Job schedules are defined in the Job Properties dialog box. SQL Server Agent communicates with SQL Server to execute the job according to the job's schedule.

Hotlist of Exam-Critical Concepts 323

Term	Definition
SQL Server Profiler	A SQL Server tool that keeps a continuous record of server activity in real time. SQL Server Profiler can monitor many different server events and event categories, filter these events with user-specified criteria, and output a trace to the screen, a file, or another SQL Server.
SQL-92	The latest version of the standard for SQL, published in 1992. The international standard is ISO/IEC 9075:1992 Database Language SQL. ANSI also published a corresponding standard (Data Language SQL X3.135-1192), so SQL-92 is sometimes referred to as ANSI SQL in the United States.
Standby server	A server that can be used quickly to take over operations if a primary server fails. Not the same as a server cluster.
Star schema	Takes advantage of typical decision support queries by using one central "fact" table for the subject area and many dimension tables containing denormalized descriptions of the facts.
Statement block	A block of Transact-SQL statements that act as a unit using BEGIN...END.
Static cursor	A cursor that shows the result set exactly as it was at the time the cursor was opened. Static cursors do not reflect updates, deletes, or inserts made to underlying data while the cursor is open. Sometimes called snapshot cursors.
Static SQL	In Embedded SQL for C or Transact-SQL, a SQL statement that is built at the time the application is compiled. It is created as a stored procedure when the application is compiled, and the stored procedure is executed when the application is run.

Term	Definition
Stored procedure	A set of commands stored as a database object for future and repeated use.
Subquery	A SELECT statement nested inside another SELECT, INSERT, UPDATE, or DELETE statement, or inside another subquery.
Symmetric multiprocessing	A technique used by NT to balance the work performed across all available processors.
Synchronization	The process of maintaining the same schema and data in a publication at a Publisher and in the replica of a publication at a Subscriber.
Syntax	The "grammar" of coding, including proper spelling, punctuation use, and statement use.
System Administrator (SA)	The login assigned for complete access to anything on a server.
System stored procedure	A SQL Server-supplied, precompiled collection of Transact-SQL statements. System stored procedures are provided as shortcuts for retrieving information from system tables or as mechanisms for accomplishing database administration and other tasks that involve updating system tables. The names of all system stored procedures begin with sp. System stored procedures are located in the master database and are owned by the System Administrator, but many of them can be run from any database. If a system stored procedure is executed in a database other than master, it operates on the system tables in the database from which it is executed.

Term	Definition
System table	System tables store SQL Server configuration information and definitions of all the objects, users, and permissions in SQL Server databases. Server-level configuration information is stored in system tables found only in the master database. Every database contains system tables defining the users, objects, and permissions contained by the database. The master database and its system tables are created during SQL Server Setup. System tables in a user database are automatically created when the database is created. SQL Server contains system stored procedures to report and manage the information in system tables. Users should use these system stored procedures rather than accessing the system tables directly. Users should not directly update any system table.
Table	A complete set of records stored in a database.
Tempdb	The database that provides a storage area for temporary tables, temporary stored procedures, and other temporary working storage needs. No special permissions are required to use tempdb (that is, to create temporary tables or to execute commands that may require storage space in the tempdb database). All temporary tables are stored in tempdb, no matter what database the user who creates them is using.
Third normal form (3NF)	A nonkey field must not depend on another nonkey field. Normalization rule #3.
Three-tier	A division of processes into user, business, and data services.
Timestamp	A column definition that, if present, represents the last time a row was changed.
Token	An identifier used by the server to uniquely identify a process.

Term	Definition
Torn page	An error in the internal data flags referring to a page of data that might not have been written correctly after a power outage or similar system crash.
Transact-SQL	An alternative form of SQL syntax used by SQL Server. Transact-SQL is the standard language for communicating between applications and SQL Server. The Transact-SQL language is an enhancement to Structured Query Language (SQL), the ANSI-standard relational database language. It provides a comprehensive language for defining tables; inserting, updating, or deleting information stored in tables; and controlling access to data in those tables. Extensions, such as stored procedures, make Transact-SQL a full programming language.
Trigger	Code that executes based on a condition that occurs when data is added to, changed in, or deleted from a table.
Truncate	The process of erasing information either completely or from a given point on.
Twisted pair	Network cabling that provides performance superior to that of 10Base2.
Two-phase commit	The process of controlling transactions that occur across multiple servers by guaranteeing that each server can complete its portion of the transaction before allowing the transaction to occur.
Unicode	Defines a set of letters, numbers, and symbols that SQL Server recognizes in the nchar, nvarchar, and ntext data types. It is related to but separate from character sets. Unicode has more than 65,000 possible values compared to a character set's 256, and it takes twice as much space to store. Unicode includes characters for most languages.
Union	A query that combines two tables by performing the equivalent of appending one table to the other.

Hotlist of Exam-Critical Concepts

Term	Definition
Unique constraint	A constraint that enforces entity integrity on a nonprimary key. Unique constraints ensure that no duplicate values are entered and that an index is created to enhance performance.
UPDATE	The SQL statement that can allow data to be changed within a table.
Update lock	A lock placed on a resource (such as a row, page, or table) that can be updated. Updated locks are used to prevent a common form of deadlock that occurs when multiple sessions are locking resources and are potentially updating them later.
User services	Services that directly interact with the user. Sometimes called interface services.
Variable	A defined entity that is assigned a value. A local variable is defined with a DECLARE@localvariable statement and assigned an initial value within the statement batch, where it is declared with either a SELECT or SET@localvariable statement. Global variables are predefined and maintained by the system.
View	A process that allows the creation of a table overlay supplying conditions that will minimize the number of columns and rows seen by the user.
Volatility	The degree and frequency with which changes are made to existing data.

Additional Terms and Concepts

CHAPTER 8 Hotlist of Exam-Critical Concepts

Additional Terms and Concepts

This is an exam preparation book. The author and publisher believe that you can't get too much practice with sample exam questions. Other study materials, such as books and software, let you practice extensively, so we recommend that you give strong consideration to using these in some form.

CHAPTER 9

Sample Test Questions

332 CHAPTER 9 Sample Test Questions

> **NOTE:** The last pages of this book have more information on New Riders' TestPrep books and New Riders' Top Score exam preparation software, as well as other New Riders certification study resources.

This chapter is a practice test designed to reflect the questions you'll probably see on an actual Microsoft exam. These questions tie in directly to the material covered in this book.

As a lead-in to the material in these preparatory questions, you should know that I took the beta version of this exam and I consider the exam to be a real-world test of SQL Server knowledge. You should also know that the exam would be difficult for an experienced SQL developer and very challenging for a rookie. The questions herein cover topics similar to what you'll find on the exam. I've tried to make the format close to what you will see on the exam. However, the questions aren't exactly like the ones you will see on the actual exam. You should use them as a learning tool to find your weaknesses in different exam-related areas.

For what it's worth, you should get all the questions right before attempting the exam. It is of no value to achieve this perfect score through memorizing answers rather than knowing the material. Each question has been designed to reflect a certain aspect of the exam, either through the type of exhibit being viewed, the format of the question, or the type of answer expected.

This sample test has 30 questions and covers each of the six objective categories.

QUESTIONS

1. *You are designing a stored procedure for use in a database application that contains very sensitive user data. In this procedure, you must execute a select query that generates a list of individuals to be updated. In the second portion of the procedure, you would like to perform the actual updates. What locking hint(s) would be used in the initial scan to guarantee that no changes can be made to the data until the entire procedure has completed?*

    A. Use TABLOCK within a transaction.
    B. Use ROWLOCK with UPDLOCK within a transaction.
    C. Use TABLOCK at statement level only.
    D. Use ROWLOCK with UPDLOCK at statement level only.

2. *You would like to obtain a listing of all customers who have placed orders within the last calendar year. You want each customer listed only once, even if he has had more than one order. Which syntax would be appropriate to solve this problem? (Select all that apply.)*

    A. `SELECT DISTINCT CustomerID FROM Customers`
       `WHERE OrderDate >= '01/01/98' and <= '12/31/98'`
    B. `SELECT CustomerID FROM Customers`
       `WHERE OrderDate BETWEEN '01/01/98' and '12/31/98' and DISTINCT`
    C. `SELECT DISTINCT(CustomerID) FROM Customers`
       `WHERE OrderDate BETWEEN '01/01/98' and '12/31/98'`
    D. `SELECT DISTINCT CustomerID FROM Customers`
       `WHERE OrderDate >= '01/01/98' or OrderDate <= '12/31/98'`
    E. `SELECT DISTINCT(CustomerID) FROM Customers`
       `WHERE DateDiff(Year, '01/01/98', OrderDate) = 0`

3. *The following exhibit represents data stored in a table. What normalization rules, if any, does this data disobey? (Choose all that apply.)*

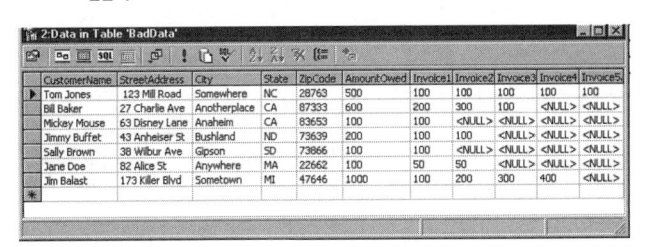

334 CHAPTER 9 Sample Test Questions

A. No decomposable columns.
B. No repeating columns.
C. No data redundancy.
D. Columns must directly relate to the primary key.

4. *You are implementing a database system that will need to be updated from several SQL Servers remotely distributed throughout the company. It is necessary that changes can be made from each of the databases and then be reflected to the original immediately upon their occurrence. Which form of replication would you implement?*

   A. MERGE replication
   B. IMMEDIATE UPDATE SUBSCRIPTION replication
   C. TRANSACTION replication
   D. SNAPSHOT replication

5. *You would like to perform some analysis on a database system that has been implemented in the company for over a year. Recently, performance in the system has been degraded when certain long-running stored procedures are executed. You would like to gather information related to table access, long-running queries, and data volatility. Which tool would you use to accommodate this information-gathering?*

   A. Performance Monitor
   B. SQL Server Profiler
   C. Network Monitor
   D. SQL Server Query Analyzer

6. *Given the following query:*
   ```
   SELECT Employees.Country, Employees.LastName,
   Employees.FirstName, Orders.ShippedDate,
   Orders.OrderID, S.Subtotal AS SaleAmount
   FROM Employees INNER JOIN
   ( Orders INNER JOIN
   [Orders Subtotals] as S ON Orders.OrderID = S.OrderID )
   ON Employees.EmployeeID = Orders.EmployeeID
   ```

   Which of the following Graphical SHOWPLAN *diagrams is the correct illustration?*

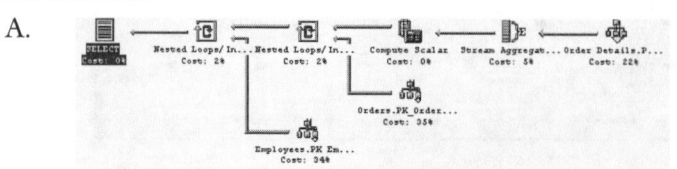

   A.

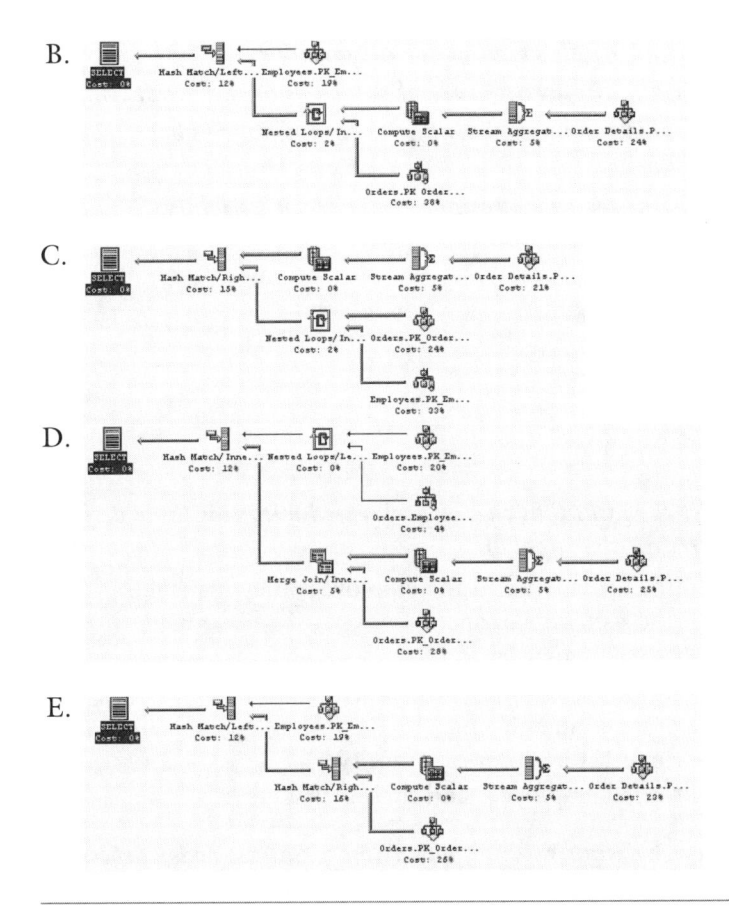

B. [query plan diagram: SELECT ← Hash Match/Left... (Cost: 12%) ← Employees.PK_Em... (Cost: 19%); Nested Loops/In... (Cost: 2%) ← Compute Scalar (Cost: 0%) ← Stream Aggregat... (Cost: 5%) ← Order Details.P... (Cost: 24%); Orders.PK_Order... (Cost: 36%)]

C. [query plan diagram: SELECT ← Hash Match/Righ... (Cost: 15%) ← Compute Scalar (Cost: 0%) ← Stream Aggregat... (Cost: 5%) ← Order Details.P... (Cost: 21%); Nested Loops/In... (Cost: 2%) ← Orders.PK_Order... (Cost: 24%); Employees.PK_Em... (Cost: 33%)]

D. [query plan diagram: SELECT ← Hash Match/Inne... (Cost: 12%) ← Nested Loops/Le... (Cost: 0%) ← Employees.PK_Em... (Cost: 20%); Orders.Employee... (Cost: 4%); Merge Join/Inne... (Cost: 5%) ← Compute Scalar (Cost: 0%) ← Stream Aggregat... (Cost: 5%) ← Order Details.P... (Cost: 25%); Orders.PK_Order... (Cost: 28%)]

E. [query plan diagram: SELECT ← Hash Match/Left... (Cost: 12%) ← Employees.PK_Em... (Cost: 19%); Hash Match/Righ... (Cost: 16%) ← Compute Scalar (Cost: 0%) ← Stream Aggregat... (Cost: 5%) ← Order Details.P... (Cost: 23%); Orders.PK_Order... (Cost: 25%)]

7. *You would like a report on network and disk statistics for a specific SQL Server. You determine that the desired statistics are totals to date and not totals for ongoing activity. Which stored procedure can be used to obtain the desired information?*
   A. sp_statistics
   B. sp_serverinfo
   C. sp_serverstatistics
   D. sp_monitor

8. *The following exhibit shows a company's employee table. You must determine if it's possible to print a listing of all managers and the employees they manage when using this table with the current organization. It must be possible to print the criteria with all the related information for employees and managers on a single row of the report. Here are the criteria for this report:*

- *Print a single manager or all managers.*
- *List a manager in order of the job he or she is working on.*
- *Provide a contact listing with the manager's home phone number.*
- *Provide for each manager in order of seniority.*

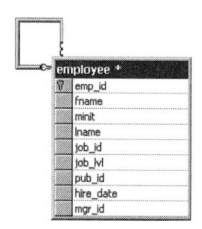

Select the tasks that can be performed with this table design. (Select all that apply.)

A. Print managers and the employees they manage.
B. Print a single manager.
C. Print all managers.
D. Print a listing in job sequence.
E. Print a contact listing.
F. Print a list in order of seniority.
G. Print all employees and their managers.

9. *You are designing an application to handle order processing. You need to write a procedure that will display product quantities. You must indicate that, for each product ordered that is present in the order details table, there are sufficient quantities of stock either on hand or on order. Which of the following queries would you use? Use the following exhibit to answer this question.*

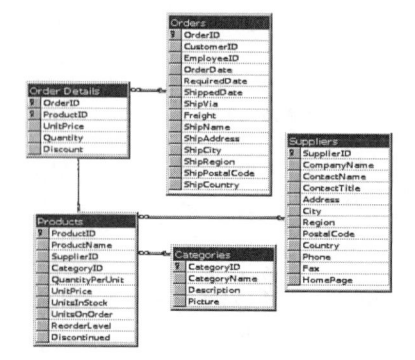

A. Select P.ProductID, Sum(Quantity) As Ordered,
   (UnitsInStock + UnitsOnOrder) * QuantityPerUnit As Total
   From [Order Details] As O
   Left Outer Join Products As P On P.ProductID = O.ProductID
   Group By P.ProductID, UnitsInStock, UnitsOnOrder,
   QuantityPerUnit
   Order By P.ProductID

B. Select P.ProductID, Sum(Quantity) As Ordered,
   (UnitsInStock + UnitsOnOrder) * QuantityPerUnit As Total
   From [Order Details] As O
   Left Outer Join Products As P On P.ProductID = O.ProductID
   Group By P.ProductID
   Order By P.ProductID

C. Select P.ProductID, Sum(Quantity) As Ordered,
   (UnitsInStock + UnitsOnOrder) * QuantityPerUnit As Total
   From [Order Details] As O
   Left Outer Join Products As P On P.ProductID = O.ProductID
   Group By P.ProductID, Quantity, UnitsInStock, UnitsOnOrder,
   QuantityPerUnit
   Order By P.ProductID

D. Select P.ProductID, Sum(Quantity) As Ordered,
   (UnitsInStock + UnitsOnOrder) * QuantityPerUnit As Total
   From [Order Details] As O
   Left Outer Join Products As P On P.ProductID = O.ProductID
   Group By P.ProductID, Quantity, Total
   Order By P.ProductID

E. Select P.ProductID, Sum(Quantity) As Ordered,
   (UnitsInStock + UnitsOnOrder) * QuantityPerUnit As Total
   From [Order Details] As O
   Left Outer Join Products As P On P.ProductID = O.ProductID
   Group By P.ProductID, Total
   Order By P.ProductID

10. *You are working on an application that has employees assigned to territories and regions for the purpose of determining the ability to relocate employees within the company. What can be said about the relationships between employees, territories, and regions according to the following exhibit? (Select two.)*

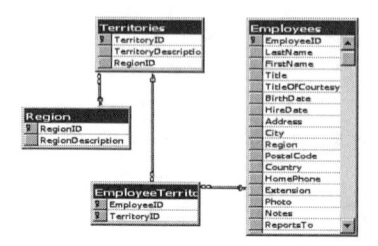

A. Each employee is responsible for a single region that is subdivided into territories.
B. Each region has a number of territories and each territory a number of employees.
C. Each employee is responsible for a single territory that is subdivided into regions.
D. Each territory has a number of regions and each region has a number of employees.
E. Employees can work in more than one territory. A territory can have more than one employee, but only one region.
F. Employees can work in more than one region, but only one territory.

11. *Users of a large database system have recently been complaining that response times for some of their queries have slowed significantly. A number of changes were made to the tables, including adding many new records and some additional columns. What could be done to improve the system's performance?*
   A. Establish normalization rules with the table structures.
   B. Create additional indexes.
   C. Have common queries placed into views.
   D. Create additional statistics.

12. *The SQL Server you are using has four individual hard drives not configured in any form of RAID. The server is used primarily to store a large corporate database in which users almost exclusively perform queries daily, although some data is added to the tables at regular intervals. How would you configure the storage files for the database?*
   A. Place the transaction log and database files on separate hard drives and configure all indexes on the same drive as the database. Place all other system files on the third and fourth drives.

B. Place the transaction log and database files on the same drive and configure the indexes to use a second drive. Place all other system files on the third and fourth drives.
C. Place the transaction log, database, and index files on separate drives. Place the other system files on the fourth drive.
D. Place the transaction log on the system drive and the database and index files on a second drive.

13. *An order entry system is configured as shown in the following exhibit.*

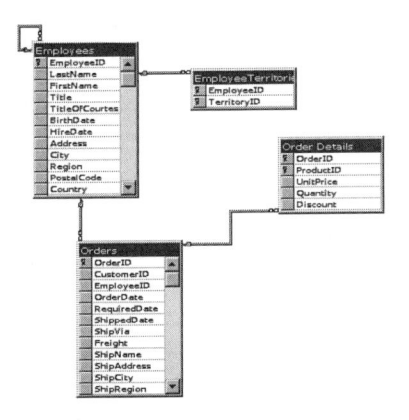

You must determine the top three selling employees based on the largest number of orders. Which of the following commands will solve the problem? (Select two.)

A. ```
Select Top 3 E.EmployeeID, Count(O.OrderID) From Employees As E
Inner Join Orders As O on E.EmployeeID = O.EmployeeID
Group By E.EmployeeID
Order By Count(OrderID) DESC
```

B. ```
Select Top 3 E.EmployeeID, Count(O.OrderID) From Employees As E
Inner Join Orders As O on E.EmployeeID = O.EmployeeID
Order By Count(OrderID) DESC
Group By E.EmployeeID
```

C. ```
Set Rowcount 3
Select E.EmployeeID, Count(O.OrderID) From Employees As E
Inner Join Orders As O on E.EmployeeID = O.EmployeeID
Group By E.EmployeeID
Order By Count(OrderID) DESC
```
```

D. Set Rowcount 3
   Select E.EmployeeID, Count(O.OrderID) From Employees As E
   Inner Join Orders As O on E.EmployeeID = O.EmployeeID
   Order By Count(OrderID) DESC
   Group By E.EmployeeID

E. Set Rowcount 3
   Select E.EmployeeID, Count(O.OrderID) From Employees As E
   Inner Join Orders As O on E.EmployeeID = O.EmployeeID
   Order By Count(OrderID) DESC

F. Select Top 3 E.EmployeeID, Count(O.OrderID) From Employees As E
   Inner Join Orders As O on E.EmployeeID = O.EmployeeID
   Order By Count(OrderID) DESC

14. *You are preparing the physical design of a customer statistics system. The current table structure is shown in the following exhibit.*

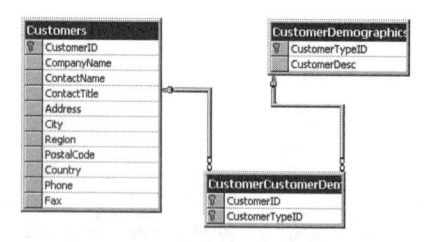

You must ensure that statistics can be presented such that any customer who referred another customer to the company can be listed. You must also allow for unlimited customer descriptions in any format. Descriptions could identify a preferred time for contacting, order discount information, subscription duration, date of birth, and so on. The descriptions must be able to accept any type of data. You decide to add a ReferredBy column to the Customers table containing the referral's CustomerID. *You create a foreign key tying the* ReferredBy *column to the primary key of the Customers table. You ensure that the column type of* CustomerDesc *is* nvarchar. *Which of the following statements are true? (Select all that apply.)*

A. Several descriptions can apply to a single customer.
B. Any type of information can be entered into the description.
C. A customer can be printed with the referral's contact name.
D. Description entries apply to specific customers.

E. A referral must be a customer already in the table or NULL.

F. A customer can only be qualified as a single type.

15. *You are developing an application for credit card purchase authorization. Purchases can be made from around the world and must be verified as quickly as possible. You would like to implement a three-tier model providing an optimum level of service to any outlets allowing the use of your card. How would you implement this network?*

    A. As a distributed application involving geographically located SQL Servers and a master server at a central head office with operations controlled using a client application that will handle a two-phase commit.

    B. As a client interface application that will communicate with geographically located subscription servers configured for merge replication with a centrally located master server.

    C. As a client application that will communicate with geographically located MTS servers. The MTS servers will communicate with centrally located SQL Servers.

    D. As a client application that will communicate with geographically located MTS servers. The MTS servers will communicate with geographically located SQL Servers.

16. *You are preparing a new index on a table that has 1,500 rows. Ten rows are added to this table every day. The table already has a primary key and the new index doesn't represent the order in which data in the table is to be stored. Updates to the table occur periodically. Which type of index would you create in this situation?*

    A. Use a CLUSTERED index with a high FILLFACTOR.

    B. Use a CLUSTERED index with a low FILLFACTOR.

    C. Use a NONCLUSTERED index with a high FILLFACTOR.

    D. Use a NONCLUSTERED index with a low FILLFACTOR.

17. *You are preparing a new index on a table that has 1,500 rows. Ten rows are added to this table every year. The table already has a primary key that represents the physical order of the data. Updates to this table are possible. Which type of index would you create in this situation?*

A. Use a CLUSTERED index with a high FILLFACTOR.
B. Use a CLUSTERED index with a low FILLFACTOR.
C. Use a NONCLUSTERED index with a high FILLFACTOR.
D. Use a NONCLUSTERED index with a low FILLFACTOR.

18. *You would like to implement full-text queries to be run by users against a database. What must you ensure for this to be possible?*
    A. Provide a unique index or primary key.
    B. Create a full-text catalog.
    C. Populate the full-text catalog.
    D. Build an application to use full-text queries.

19. *You have set up full-text queries for a table in the database, but users report that correct results are not being received from the results of their previously successful queries. What is the problem likely to be?*
    A. The users have not been trained in the use of Transact SQL.
    B. The catalog has not been repopulated.
    C. The catalog was not initially populated.
    D. The users lack the appropriate access permissions.

20. *You are developing a procedure for a small airline. The procedure must insert reservations for the flight requested and the connecting flight. The procedure must not enter any records if errors occur. The following exhibit represents the database layout, and the sample code illustrates the procedure to be used.*

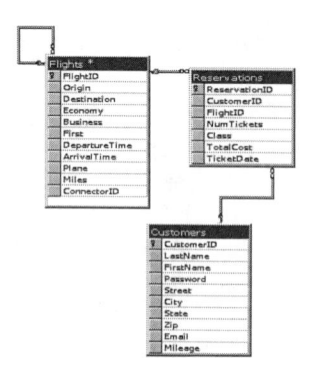

```
Declare @ConnID varchar(10)
Declare @Myerr int
Begin Transaction
 Insert Reservations Values (@ResID, @CusID, @FlID, @NoTick,
@Clss, NULL, Getdate())
```

```
Select @Myerr = @Error
Select @ConnID = ConnectorID from Flights where FlightID = @FlID
If not isnull(@ConnID, '0') > '0'
  Insert Reservations Values (@ResID+1, @CusID, @ConnID, @NoTick,
↪@Clss, NULL, Getdate())
  If @Error > @MyErr
    Select @MyErr = @Error
  If @MyErr > 0
    Rollback Transaction
Commit Transaction
```

Based on this code, which of the following statements is true? (Select all that apply.)

A. A record is added for the requested flight.
B. A record is added for the connecting flight.
C. Errors are properly trapped for possible errors on INSERT.
D. If an error occurs, the transaction is rolled back.
E. The total cost of the flight is calculated and updated to the initial flight record.
F. If no errors occur, the transaction is committed.

21. *You want to create a new SQL Server application using OLE DB or ADO. You need complete control over the application's behavior and performance. Which technique would you select?*

A. Either method is equally appropriate under these circumstances.
B. Neither technique would give you the desired control.
C. ADO.
D. OLE DB.

22. *You would like to run a captured trace that was created on the Shipping server. The server is unavailable, so you decide to run the query on the Invoicing server, which is currently available and is experiencing limited activity. Which of the following are true and might prevent you from running the captured trace? (Select all that apply.)*

A. You can't run a trace on a server other than the one originally used.
B. The original trace can't contain replication events.
C. If the original trace contains bcp captured information, it may not be replayed.
D. You can't replay a trace that traps application events.
E. You can't replay a trace captured using SQL Server authentication.

23. **You are preparing a trigger for execution when updates occur within a database. Here is the code to be used:**

    ```
    BEGIN TRANSACTION
    INSERT INTO SalesBackup
     SELECT * FROM inserted
    IF @@Error > 0
     ROLLBACK TRANSACTION
    COMMIT TRANSACTION
    INSERT INTO OrdersBackup
     SELECT * FROM Sales
    IF @@Error > 0
     ROLLBACK TRANSACTION
    ```

    If the insert to `SalesBackup` was functioning properly but the insert for the `OrdersBackup` produced an error, what would be the end result of the two tables?

    A. Only the `SalesBackup` table would have new records inserted.
    B. Neither table would have new records inserted.
    C. Only the `OrdersBackup` would have new rows inserted.
    D. Both tables would have new records inserted.

24. **You are preparing an update trigger that will take the information from the update and place it into two other tables. Which set of commands will perform the desired process?**

    A. `Insert Into OldData Select * From Deleted`
        `Insert Into NewData Select * From Inserted`
    B. `Insert Into OldData Select Updated From Deleted`
        `Insert Into NewData Select Updated From Inserted`
    C. `Insert Into OldData Select * From Updated`
        `Insert Into NewData Select * From Updated`
    D. `Insert Into OldData Select * From Sales`
        `Insert Into NewData Select * From Updated`

25. **You are implementing a procedure within an existing system. You have been assigned to create a single stored procedure that will allow for the copying of information into historical tables. Currently, all data for the last 15 years of business is stored in a single table.**

    The procedure needs to produce two tables that will be regenerated each time the procedure is executed. The first table will contain all data for the last two years. The two years will begin three months prior to the current system month when the procedure is executed and go back two years from that point. Using that point as a marker, all other historical information older than that will be placed in the second new table.

The entire process must be executed under the scope of a transaction. If any errors occur, all changes must be rolled back and the original system configuration must be restored from the point prior to the procedure's execution.

The code for this procedure currently looks like this:

```
Begin Transaction
Use Northwind
if EXISTS (Select Name From sysobjects Where Name = "TwoYear" and
↪Type="U")
 Drop Table TwoYear
if EXISTS (Select Name from sysobjects Where Name = "OverTwo" and
↪Type="U")
 Drop Table OverTwo
select * into TwoYear from orders
 where Datediff(month, OrderDate, getdate()) > 3
   and Datediff(month, OrderDate, getdate()) <= 27
If @@Error > 0
 Rollback Transaction
select * into OverTwo from orders
 where Datediff(month, OrderDate, getdate()) > 27
If @@Error > 0
 Rollback Transaction
Commit Transaction
```

Which of the following statements about this procedure is true? (Select all that apply.)

A. The two tables are regenerated each time the procedure is executed.
B. The first table contains the appropriate two-year data.
C. The second table contains the appropriate remaining data.
D. The transaction is formatted correctly.
E. All changes are rolled back and the original configuration is maintained.

26. *You are designing an application that will utilize a cursor to perform its operations. What is the proper order for statement execution related to cursor usage?*

  A. Declare / Open / Fetch / Deallocate
  B. Open / Fetch / Deallocate / Close
  C. Declare / Fetch / Deallocate / Close
  D. Open / Assign / Fetch / Close

27. *You are designing an application that will monitor table activity. When an order is placed that requires confirmation from the credit manager, the details of that order must be sent to the credit manager for his or her approval. What command would be used to accomplish this task?*

A. `xp_processmail`
B. `xp_readmail`
C. `xp_sendmail`
D. `sp_processmail`
E. `sp_readmail`
F. `sp_sendmail`

28. *You have created a database that you expect to have a high level of INSERT, UPDATE, and DELETE activity. What can you do to increase the database's performance? (Select two.)*
    A. Define additional indexes.
    B. Implement filegroups.
    C. Use disk striping.
    D. Define additional triggers.

29. *You would like to implement nested and recursive triggers on a table. What actions must you take to allow this to occur? (Select all that apply.)*
    A. Ensure that the setting "Allow triggers to be fired which fire other triggers" for the server has been set.
    B. Ensure that the database option for "Allow Nested Triggers" has been set.
    C. Ensure that the setting "Allow triggers to recurse" for the server has been set.
    D. Ensure that the database option for "Recursive Triggers" has been set.

30. *You are preparing the logical design of a database that will be used to track weather statistics. Information for this system will be received via direct feed from weather stations throughout the territory. Each territory is divided into regions. Each region can have one or more weather stations. Each weather station will send readings to the server every hour. How would you set up the entities for this system to conform to normalization standards?*
    A. Set up one entity.
    B. Set up two entities.
    C. Set up three entities.
    D. Set up four entities.
    E. Set up five entities.

Answers and Explanations

1. **B**   Locks must be set within a transaction to be held from the original SELECT over to the completion of the procedure. A TABLOCK would unnecessarily lock the entire table.

2. **A, C, E**   The correct format is SELECT DISTINCT. In answer D, the or would force the entire recordset, not the desired dates.

3. **A, B, C**   The name column is decomposable: It can be divided into first and last names. The invoice amounts should be kept in a separate table; they are repeating columns. Provision of the total with the invoice amounts represents data redundancy.

4. **A**   A MERGE replication is the only form of replication that allows subscribers to update the original table.

5. **B**   SQL Server Profiler is used to trap information relating to the applications within the database. Performance Monitor is used to trap information relating to the server. Network Monitor is used to trap packet information to and from the server. SQL Server Query Analyzer is used to view the SHOWPLAN information for a specific query.

6. **A**   B represents the Graphical SHOWPLAN for a LEFT, INNER join combination. C represents the Graphical SHOWPLAN for an INNER, LEFT join combination. D represents the Graphical SHOWPLAN for a similar query with a subquery added. E represents the Graphical SHOWPLAN for a LEFT, LEFT join combination.

7. **D**   sp_monitor provides this report specifically. The other answers just look good.

8. **A, B, C, D, F, G**   There is no information available to provide phone numbers. Beware of this style of question. Sometimes it's the obvious thing that is missing from the complete picture.

9. **A**   All non-aggregate columns from the select list must be included in the group list with no provision in SQL Server to use alias names or computed names.

10. **B, E** Watch carefully the one-to-many- and many-to-many-style relationships. They are covered in a number of involved situations on the exam, without being referred to using those terms.

11. **D** If you create additional statistics, the server has a wider variety of information to base query plans on. Performance might improve as changes to a table's structure and content occur.

12. **C** If possible, all elements should be maintained on separate drives attached to separate controllers or to a controller that has its own processor. This will allow the drive heads to remain in position longer for sequential procedures.

13. **A, C** Although the SQL Server documentation states erroneously that there is no equivalent to the ACCESS top-three coding, both of these will work.

14. **A, B, C, E** Description entries apply to customer types, not directly to customers. A customer can have a number of types.

15. **D** For the fastest possible response in this situation, multiple transaction servers and multiple SQL Servers is the best solution, even though all of the answers are theoretically possible.

16. **D** The primary key is usually the clustered index of a table. The clustered index indicates the physical order of the data. A low FILLFACTOR leaves more room for updates.

17. **C** See the explanation for question 16.

18. **A** A unique index or primary key must be provided before you can set up full-text queries. The remaining steps would then follow.

19. **B** It appears that the catalog was initially populated. However, unlike standard indexes, full-text indexes must be repopulated either manually or by scheduled events.

20. **A, B, F** There is no calculation in the procedure. Also, @Error is not valid. It must be @@Error.

21. **D** OLE DB provides better control over application performance and behavior, although ADO is used for most business-related applications.

22. **B, C** To replay a trace on a server other than the one that originally captured the data, the trace can't contain bcp events or replication events.

23. **B** The second rollback transaction command will roll back the entire trigger.

24. **A** The deleted table is used during a DELETE or UPDATE process to hold the data being removed from the server. The inserted table holds the new data going into a table for an INSERT or UPDATE operation. There is no such thing as an updated table.

25. **A, B, C, D** The original configuration would not be maintained, because you can't roll back from a Drop Table command.

26. **A** This is the only possible order. You can substitute Close for Deallocate if you want to reuse the cursor in the same procedure without having to redeclare it.

27. **C** Extended stored procedures access DLLs to perform functionality not normally available to SQL Server.

28. **B, C** Defining additional triggers and/or indexes will actually decrease performance.

29. **A, D** Nested triggers is a server setting, while recursive triggers is a database setting.

30. **D** One entity should be set up for Territories, one for Regions, one for Weather Stations, and one for Weather Readings.

Not every interesting item that the instructor shares with the class is necessarily directly related to the exam. This is the case with "Did You Know?" Think of this information as an intriguing sidebar or the interesting diversion you might wish the instructor would share with you during an aside.

CHAPTER 10

Did You Know?

The following are interesting items not directly relevant to the exam:

1. The code base for Sybase SQL Server and Microsoft SQL Server was identical through their respective 4.2 versions. They still have a very similar architecture, although differences were introduced in each subsequent release of both products. Both databases use Transact-SQL as a common procedural language, although the dialects have considerably changed since the 4.2 versions.

2. Microsoft released version 6 after version 4.21. There was no version 5.

3. The Microsoft Access 2000 product uses a SQL Server-compatible engine, making it possible to use a common friendly user interface as a front end to SQL Server versions 6.5 and 7.

4. With the release of the SQL Server 7 single-user desktop version, SQL Server can now be used on a Windows 95 or 98 machine with essentially the same interface and features as the full-blown server version. This gives Microsoft three competing desktop database tools: Access, FoxPro, and SQL Server. Microsoft's official line is that all three products will continue to be released because each provides advantages specific to the product.

5. SQL Server 6.5 now has available Service Pack 5 (released in December 1998). Microsoft is phasing out future development and engineering efforts for the MIPS and PowerPC platforms. Service Pack 5 is not available for these platforms.

6. Evaluation copies of SQL Server 7 and all other Microsoft BackOffice products (120-day licenses) are available for free download from the Microsoft Web site:

   http://backoffice.microsoft.com/downtrial/default.asp

   You can install copies of these products at home and study with the actual software at your leisure.

7. SQL Server 7 has two sample databases that you can practice your skills on. Access users will be familiar with the NorthWinds database now included with the server. Previous versions of SQL Server provided the Pubs database. It is still available.

8. It doesn't make much sense to configure tempdb in RAM (SQL Server 6.x), because the NT caching environment will probably already have it placed into RAM. In SQL Server 7, this configuration option has been removed because tempdb will grow dynamically as needed for a given result set.

INDEX

SYMBOLS

1NF (first normal form), 18, 311
2NF (second normal form), 18
3NF (third normal form), 325
10Base2, description of, 304
@@Error, review of, 285
@@ERROR statement, 120
@@FETCH_STATUS statement, 50

A

accessing data, 142
    CONTAINSTABLE clause, 145
    FREETEXTTABLE clause, 146
    linked server configuration, 144
    OPENQUERY method, 145
    OPENROWSET method, 145
    parameters, database files, 161-164
    remote stored procedures, 143-144
    static/dynamic sources, 143

ACID (atomicity, consistency, isolation, and durability), 304
    atomicity, 57
    consistency, 57-58
    durability, 59
    isolation, 59
    overview of, 57
ADO, sample test questions, 343
aggregate functions, 111, 304
aliases, subqueries, 97
alphanumeric, description of, 304
ALTER DATABASE statement
    accessibility parameters, 162
    configuration parameters, 165
    examples of, 158
    permissions for, 158
    syntax, 158
ALTER VIEW statement, 122
altering
    database files, 158
    views, 122
ANSI, 304

ANSI NULL CONTENT
  option, 166
application programming
  interfaces (APIs), OLE, 317
arithmetic errors, INSERT,
  UPDATE, or DELETE
  operations, 79
ASCII, description of, 304
associative entities, description
  of, 15, 304
atomicity
  description of, 304
  transactions, 57
Attention event class, 251
attributes, description of, 15,
  282, 304
Autoclose, description of, 304
AUTOCLOSE parameter, 166
automatic database recovery,
  304, 60
automatic file expansion, 152
AUTOSHRINK parameter,
  165, 304
availability, description of,
  39, 304
AvgBalance column,
  example of, 178
avoiding deadlocks, 73-74

B

backing up, differential
  option, 309
BACKUP DATABASE
  statement, 164
BACKUP LOG statement, 164
BACKUP statement, 60-62, 157
  differential backups, 63
  full backups, 62
  log backups, 62

backups
  creating, 196
  criteria for using, 196
  optimizing performance, 235
bcp utility, 197-198, 236
BEGIN DISTRIBUTED
  TRANSACTION
  statement, 106
BEGIN TRANSACTION
  statement, 54
BEGIN...END statement, 101
bind tokens, 71
bitwise operators, 127, 305
Boolean operators, 305
bound connections, 71-72, 305
BREAK statement, 104
bulk copy operations,
  optimizing performance,
  236-237
BULK COPY statement, 164
bulk copy transfers,
  197-198, 305
  fast bcp, 199
  slow bcp, 199
BULK INSERT statement,
  164, 236
business rule 22, 305

C

cabling
  10Base2, 304
  performance, 33
  twisted-pair, 326
caching, 305
calculations
  order of operations, 127
  performing, 125-127
captured event data
  SQL Server Profiler, 249
  trace, sample test
    questions, 343

Cartesian product, 95
cascading updates and deletes, 132, 305
CASE statement, 104
case study questions, 301
character strings, concatenating, 306
character-related data types, selecting, 171
characteristic entities, 15, 305
CHECK constraints, 180-181, 305
CHECKIDENT parameter, 174
checkpointing, 64, 305
Client Configuration utility, 31, 305
client-side cursor, 306
CLUSTERED indexes, 183-184, 188-190, 348
   creating, 306
   organization, 184, 186
code base
   exam questions, 289
   Sybase versus Microsoft SQL Server, 352
columns
   constraints, 180
   description of, 306
   identifier, 313
   loading value into, 79
   selecting for indexes, 191
combining backup strategies, 235
commands
   DBCC, 286
   sample test questions, 339, 345
   SAVE TRANSACTION, 71
comments, Transact-SQL scripts, 105
commit command, distributed transactions, 56
COMMIT TRANSACTION statement, 54

COMMIT WORK statement, 54
committal phase, 306
comparison operators, 98-99, 306
compound key, 306
COMPUTE BY clause, SELECT statement, 136
   syntax, 90
   uses of, 90-91
computed column expressions, 178
concatenation, 306
conditional error check example, 146
configuring
   database files, parameters, 165-167
   functions, 112-113
   storage files, sample test questions, 338
connect event, 250
consistency
   description of, 306
   transactions, 57-58
constants, 306
constraints, 306
   CHECK, 181
   classifications, 180
   comparing to rules, 132
   FOREIGN KEY, 180, 190
   implementing, 179
   modeling, Database Diagram, 23-24
   NOT NULL, 180
   PRIMARY KEY, 181, 184
   UNIQUE, 181, 191, 327
CONTAINS parameter, advanced text searches, 207
CONTAINS predicate, 205
CONTAINSTABLE clause, SELECT statement, 145

contention, 307
CONTINUE statement, 104
control of flow
  description of, 307
  Transact-SQL scripts, 100
    aggregate functions, 111
    BEGIN...END statement, 101
    BREAK statement, 104
    CASE statement, 104
    comments, 105
    CONTINUE statement, 104
    DECLARE statement, 105
    EXECUTE statement, 106-107
    functions, 110
    GOTO statement, 101
    IF...ELSE statement, 101
    PRINT statement, 106
    RETURN statement, 102-103
    rowset functions, 110
    scalar functions, 111-120
    variables, 108-109
    WAITFOR statement, 103
    WHILE statement, 103
convergence
  description of, 307
  transactions, 58
cost-base query analyzer, 224
CREATE DATABASE statement, 152-154
  parameters
    accessibility, 162
    configuration, 165
  examples of, 155
  MAXSIZE option, 157
  permission for, 155
  syntax for, 153
CREATE DEFAULT statement, 179

CREATE INDEX statement, 182
CREATE PROCEDURE statement, 124
Create Relationship dialog box, 21-22
CREATE RULE statement, 132
CREATE STATISTICS statement, 221
CREATE TABLE statement
  examples of, 175
  syntax for, 174
CREATE TRIGGER statement, 131
CREATE VIEW statement, 121
creating
  database files, 153, 155
  filegroups, 156
  indexes, 182-183
    CLUSTERED, 184, 186
    NONCLUSTERED, 188
    strategies for, 183-184
  relationships, 21
  stored procedures, 124
  triggers, 131
  user-defined data types, 172
  views, 121
cross-joins, 95
CUBE keyword, 136, 307
Current Activity object, locking diagnosis, 241
CURSOR CLOSE ON COMMIT parameter, 167
cursors, 113, 307
  client-side, 306
  concurrency options, SCROLL LOCKS behavior, 246
  description of, 47
  dynamic, 310
  execution plans, 210
  forward-only, 312
  insensitive, 314

DATABASES 357

Insensitive type, 52
keyset, 314
performance, sample test
  questions, 345
Read-Only type, 52
repeatable read, 320
scope, 53
scrollable, 321
scrollable and navigation, 52
selecting, 49
  cursor features, 51
  data volatility, 50
  functionality, 52
  performance, 51
  response, 51
  resultset size, 49
sensitive, 321
server-side, 322
static, 323
types of, 47-48
Cursors event classes, 251
**customer lists, sample test
  questions, 333**

D

data
  accessing, 142
    CONTAINSTABLE
      clause, 145
    FREETEXTTABLE
      clause, 146
    linked server
      configuration, 144
    OPENQUERY method, 145
    OPENROWSET method, 145
    remote stored procedures,
      143-144
    static/dynamic sources, 143
  alphanumeric, 304

consistency (ACID), 57
  atomicity, 57
  consistency, 57-58
  durability, 59
  isolation, 59
integrity
  business rules, 22
  description of, 307
  maintaining, 170
services, 284, 307
summarizing, 133-134,
  36-137
types, 108-109
  equivalencies, 109
  selecting, 170-171
volatility, cursor selection, 50
warehousing schemas,
  denormalization, 26, 307
Data Source Name, 309
Data Transformation Services,
  see **DTS**
Database Consistency Checker,
  see **DBCC**
databases
  backing up, syntax for, 60
  columns, 306
  convergence, 307
  description of, 14, 307
  designing
    exam, 289
    normalization rules, 282
    sample test questions, 342
  diagrams, 23-24, 282
  elements of, 14, 16
  files
    Autoshrink, 304
    creating, 153, 155
    database parameters, 161
    accessibility, 161-164
    configuration, 165-167

358 DATABASES

informational, 168
managing, 157
altering, 158
shrinking, 159-160
interaction statements, Transact-SQL, 55
log file (LDF), 315
maintaining, 286
master, 316
model, 316
MSDB, 316
normalization, 316
ODBC, 317
offline, 317
performance, optimizing, 237
physical model, 318
populating, bulk copy, 197-198
  fast bulk copy, 199
  slow bulk copy, 199
primary data file, 318
replication, denormalization, 25
scalability, 320
secondary data file (NDF), 321
tempdb, 325
theories, 289
Data Transformation Services
  Import Wizard, 200
  overview of, 199
  package design, 201, 203
overview of, 196
date and time functions, 113
datetime data type, 170
DB-Library, 308
DBCC (Database Consistency Checker), 216-217, 286, 307
DBCC MEMUSAGE, 213
DBCC SHOW STATISTICS statement, 226
DBCC SHOWCONTIG statement, 213

DBCC statement, parameters
  CHECKIDENT, 174
  SHRINKDATABASE, 159-160
  SHRINKFILE, 159-161
DBCC UPDATEUSAGE, 184
DBO (Database Owner), USE ONLY option, 164, 308
db_option statement
  AUTOCLOSE parameter, 166
  MERGE PUBLISH parameter, 166
  PUBLISHED parameter, 166
  RECURSIVE TRIGGER parameter, 167
  trunc. log on chkpt. parameter, 167
deadlocks, 72, 240, 308
  avoiding, 73-74
  victims, selecting, 245
DECLARE CURSOR statement, 247
  SQL-92, 47
  Transact-SQL Extended, 47
DECLARE statement, 105
DEFAULT TO LOCAL CURSOR parameter, 167
default values, 50, 178, 308
DELETE statement, 81
  cascading, 305
  description of, 308
  errors, 79
  examples of, 45, 82
  joins, 79
  review of, 284
  subqueries, 98
  syntax for, 80-81
denormalization
  data warehousing schemas, 26
  description of, 17, 25, 283, 308
  planned, 25

dependencies, 15-16, 282, 308
designing views, 121
device files, 152, 308
dialog boxes
   Create Relationship, 21-22
   Properties, 22
   Trace Properties, 250
differential database backups, 63, 235, 309
dirty reads, 69, 309
dirty writes, 309
disaster recovery plan, 309
disconnect event, 250
disk controllers, performance, 33
disk striping, 309
distributed transactions, 56, 309
domain error, 125
drivers
   DB-Library, 308
   performance, 32
DROP_EXISTING parameter, 194
DSN (Data Source Name), 309
DTS (Data Transformation Services), 197, 199, 307, 310
   Import Wizard, 200
   package design, 201, 203
dtsrun utility, 201-202
DUMP statement, 157
durability, 59, 310
Dynamic cursor type, 48, 310
dynamic data sources, 143
dynamic link library, 310
dynamic row-level locking, 310
Dynamic SQL, 45-46, 310

E

entities, 14, 282, 310
   associative, 15
   characteristic, 15
   dependencies, 15
   kernel, 314
equi-joins, 93, 310
errors
   event classes, 251
   mathematical operations, 125
   sample test questions, 342
   torn page, 326
   Transact-SQL scripts, 120
evaluating query plans, 225-234
evaluation copies, 352
events, identifying with SQL Server Profiler, 249, 251-253
exam, 288
   code, 289
   content, 38, 289
   failure
      rates, 289
      procedures for, 300
   Microsoft mind-set, 290-291
   multiple-answer questions, 297
   multiple-choice questions, types of, 289
   navigating, 296, 298
   overview of, 288
   procedures for, 294-295
   questions, 288, 301
   retaking, 300
   sample questions, 296-298, 331-332
   score report, 299
   time frame of, 291-292
   time limits and, 293
examples, self-joins, 254-256
exclusive locks, 65, 310
execute immediate statement, 46
EXECUTE statement, 106-107, 125
executing stored procedures, 125

execution plans, 210
    description of, 212
    evaluation of, 213
    example of complex, 210
    hash joins, merge joins, and
        parallel queries, 212
    index intersection and union
        techniques, 213
    optimizing
        performance, 213
            Database Consistency Checker,
                216-217
            graphical SHOWPLAN
                mechanism, 217
            hash joins, 215
            merge joins, 214
            semi-joins, 216
            SET SHOWPLAN ALL
                statement, 219-220
            SET SHOWPLAN TEXT
                statement, 218
            UPDATE STATISTICS
                statement, 221-223
    performance improvements
        in, 212
    Query Processor, 224-225
Execution Warnings event
    class, 251
existing connection event, 250
EXISTS, subqueries, 99
explicit transactions, 54, 310
extended stored procedures, 310
extensibility, 37, 311

F

fact table design,
    performance, 35
fact tables, 311
failure rates for exam, 289, 300
fast bulkcopy, 311

fault tolerance, 311
fetch command, cursor
    navigation options, 52
file management
    database files, 157, 161
        altering, 158
        creating, 155
        database accessibility
            parameters, 161-1645
        database configuration
            parameters, 165-167
        database informational
            parameters, 168
        shrinking, 159-160
    log files, 169, 315
    overview of, 152
filegroups, 311
    creating, 155-156
    description of, 153
FILLFACTOR property,
    192-193, 285, 311
first normal form, 18, 311
floating-point underflow
    error, 125
FOR ATTACH option, 163
FOR BROWSE option,
    locking, 68
FOR LOAD option, 154, 163
foreign keys
    constraints, 180, 190
    description of, 312
    selecting, 20
FORMSOF( ) function, 205
Forward-only cursor type, 48
forward-only cursors, 312
fourth and fifth normal
    forms, 19
FREETEXTTABLE clause,
    SELECT statement, 146
FROM clause, joins, 93

full backups, 62
full-text catalog, 312
full-text implementation, 203-206
Full-Text Indexing Wizard, 203, 312
full-text queries, 312
   maintainability, 36-37
   sample test questions, 342
full-text service, starting, 203
FULLSCAN option, 222, 312
functionality, cursor selection, 52
functions, 312
   aggregate, 304
   cube, 307
   exam, 111
   scalar, 321
   Transact-SQL scripts, 110
      aggregate, 111
      rowset, 110
      scalar, 111-120
FUTUREONLY parameter, 179

G

generated values, 173
   computed column expressions, 178
   default values, 178
   IDENTITY columns, 173-175
   unique identifiers, 176-177
      as constants, 176
      NEWID function, 178
GIGO (Garbage In gives Garbage Out), 170
global cursors, 53
global variables, 327
globally unique identifier, *see* GUID
GOTO statement, 101
grace hash joins, 215

granularity, 240, 312
graphical SHOWPLAN mechanism, 217
   exam, 288
   sample test questions, 313, 334
GROUP BY clause, SELECT statement, 89, 134
grouping, 313
growth increment size
   CREATE DATABASE statement, 154
GUID (globally unique identifier)
   as constant, 176
   description of, 173, 176-177, 313
   NEWID function, 178

H

hard drives
   device file, 308
   disk striping, 309
   disk striping with parity, 309
hardware, performance, 33
HASH, ( ) predicate, 215
hash joins, 212-215
Hash Warning event class, 251
HAVING clause, SELECT statement, 89, 134
heap, 313
hold locks, 68, 313
HOLDLOCK command, 286
hubs, 313

I

identifiers, 14-15, 313
identifying
   events with SQL Server Profiler, 249, 251-253
   primary keys, 19

IDENTITY columns, 313
    creating, 175
    description of, 173
    indicating, 174
    review of, 285
IF...ELSE statement, 101
immediate guaranteed
    consistency, 58, 313
implementation exam, 289
    optimizing and tuning, 210
    physical design, 41
    rules, 132
implicit transactions, 55, 313
IN, inner queries, 98
in-memory hash joins, 215
Index Create Memory
    configuration option, 239
indexes
    characteristics, 191
        DROP_EXISTING
            parameter, 194
        FILLFACTOR property,
            192-193
        PAD_INDEX parameter, 194
    CLUSTERED, 184-186, 306
    columns, selecting, 191
    creating, 182-184
    description of, 17, 313
    fill factor and, 311
    full-text, 312
    Index Tuning Wizard, 194-195
    leaf level page, 315
    nodes, 194
    NONCLUSTERED, 188, 316
    purposes of, 181
    sample test questions, 341
    selecting, 188, 190, 225
    SQL Server Profiler, 195
informational parameters
    (database files), 168

inner-joins, 93, 314
inner queries, 96
input parameters, 127, 314
Insensitive cursors, 52
INSERT statement, 197,
    284, 314
    errors, 79
    examples of, 80
    joins, 79
    subqueries, 98
    syntax for, 77
    uses of, 78-79
inserting rows, 79
installations, optimizing
    performance, 234
    backup and restore
        operations, 235
    bulk copy operations, 236-237
    database and transaction log
        operations, 237
    server operations, 238-239
    temporary operations, 236
integrity, 170
intent locks, 66, 314
intermediate level nodes, 186
isolation, 64-66, 314
    exclusive locks, 65
    intent locks, 66
    Lock Manager, 67
    locking configuration, 68
    schema locks, 66
    serializable levels, 322
    share locks, 65
    SQL-92, 69
        read committed, 69
        read uncommitted, 69
        repeatable read, 70
        serializable, 70
    syntax, 70
    transactions, 59, 68
    update locks, 65

J

joins, 92, 314
  cross-joins, 95
  denormalization, 26
  equi-joins, 310
  inner-joins, 93, 314
  INSERT, UPDATE, or
    DELETE statement, 79
  outer-joins, 94, 317
  self-joins, 321

K

kernel entities, 14, 314
keys
  compound, 306
  foreign, 312
  primary, 318
keyset cursors, 48, 314
keywords, control-of-flow, 307

L

latent guaranteed consistency, 58, 315
LDF (log file), 315
leaf level page, 315
left anti semi-joins, 216
linked servers, 144, 315
LOAD statement, 157
loading values, 79, 315
local cursors, 53
local variables, 327
Lock Manager, 67
LOCK TIMEOUT, 246
LOCKCC option (SET CONCURRENCY statement), 75
locking, 64-68, 240, 315
  diagnosing, 241-244
  dynamic row-level, 310
  exclusive, 310
  groups, 65-66
  hold lock, 313
  implementing, 66
  intent, 314
  isolation level, 314
  optimistic, 75
  pessimistic, 75, 318
  sample test questions, 333
  schema, 321
  shared, 322
  SQL Server Profiler, 244
  types of, 74
  resolving, 245-246
  update, 327
log files
  backups, 62
  managing, 169
logical data model, 282, 315
  physical design, 318
  sample test questions, 346
logical operators, 99, 315
LoginFailed event class, 251
logins, System Administrator, 324
logs, description of, 315

M

maintaining data and referential integrity, 170
  data and referential
    type, 170
  data type selection, 170-171
  full-text queries, 36-37
  generated values, 173
    computed column expressions, 178
    default values, 178
    IDENTITY columns, 173-175
    unique identifiers, 176-178

NULL and NOT NULL, 173
  user-defined data types, 172
managing
  database files, 157
    altering, 158
    shrinking, 159-160
  log files, 169
many-to-many dependencies, 284, 316
MANY-TO-MANY MERGE, ( ) predicate, 216
master databases, 316
mathematical functions, 114
mathematical operators, 126, 316
Max Async IO configuration option, 239
Max Server Memory configuration option, 238
Max Worker Threads configuration option, 238
MAXSIZE option, CREATE DATABASE statement, 157
mbps (megabits per second), 316
media, removable, 319
megabits per second, 316
memory, cache, 305
merge joins, 212-241
MERGE PUBLISH parameter, 166
MERGE replication, 347
metadata, 37, 115
Microsoft
  BackOffice products Web site, 352
  competing desktop database tools, 352
Microsoft Access 2000, SQL Server interface, 352
Microsoft mind-set and exam questions, 290-291

Microsoft SQL Server, code base, 352
Min Memory Per Query configuration option, 239
Min Server Memory configuration option, 238
miscellaneous event classes, 251
modeling
  logical database design, 315
  physical database design, 40
    three-tier object, 40
    two-tier object, 41
  rules and constraints, Database Diagram, 23-24
modifying data, views, 122
MSDB database, 316
multigranular locks, 244
multiple backup devices, benefits of, 235
multiple-choice questions, exam, 289, 297, 300
multiprocessor servers, performance, 34

N

named pipe, 316
navigating exam, 296, 298
NEAR( ) function, 206
nested triggers, sample test questions, 346
nesting, 106
networks
  hubs, 313
  named pipe, 316
NEWID function, 178
non-logged operations, 164
NONCLUSTERED indexes, 183, 316
  bulk copies, 237
  organization, 188
  selecting, 188, 190

NORECOMPUTE option, UPDATE STATISTICS statement, 222
normal forms, 18, 316
normalization, 17, 316
   first normal form, 18
   fourth and fifth normal forms, 19
   second normal form, 18, 321
   third normal form, 19, 325
normalization rules, database design, 282
   sample test questions, 333, 346
NOT EXISTS subqueries, 99
NOT IN inner queries, 98
NOT NULL constraints, 180
NULL constraints, 173
nullability, data types, 172
numeric data types, selecting, 171

O

objects
   event classes, 252
   global, 312
   granularity, 312
   GUID, 313
ODBC (Open Database Connectivity), 32, 317
OFFLINE option, 164, 317
OLE DB objects, 317
   rowsets, 320
   sample test questions, 343
one-to-many dependencies, 16, 317
one-to-one dependencies, 16, 317
Open Database Connectivity, 32, 317
OPENQUERY, 145
OPENROWSET, 145
operations
   isolating, 314
   nonlogged, 316
operators
   bitwise, 127
   comparison, 306
   logical, 315
   mathematical, 126, 316
   rollup, 320
   unary, 126
OPTCC option (SET CONCURRENCY statement), 76
OPTCCVAL option (SET CONCURRENCY statement), 76
optimistic locking, 74-75
OPTIMISTIC WITH ROW VERSIONING behavior, 246
OPTIMISTIC WITH VALUES behavior, 246
optimizing performance
   backup and restore operations, 235
   bulk copy operations, 236-237
   database and transaction log operations, 237
   Database Consistency Checker, 216-217
   graphical SHOWPLAN mechanism, 217
   hash joins, 215
   installations, 234
   merge joins, 214
   overview of, 213
   sample test questions, 334, 338, 346
   semi-joins, 216
   server operations, 238-239

SET SHOWPLAN ALL
  statement, 219-220
SET SHOWPLAN TEXT
  statement, 218
temporary operations, 236
UPDATE STATISTICS
  statement, 221-223
ORDER BY clause
  comparing to index, 182
  SELECT statement, syntax, 90
order of operations,
  mathematical calculations, 127
order processing, sample test
  questions, 336
outer joins, 94, 317
OUTPUT parameter, 167
output parameters, 127, 317
ownership, CREATE
  DATABASE statement, 154

P

package objects, 201
PAD_INDEX parameter, 194
PAGELOCK command, 286
parallel queries, 212, 317
parameters, 46, 317
  database, 161
    accessibility, 161-164
    configuration, 165-167
    informational, 168
  input, 314
  output, 317
  sp_dboption statement,
    162-163
parsing, 317
performance, 30-31, 318
  cabling, 33
  cursor selection, 51
  disk controllers, 33
  drivers, 32

fact table design, 35
hardware and, 33
multiprocessor servers, 34
optimizing, 213
  backup and restore
    operations, 235
  bulk copy operations, 236-237
  database and transaction log
    operations, 237
  Database Consistency Checker,
    216-217
  graphical SHOWPLAN
    mechanism, 217
  hash joins, 215
  installations, 234
  merge joins, 214
  sample test questions, 334,
    338, 346
  semi-joins, 216
  server operations, 238-239
  SET SHOWPLAN ALL
    statement, 219-220
  SET SHOWPLAN
    TEXT, 218
  temporary operations, 236
  UPDATE STATISTICS
    statement, 221-223
RAM, 34
stored procedures, 32
triggers, 35
Performance Monitor, 30,
  286, 318
performing calculations,
  125-127
pessimistic locking, 74-75, 318
phantom data, 69
physical database, creating, 285
physical design
  @@trancount object, 76
  accessing data, 142

PHYSICAL DESIGN ISSUES 367

CONTAINSTABLE
   clause, 145
FREETEXTTABLE
   clause, 146
   linked server
     configuration, 144
   OPENQUERY method, 145
   OPENROWSET method, 145
   remote stored procedures,
     143-144
   static/dynamic sources, 143
cursors, 318
   scope, 53
   scrollable and
     navigation, 52
data consistency, 57
   atomicity, 57
   consistency, 57-58
   durability, 59
   isolation, 59
deadlocks, avoiding, 72
   by accessing objects in same
     order, 73
   by avoiding user
     interaction, 73
   by minimizing
     transaction size, 74
   by using bound
     connections, 74
   by using low isolation levels, 74
dynamic SQL model, 45-46
isolation, 64
   exclusive locks, 65
   implementing locking, 66
   intent locks, 66
   Lock Manager, 67
   locking configuration, 68
   schema locks, 66
   share locks, 65
   update locks, 65

locking, 74-75
recoverability, 59
   automatic database
     recovery, 60
   Backup and Restore
     statements, 60-62
   checkpointing, 64
   differential backups, 63
   full backups, 62
   log backups, 62
   standby servers, 63
sample test questions, 340
session level configuration,
   139-142
SQL-92 cursors, Insensitive
   type, 52
stored procedures model, 46-47
summarizing data, creating
   resultsets, 133-134, 136-137
Transact-SQL cursors, 47
   cursor types, 47-48
   Insensitive type, 52
   Read-Only type, 52
   selection, 49-52
transactions, 53
   control, 70-72
   isolation, 68-70
   management, 54-56
views, 121-123
physical design issues, 30
   availability, 39
   extensibility, 37
   maintainability, 35-37
   models, 40
     three-tier object, 40
     two-tier object, 41
   performance, 30-31
     cabling, 33
     disk controllers, 33
     drivers, 32

368 PHYSICAL DESIGN ISSUES

fact table design, 35
hardware, 33
multiprocessor servers, 34
RAM, 34
stored procedures, 32
triggers, 35
scalability, 38-39
security, 40
physical implementation
   constraints, 179
      CHECK, 181
      classifications of, 180
      FOREIGN KEY, 180
      NOT NULL, 180
      PRIMARY KEY, 181
      UNIQUE, 181
   database population, 196
      bulk copy, 197-198
      Data Transformation Services, 199
      Data Transformation Services Import Wizard, 200
      Data Transformation Services package design, 201, 203
      fast bulk copy, 199
      slow bulk copy, 199
   file management, 152
      database accessibility parameters, 161-164
      database configuration parameters, 165-167
      database files, altering, 158
      database files, creating, 153, 155
      database files, shrinking, 159-160
      database parameters, 161, 168
      filegroups, creating, 156
      log files, 169

full-text implementation
   advanced text searches, 205-206
   overview of, 203-205
index maintenance, 181, 194
   CLUSTERED indexes, 184, 186
   columns, selecting, 191
   index characteristics, 191-194
   Index Tuning Wizard, 195
   indexes, creating, 182-183
   indexes, strategies for, 183-184
   NONCLUSTERED indexes, 188
   selecting form of indexes, 188, 190
   SQL Server Profiler, 195
maintaining integrity
   computed column expressions, 178
   data and referential type, 170
   data type selection, 170-171
   default values, 178
   generated values, 173
   IDENTITY columns, 173-175
   NULL and NOT NULL, 173
   unique identifiers, 176-178
   user-defined data types, 172
physical modeling, 318
physical relationships, 284
placeholders, question mark, 46
practicing for exam, 294
preparation phase, description of, 318
prepare command, distributed transactions, 56
prepared execution, 318
primary data files (MDF), 318, 153

PRIMARY KEY constraints, 180-181, 184
primary keys, 318
  identifying, 19
  overview of, 348
PRINT statement, 106
printing from tables, sample test questions, 335
procedures
  extended stored, 310
  parameters, 317
  prepared, 318
  return code, 320
  stored, 324
Profiler, 32, 318
Properties dialog box, 22
PUBLISHED parameter, 166

Q

queries
  description of, 318
  distributed, 309
  execution plan, 319
  full-text, 312
  graphical showplan, 313
  optimizing, 319
  parallel query execution, 317
  parameters, 317
  plans
    evaluation of, 225
    system tables, 226-229, 234
  sample test questions, 336
  subqueries, 96-99
  union, 326
  views, 123
Query Optimizer, 213
  hash joins, 215
  merge joins, 214
  semi-joins, 216
Query Processor, statistics, 224-225

question mark placeholder, 46
questions, exam
  case study type, 301
  code, 289
  Microsoft mind-set, 290-291
  multiple-answer, 297
  ranking type, 301
  samples, 296-298, 331-332
  simulation type, 301
  source of, 300
  time frame, 291-292

R

RAID (Redundant Array of Inexpensive Drives), 319
RAISERROR statement, 120, 128-129
raising errors, 128
RAM, performance, 34
range error, 125
range lock, 70
ranking questions, 301
read ahead, 319
read committed, 319
read committed isolation level, SQL-92, 69
READ ONLY option, 164, 246
read uncommitted isolation level, 319
Read-Only cursor, 52
READCOMMITTED command, 286
READONLY option (SET CONCURRENCY statement), 76
recompiling stored procedures, 130
records, 319
recoverability, 59
  automatic database recovery, 60

Backup and Restore
  statements, 60-62
  differential backups, 63
  full backups, 62
  log backups, 62
  checkpointing, 64
  standby servers, 63
Recovery Interval configuration option, 239
recursive hash joins, 215
RECURSIVE TRIGGER parameter, 167
recursive triggers
  description of, 319
  sample test questions, 346
Redundant Array of Inexpensive Drives, 319
referential integrity, 319
  example, 147
  foreign key constraints, 20
  maintaining, 170
relationships, 319
  creating, 21
  many-to-many, 316
  one-to-many, 317
  one-to-one, 317
  sample test questions, 337
remote servers, 319
remote stored procedures, 319
  executing, 144
  setting up, 143
removable media, 319
repeatable read isolation level, SQL-92, 70
replication, 320
  sample test questions, 334
reserved return values, 102
RESIDUAL, ( ) predicate, 216
resource lock types, 243
resource timeout, 74

response, cursor selection, 51
restore operations
  database files, 154
  loading, 315
  optimizing performance, 235
RESTORE statement, 60-62, 157
  differential backups, 63
  full backups, 62
  log backups, 62
resultsets, 320
  cursor selection, 49
  summarizing data, 133-134, 136-137
retaking exam, 300
return code, 320
RETURN statement, 102-103
right anti semi-joins, 216
ROLLBACK (or ROLLBACK WORK) statement, 54, 320
ROLLBACK TRANSACTION statement, 54
ROLLUP keyword
  description of, 320
  SELECT statement, 137
root nodes, 186
row-level locking, 240
ROWGUIDCOL property, 177
ROWLOCK command, 286
rows, inserting, 79
rowset functions, 110, 320
rules, 320
  implementing, 132
  modeling, Database Diagram, 23-24

S

SA (System Administrator), 324
sample databases, 352
save point, 320

SAVE TRANSACTION
  command, 71
savepoints, implementing, 71
scalability, 38-39, 320
scalar functions, 111-112
  configuration, 112-113
  cursor, 113
  date and time, 113
  mathematical, 114
  metadata, 115
  security, 116
  string, 116-117
  system, 117-119
  system statistical, 119
  text and image, 120
scale event classes, 252
schemas
  locks, 66, 321
  snowflake, 322
  star, 323
score report, exam, 299
scripts
  description of, 321
  Transact-SQL, 100
    aggregate functions, 111
    *BEGIN...END
      statement, 101*
    BREAK statement, 104
    CASE statement, 104
    comments, 105
    CONTINUE statement, 104
    control of flow, 100
    DECLARE statement, 105
    error-handling methods, 120
    *EXECUTE statement,
      106-107*
    functions, 110
    GOTO statement, 101
    IF...ELSE statement, 101
    PRINT statement, 106
    RETURN statement, 102-103

  rowset functions, 110
  scalar functions, 111-120
  variables, 108-109
  WAITFOR statement, 103
  WHILE statement, 103
SCROLL LOCKS behavior, 246
scrollable cursors, 52, 321
SCSIs, 321
searching (text), advanced
  methods, 205-206
second normal form, 18
secondary data files, 153, 321
security, 40, 116
SELECT DISTINCT
  statement, 285
SELECT INTO statement,
  88-89, 164
SELECT statement, 321
  COMPUTE BY clause, 90-91
  CONTAINSTABLE clause, 145
  examples of, 91
  FREETEXTTABLE clause, 146
  GROUP BY and HAVING
    clauses, 89
  joins, 93
  ORDER BY clause, syntax, 90
  result sets, 320
  summarizing data, 133
    COMPUTE BY clause, 136
    CUBE keyword, 136
    GROUP BY clause, 134
    HAVING clause, 134
    ROLLUP keyword, 137
    TOP clause, 134
  syntax, 85-86
selecting
  columns for indexes, 191
  data type, 170-171
  foreign keys, 20
  indexes, 188, 190

self-join relationships, 283, 321
  description, 92
  example, 254-256
semi-joins, Query
  Optimizer, 216
serializable isolation level, 322
  SQL-92, 70
server-side cursors, 322
servers
  clusters, 322
  linked, 315
  optimizing performance,
    238-239
  remote, 319
  standby, 323
session level configuration,
  139-142
sessions, 322
SET ANSI_PADDING
  statement, 79
SET ARITHABORT ON
  statement, 126
SET CONCURRENCY
  statement, options, 75
SET DEADLOCK_PRIORITY
  statement, 72
SET FETCH_BUFFER
  statement, 48
SET IMPLICIT_
  TRANSACTIONS ON
  statement, 55
SET LOCK_TIMEOUT
  statement, 73
SET SHOWPLAN ALL
  statement, 213, 217
    optimizing performance,
      219-220
SET SHOWPLAN TEXT
  statement, 213, 217-218
SET statement, 139-142
share locks, 65, 322

SHOWCONTIG statement, 216
SHOWPLAN option, SQL
  Server Query Analyzer, 286
shrinking database files,
  159-160
simulation questions, 301
single character type
  identifiers, 129
SINGLE USER option, 164
slow bulkcopy, 322
smalldatetime data type, 170
snowflake schema, 212, 322
Sort Warnings event class, 251
sp autostats stored
  procedure, 223
sp createstats system stored
  procedure, 224
sp dboption system stored
  procedure, 224
sp lock stored procedure, 242
spaghetti code, 101
sp_addmessage, 130
sp_addtype stored
  procedure, 172
sp_altermessage, 130
sp_attach_db stored
  procedure, 164
sp_bindefault, syntax, 179
sp_bindsession, 72
sp_certify_removable stored
  procedure, 164
sp_configure, locking, 68
sp_create_removable stored
  procedure, 164
sp_dboption statement
  AUTOCLOSE parameter, 166
  AUTOSHRINK parameter, 165
  examples, 163
  parameters, 162-163
  TORN PAGE DETECTION
    parameter, 168

STATEMENTS 373

sp_detach_db stored procedure, 164
sp_dropmessage, 130
sp_fulltext_catalog stored procedure, 204
sp_fulltext_column stored procedure, 204
sp_fulltext_database stored procedure, 204
sp_fulltext_table stored procedure, 204
sp_getbindtoken, 71
sp_helpdb statement, 162, 168
sp_helpindex stored procedure, 183
sp_recompile system procedure, 46
sp_spaceused stored procedure, 183-184
sp_unbindrule, 132
SQL operators event classes, 252
SQL Server 6.5, Service Pack 5, 352
SQL Server Agent, 322
SQL Server Profiler, 194-195, 247, 323
  identifying events using, 249, 251-253
  locking diagnosis, 244
  uses of, 249, 286
SQL Server Query Analyzer, SHOWPLAN option, 286
SQL-92, 323
stacking, 106
standards
  ASCII, 304
  SQL-92, 323
standby servers, 63, 323
star schema, 212, 323
starting full-text service, 203

statements, 92, 164
  @@ERROR, 120
  @@FETCH_STATUS, 50
  ALTER DATABASE
    accessibility parameters, 162
    configuration parameters, 165
    examples, 158
    permissions, 158
    syntax, 158
  ALTER VIEW, 122
  BACKUP, 60-62
    differential backups, 63
    full backups, 62
    log backups, 62
    use of, 157
  BACKUP DATABASE, 164
  BACKUP LOG, 164
  BEGIN DISTRIBUTED TRANSACTION, 106
  BEGIN TRANSACTION, 54
  BEGIN...END, 101
  blocks, 146-147, 323
  BREAK, 104
  BULK COPY, 164
  BULK INSERT, 164
  CASE, 104
  COMMIT TRANSACTION, 54
  COMMIT WORK, 54
  CONTINUE, 104
  CREATE DATABASE, 152
    accessibility parameters, 162
    configuration parameters, 165
    examples, 155
    MAXSIZE option, 157
    permission, 155
    syntax, 153
    uses of, 154

CREATE DEFAULT, 179
CREATE INDEX, 182
CREATE PROCEDURE, 124
CREATE RULE, 132
CREATE TABLE, 174-175
CREATE TRIGGER, 131
CREATE VIEW, 121
database interaction,
  Transact-SQL, 55
DBCC
  CHECKIDENT
    parameter, 174
  SHRINKDATABASE or
    SHRINKFILE
    parameters, 159
  SHRINKDATABASE
    parameter, 160
  SHRINKDATABASE
    paramter, 159
  SHRINKFILE parameter,
    160-161
DBCC UPDATEUSAGE, 184
db_option
  AUTOCLOSE
    parameter, 166
  MERGE PUBLISH
    parameter, 166
  PUBLISHED parameter, 166
  RECURSIVE TRIGGER
    parameter, 167
  trunc. log on chkpt.
    parameter, 167
DECLARE, 105
DECLARE CURSOR, 47
DELETE, 308
  errors, 79
  examples, 82
  joins, 79
  subqueries, 98
  syntax, 80-81

developing prior to exam, 282
DUMP, 157
EXECUTE, 106-107, 125
EXECUTE IMMEDIATE, 46
GOTO, 101
IF...ELSE, 101
INSERT, 197, 314
  errors, 79
  examples, 80
  joins, 79
  subqueries, 98
  syntax, 77
  uses, 78-79
LOAD, 157
nested, 316
parameters, 46
PRINT, 106
RAISERROR, 120, 128-129
replaceable parameters, 45
RESTORE, 60-62
  differential backups, 63
  full backups, 62
  log backups, 62
  use of, 157
RETURN, 102-103
ROLLBACK (or ROLLBACK
  WORK), 54
ROLLBACK
  TRANSACTION, 54
SELECT, 87-88, 321
  COMPUTE BY clause,
    90-91, 136
  CONTAINSTABLE
    clause, 145
  CUBE keyword, 136
  examples, 91
  FREETEXTTABLE
    clause, 146
  GROUP BY and HAVING
    clauses, 89

STORED PROCEDURES 375

GROUP BY clause, 134
HAVING clause, 134
joins, 93
ORDER BY clause, 90
result set, 320
ROLLUP keyword, 137
summarizing data, 133
syntax, 85-86
TOP clause, 134
SELECT INTO, 164
SET, 139
   date and time
     statements, 139
   locking statements, 139
   miscellaneous statements, 140
   query execution
     statements, 140
   SQL-92 settings statements, 141
   statistics statements, 141
   transactions
     statements, 142
SET ANSI_PADDING, 79
SET ARITHABORT ON, 126
SET CONCURRENCY,
   options, 75
SET DEADLOCK_
   PRIORITY, 72
SET FETCH_BUFFER, 48
SET IMPLICIT_
   TRANSACTIONS ON, 55
SET LOCK_TIMEOUT, 73
showplan, 322
sp_dboption
   AUTOCLOSE
     parameter, 166
   AUTOSHRINK
     parameter, 165
   configuration
     parameters, 165

   examples of, 163
   parameters for, 162-163
   TORN PAGE DETECTION
     parameter, 168
sp_helpdb, 162, 168
static versus dynamic
   mechanism, 45
UPDATE, 83-84, 327
   errors, 79
   examples, 84
   joins, 79
   subqueries, 98
   syntax, 82-83
UPDATETEXT, 164
WAITFOR, 103
WHILE, 103
WRITETEXT, 164
static cursors, 48, 323
static data sources, 143
Static SQL, 323
statistics
   errors, 223
   Query Processor, 224-225
   sample test questions, 335
STATISTICS_
   NORECOMPUTE option, 182
storage files
   configuring, 338
   sample test questions, 333
stored procedures, 123, 130
   calculations, performing,
     125-127
   creating, 124
   description, 324
   event classes, 252
   exam, 288
   executing, 125
   input and output
     parameters, 127
   performance, 32

RAISERROR, 128-129
  recompiling, 130
  sample test questions, 333, 344
strings
  functions, 116-117
  variables, concatenating, 306
subqueries, 92, 96-97
  aliases, 97
  comparison operators, 98-99
  description, 324
  EXISTS or NOT EXISTS, 99
  implementations, 97
  IN or NOT IN, 98
  INSERT, UPDATE, or
    DELETE, 98
  logical operators, 99
  UNION, 99
summarizing data, 133-137
super-aggregate rows, 136
Sybase SQL Server, code
  base, 352
Sylvan Prometric Web site, 294
symmetric multiprocessing, 324
synchronization, 324
syntax, 288, 324
syntax-based optimizer, 224
sysindexes table, 184-186
System Administrator, 324
system failures
  automatic recovery and, 304
  fault tolerance, 311
  rollback, 320
system functions, 117-119
system statistical functions, 119
system stored procedures, 324
system tables, 325
  every database, 227-228
  master database only, 227
  MSDB database, 228
  new to SQL Server, 229-234

query plans, 226
SQL Server Agent Tables in
  MSDB Database, 228
storing, 228-229
types of, 227
uses of, 234

T

tables
  constraints, 180
  description of, 325
  heap, 313
  printing from, sample test
    questions, 335
  sample test questions, 344
  size limitations, 175
  system, 325
TABLOCK command, 286
TABLOCK hint, bulk copy, 237
tempdb
  description, 325
  SQL Server 6.x versus
    SQL Server 7, 352
temporary operations,
  optimizing performance, 236
text and image functions, 120
third normal form, 325
  description of, 19
three-tier object model, 40, 325
  sample test questions, 341
time limits, exam, 293
timeout value, 73
timestamp data type, 170, 325
tokens, 325
toolbars, execution plans, 210
TOP clause, SELECT
  statement, 134
torn pages, 326
TORN PAGE DETECTION
  parameter, 168

Trace Properties dialog box, 250
Transact-SQL
   cursors, 47-48
      Insensitive type, 52
      Read-Only type, 52
      selecting, 47-52
   database interaction
      statements, 55
   description of, 326
   scripts, 100
      aggregate functions, 111
      BEGIN...END statement, 101
      BREAK statement, 104
      CASE statement, 104
      comments, 105
      CONTINUE statement, 104
      control of flow, 100
      DECLARE statement, 105
      error-handling methods, 120
      EXECUTE statement,
        106-107
      functions, 110
      GOTO statement, 101
      IF...ELSE statement, 101
      PRINT statement, 106
      RETURN statement,
        102-103
      rowset functions, 110
      scalar functions, 111-120
      variables, 108-109
      WAITFOR statement, 103
      WHILE statement, 103
   stored procedures, 123
      creating, 124
      executing, 125
transactions
   atomicity, 304
   controlling
      bound connections, 71-72
      overview, 70-71
   distributed, 309
   event classes, 253
   explicit, 310
   immediate guaranteed
      consistency, 313
   implicit, 313
   isolation
      overview of, 68
      SQL-92, 69-70
      syntax example, 70
   latent guaranteed
      consistency, 315
   log operations
      backing up, syntax, 61
      optimizing
        performance, 237
   managing
      distributed
        transactions, 56
      explicit transactions, 54
      implicit transactions, 55
   review of, 285
   save point, 320
transformations, 200
triggers, 285
   cascading updates and deletes,
      132
   creating, 131
   description of, 326
   nested and recursive, sample
      test questions, 346
   overview of, 130
   performance, 35
   recursive, 319
   sample test questions, 344
   update, sample test questions,
      344
truncating, 326
TSQL event classes, 253
twisted-pair, description of, 326

two-phase commit, 318
  description of, 56, 326
  preparation phase, 318
two-tier object model, 41

U

unary operators, 126
unicode, 326
UNION, 326
  subqueries, 99
UNIQUE constraints,
  180-181, 327
  indexes, 191
uniqueidentifier data type,
  example, 177
unrestricted joins, 95
UPDATE statement, 284, 327
  errors, 79
  examples of, 84
  joins and, 79
  locks, 65
  subqueries, 98
  syntax for, 82-83
  uses of, 83-84
UPDATE STATISTICS
  statement, 213, 221-223
updates
  cascading, 305
  triggers, 132
  sample test questions, 344
UPDATETEXT statement, 164
user services, 327
user-defined data types,
  creating, 172
utilities
  Client Configuration, 31, 305
  ODBC, 32
  Performance Monitor, 318
  Profiler, 318

V

variables, 171
  description of, 327
  property, 318
  Transact-SQL scripts, 108-109
views, 327
  altering, 122
  creating, 121
  description of, 16
  designing, 121
  modifying data, 122
  overview of, 121
  querying data, 123
volatility, description of, 327

W-Z

WAITFOR statement, 103
warnings
  errors, 223
  event classes, 251
Web sites
  Microsoft BackOffice
    products, 352
  sample exams, 294
  Sylvan Prometric, 294
  weighted values, advanced text
    searches, 207
WHILE statement, 103
wildcards, advanced text searches, 206
Windows NT Performance
  Monitor, locking
  diagnosis, 244
WRITETEXT statement, 164
writing statement blocks, 146
  conditional error check, 146
  referential integrity, 147

NEW RIDERS TITLES

MCSE Fast Track: Networking Essentials

1-56205-939-4, $19.99, 9/98

MCSE Fast Track: TCP/IP

1-56205-937-8, $19.99, 9/98

MCSE Fast Track: Windows 98

0-7357-0016-8, $19.99, 12/98

MCSE Fast Track: Internet Information Server 4

1-56205-936-X, $19.99, 9/98

MCSE Fast Track: Windows NT Server 4

1-56205-935-1, $19.99, 9/98

MCSD Fast Track: Solution Architectures

0-7357-0029-X, $29.99, Q3/99

MCSE Fast Track: Windows NT Server 4 Enterprise

1-56205-940-8, $19.99, 9/98

MCSD Fast Track: Visual Basic 6, Exam 70-175

0-7357-0018-4, $19.99, 12/98

MCSE Fast Track: Windows NT Workstation 4

1-56205-938-6, $19.99, 9/98

MCSD Fast Track: Visual Basic 6, Exam 70-176

0-7357-0019-2, $19.99, 12/98

NEW RIDERS CERTIFICATION TITLES

TRAINING GUIDES

Complete, Innovative, Accurate, Thorough

Our next generation Training Guides have been developed to help you study and retain the essential knowledge that you need to pass your certification exams. We know your study time is valuable, and we have made every effort to make the most of it by presenting clear, accurate, and thorough information.

In creating this series, our goal was to raise the bar on how certification content is written, developed, and presented. From the two-color design that gives you easy access to content to the new software simulator that allows you to perform tasks in a simulated operating system environment, we are confident that you will be well-prepared for exam success.

Our New Riders Top Score Software Suite is a custom-developed set of full-functioning software applications that work in conjunction with the Training Guide by providing you with the following:

Exam Simulator tests your hands-on knowledge with over 150 fact-based and situational-based questions.
Electronic Study Cards test your knowledge with explanations that are linked to an electronic version of the Training Guide.
Electronic Flash Cards help you retain the facts in a time-tested method.
An Electronic Version of the Book provides quick searches and compact, mobile study.
Customizable Software adapts to the way you want to learn.

MCSE Training Guide: Networking Essentials, Second Edition
1-56205-919-X, $49.99, 9/98

MCSE Training Guide: Windows NT Server 4, Second Edition
1-56205-916-5, $49.99, 9/98

MCSE Training Guide: Windows NT Server 4 Enterprise, Second Edition
1-56205-917-3, $49.99, 10/98

MCSE Training Guide: Windows NT Workstation 4, Second Edition
1-56205-918-1, $49.99, 9/98

MCSE Training Guide: Windows 98
1-56205-890-8, $49.99, 1/99

MCSE Training Guide: TCP/IP, Second Edition
1-56205-920-3, $49.99, 11/98

Training Guides

Training Guides
First Editions

Your Quality Elective Solution

MCSE Training Guide: SQL Server 7 Administration
0-7357-0003-6, $49.99, 5/99

MCSE Training Guide: SQL Server 7 Database Design
0-7357-0004-4, $49.99, 5/99

MCSD Training Guide: Solution Architectures
0-7357-0026-5, $49.99, Q3/99

MCSD Training Guide: Visual Basic 6 Exams 70-175
0-7357-0002-8, $69.99, 3/99

MCSD Training Guide: Visual Basic 6 Exams 70-176
0-7357-0002-8, $69.99, 3/99

MCSE Training Guide: Systems Management Server 1.2, 1-56205-748-0

MCSE Training Guide: SQL Server 6.5 Administration, 1-56205-726-X

MCSE Training Guide: SQL Server 6.5 Design and Implementation, 1-56205-830-4

MCSE Training Guide: Windows 95, 70-064 Exam, 1-56205-880-0

MCSE Training Guide: Exchange Server 5, 1-56205-824-X

MCSE Training Guide: Internet Explorer 4, 1-56205-889-4

MCSE Training Guide: Microsoft Exchange Server 5.5, 1-56205-899-1

MCSE Training Guide: IIS 4, 1-56205-823-1

MCSD Training Guide: Visual Basic 5, 1-56205-850-9

MCSD Training Guide: Microsoft Access, 1-56205-771-5

NEW RIDERS CERTIFICATION TITLES

TESTPREP SERIES
Practice, Check, Pass!

Questions. Questions. And more questions. That's what you'll find in our New Riders *TestPreps*. They're great practice books when you reach the final stage of studying for the exam. We recommend them as supplements to our *Training Guides*.

What makes these study tools unique is that the questions are the primary focus of each book. All the text in these books support and explain the answers to the questions.

Scenario-based questions challenge your experience.

Multiple-choice questions prep you for the exam.

Fact-based questions test your product knowledge.

Exam strategies assist you in test preparation.

Complete yet concise explanations of answers make for better retention.

Two practice exams prepare you for the real thing.

Fast Facts offer you everything you need to review in the testing center parking lot.

MCSE TestPrep: Networking Essentials, Second Edition

0-7357-0010-9, $19.99, 12/98

MCSE TestPrep: Windows 95, Second Edition

0-7357-0011-7, $29.99, 12/98

MCSE TestPrep: Windows NT Server 4, Second Edition

0-7357-0012-5, $19.99, 12/98

MCSE TestPrep: Windows NT Server 4 Enterprise, Second Edition

0-7357-0009-5, $19.99, 11/98

MCSE TestPrep: Windows NT Workstation 4, Second Edition

0-7357-0008-7, $19.99, 12/98

MCSE TestPrep: TCP/IP, Second Edition

0-7357-0025-7, $19.99, 12/98

MCSE TestPrep: Windows 98

1-56205-922-X, $19.99, 11/98

TESTPREP SERIES
FIRST EDITIONS

MCSE TestPrep: SQL Server 6.5 Administration, 0-7897-1597-X

MCSE TestPrep: SQL Server 6.5 Design and Implementation, 1-56205-915-7

MCSE TestPrep: Windows 95 70-64 Exam, 0-7897-1609-7

MCSE TestPrep: Internet Explorer 4, 0-7897-1654-2

MCSE TestPrep: Exchange Server 5.5, 0-7897-1611-9

MCSE TestPrep: IIS 4.0, 0-7897-1610-0

How to Contact Us

IF YOU NEED THE LATEST UPDATES ON A TITLE THAT YOU'VE PURCHASED:

1) Visit our Web site at www.newriders.com.

2) Click on Product Support, and enter your book's ISBN number located on the back cover in the bottom right-hand corner.

3) There you'll find available updates for your title.

IF YOU ARE HAVING TECHNICAL PROBLEMS WITH THE BOOK OR THE CD THAT IS INCLUDED:

1) Check the book's information page on our Web site according to the instructions listed above, or

2) Email us at support@mcp.com, or

3) Fax us at (317) 817-7488 attn: Tech Support.

IF YOU HAVE COMMENTS ABOUT ANY OF OUR CERTIFICATION PRODUCTS THAT ARE NON-SUPPORT RELATED:

1) Email us at certification@mcp.com, or

2) Write to us at New Riders, 201 W. 103rd St., Indianapolis, IN 46290-1097, or

3) Fax us at (317) 581-4663.

IF YOU WANT TO PREVIEW ANY OF OUR CERTIFICATION BOOKS FOR CLASSROOM USE:

Email us at pr@mcp.com. Your message should include your name, title, training company or school, department, address, phone number, office days/hours, text in use, and enrollment. Send these details along with your request for desk/examination copies and/or additional information.

IF YOU ARE OUTSIDE THE UNITED STATES AND NEED TO FIND A DISTRIBUTOR IN YOUR AREA:

Please contact our international department at international@mcp.com.

We Want To Know What You Think

To better serve you, we would like your opinion on the content and quality of this book. Please complete this card and mail it to us or fax it to 317-581-4663.

Name _____

Address _____

City _____ State _____ Zip _____

Phone _____ Email Address _____

Occupation _____

Which certification exams have you already passed? _____
_____
_____

Which certification exams do you plan to take? ___
_____
_____
_____

What influenced your purchase of this book?
❏ Recommendation ❏ Cover Design
❏ Table of Contents ❏ Index
❏ Magazine Review ❏ Advertisement
❏ Publisher's reputation ❏ Author Name

How would you rate the contents of this book?
❏ Excellent ❏ Very Good
❏ Good ❏ Fair
❏ Below Average ❏ Poor

What other types of certification products will you buy/have you bought to help you prepare for the exam?
❏ Quick reference books ❏ Testing software
❏ Study guides ❏ Other

What do you like most about this book? Check all that apply.
❏ Content ❏ Writing Style
❏ Accuracy ❏ Examples
❏ Listings ❏ Design
❏ Index ❏ Page Count
❏ Price ❏ Illustrations

What do you like least about this book? Check all that apply.
❏ Content ❏ Writing Style
❏ Accuracy ❏ Examples
❏ Listings ❏ Design
❏ Index ❏ Page Count
❏ Price ❏ Illustrations

What would be a useful follow-up book to this one for you? _____

Where did you purchase this book? _____

Can you name a similar book that you like better than this one, or one that is as good? Why? _____
_____
_____

How many New Riders books do you own? _____

What are your favorite certification or general computer book titles? _____
_____

What other titles would you like to see us develop? _____
_____

Any comments for us? _____
_____

Fold here and tape to mail

Place
Stamp
Here

New Riders
201 W. 103rd St.
Indianapolis, IN 46290